# A Smart Energy Policy

# A Smart Energy Policy

## An Economist's Rx for Balancing

## Cheap, Clean, and Secure Energy

James M. Griffin

Yale University Press

New Haven & London

Published with assistance from the Louis Stern Memorial Fund.

Set in Adobe Garamond type by The Composing Room of Michigan, Inc.
Printed in the United States of America by Sheridan Books, Ann Arbor, Michigan.

Library of Congress Cataloging-in-Publication Data

Griffin, James M., 1944–
    A smart energy policy : an economist's Rx for balancing cheap, clean, and secure
energy / James M. Griffin.
        p.    cm.
    Includes bibliographical references and index.
    ISBN 978-0-300-14985-2 (cloth : alk. paper)    1. Energy policy—United States.
2. Climatic changes—United States.    I. Title.
    HD9502.U52G75 2009
    333.790973—dc22                                              2008052784

A catalogue record for this book is available from the British Library.

This paper meets the requirements of ANSI/NISO Z39.48-1992 (Permanence
of Paper). It contains 30 percent postconsumer waste (PCW) and is certified by
the Forest Stewardship Council (FSC).

10 9 8 7 6 5 4 3 2 1

# Contents

# Preface

When it comes to U.S. energy policy, a survey of consumers would no doubt reveal a broad consensus that it is badly off course. Not many would agree, however, on what the problems are and how they can be solved. By contrast, the same survey conducted among economists, of whatever political persuasion, would probably show much greater agreement on both the key issues and the policy solutions. The reason is that economics provides a common framework for the analysis of many social problems. Unfortunately, economists spend too much of their time talking to one another, and not to the general public, about what economic principles can teach us. This book is an attempt to remedy that by offering an economist's prescription for energy policy in a more accessible form. For a person trained to write in the language of economics, this task has been a challenge. You can judge for yourself how successful I have been.

To the extent that I have succeeded, I owe thanks to a number of friends and colleagues who have offered numerous suggestions. At the top of my list is my wife, Pat, a political scientist by training, who offered encouragement and occasional harsh but constructive criticism. Ken Vincent (of the Scowcroft Institute) offered invaluable day-to-day assistance, and Rebecca Willis, Leslie McDonald, David Nyquist, and Heather Thomson provided careful editorial assistance. Special thanks are in order to professors Marian Radetzki of Luleå University of Technology and John Tilton of the Colorado School of Mines for their insightful suggestions.

The first draft of this book benefited considerably from the comments of a number of able reviewers from diverse backgrounds. The list of reviewers included an eclectic group consisting of representatives from academia (Robert Mendelsohn of Yale University and David Victor of Stanford University), government (Howard Gruenspecht, with the Department of Energy, and Jim Woolsey, former director of the Central Intelligence Agency), think tanks (William Pizer of Resources for the Future, Michael Toman of the Rand Corporation, and Henry Olsen of the American Enterprise Institute), industry (Ed Porter and Art Wiese of the American Petroleum Institute and Anthony Corridore of Lafarge), and the media (Bill Tucker of the *New York Post*). I also wish to thank the editor of my energy textbook, Boyd Griffin, for some excellent suggestions. Karen Schoen provided outstanding editorial assistance. Finally, the editorial staff at Yale University Press has been a pleasure to work with.

# Introduction: An Overview
# from 30,000 Feet

## A WORLDWIDE NEED FOR A SMART
## ENERGY POLICY

A key premise of this book is that energy policy, especially in the United States, is fatally flawed both in the *process* by which problems are identified and in the *solutions* that are chosen. The process is guided largely by whatever interest groups are most vocal. The solutions often feature either command-and-control mandates or a grab bag of governmental goodies in the form of subsidies, tax credits, and grants. The result is a mishmash of legislation that is inconsistent, ineffective, and ill conceived. What is needed—in the United States and throughout the world—are policies that encourage the kind of behavior, by both consumers and businesses, that will achieve clearly defined, worthy goals.

Much debate could be generated about what the goals should be, but, for the sake of the arguments presented in this book, the energy goal for the United States and other countries—indeed for the whole world economy—should be energy that is *cheap, clean,* and *secure.* These goals are intertwined and related; for example, we know that energy produced from high-sulfur coal may seem cheap to a power producer, but it fails the cleanliness test, creating a number of environmental costs to the public that are not reflected in the price of the dirty coal.

The goal of cheap energy is based on the fact that energy is the lifeblood of a growing, healthy economy. The cost of a unit of energy is an important factor in the productivity of businesses and in the standard of living of the world's consumers. The lower the cost of a unit of clean energy, the greater the potential for the heat, light, and power needed by people and businesses. The greater the percentage of a household budget required for energy, the less that can be spent on food, medicine, housing, and discretionary items that enhance the quality of life. Cheap energy that is also clean and secure would be a great thing for the world economy.

With the pressing problems of climate change and dirty air and water, we know that clean energy is essential to the continued health and prosperity of all nations. Given the choice between dirty energy and clean energy at a moderately higher price, clean energy wins hands down. The more affluent a society becomes, the greater the premium it is willing to pay for clean energy. General awareness and appreciation for clean energy has a long history. Today, even schoolchildren understand that there are serious environmental costs associated with dirty sources of energy, particularly those resulting in greenhouse-gas emissions. New combined-cycle natural-gas-fired power plants emit one-third the carbon dioxide ($CO_2$) as state-of-the-art coal-fired power plants. Nevertheless, throughout the world, the prevailing market price for a unit of natural gas, the much cleaner fossil fuel, exceeds that of the dirtier alternatives such as coal; this could be viewed as an example of the market's failure to include the true cost of dirty energy in its price to the likely users (for example, electrical power plants). But under the threats of climate change and environmental degradation, clean energy must be part of the goal, and a sound policy will include a mechanism to price any given source of energy at a level that reflects its true cost to society.

Lastly, energy should be secure because it is a critical condition for a high living standard and has few substitutes in the short run. Just as with clean energy, the more affluent a society is, the greater importance it will attach to secure energy. When people talk about energy security, usually what they really mean is oil security, because of the political instability of the Middle East and its key role in the world oil market. However, security concerns apply to other areas of the world too, as evidenced by events in Venezuela and Nigeria and the reliance of much of Europe on natural-gas supplies from Russia. Oil security has two important ramifications. The first is the economic havoc that a major disruption of Middle East oil supplies would have on the world economy. But even in the absence of a disruption, oil revenues in the hands of certain Middle East countries may go to finance terrorist organizations.

There are inherent conflicts in the quest to realize cheap, clean, and secure energy. Ideally, the cheapest energy sources would also be the cleanest and most secure; unfortunately, that is not the case. Coal, for example, may seem to be the cheapest and the most secure given current market prices, but it is certainly not clean, and when proven technologies for sequestering its carbon emissions are used, it is no longer cheap. In the mix of world energy sources as of 2005, fossil fuels—the primary source of $CO_2$ emissions—dominated, accounting for 87 percent of the total.[1] Other sources included hydropower (6 percent), nuclear power (6 percent), and other forms of renewable energy, such as firewood, biomass, and solar power (which together account for only 1 percent). Among fossil fuels, petroleum accounts for the lion's share, with 38 percent of consumption, and coal and natural gas account for 26 percent and 23 percent, respectively.

When we look at all the possibilities for cheap, clean, and secure energy, the challenges become clear. Hydropower, arguably one of the cheapest, cleanest, and most secure sources of energy where it exists, offers very little potential for expansion; most opportunities have already been developed. Nuclear energy is certainly not cheap and presents a number of questions about cleanliness and security. Renewable fuels from biomass are not yet cheap, especially without subsidies, and are not always clean (for example, there are water issues with ethanol), and although the use of biofuels can be expected to grow, it is unlikely that renewable fuels from current technologies will replace fossil fuels as the dominant source of energy in the foreseeable future. Solar and wind energy have shown impressive growth where conditions are favorable but are not yet cheap compared with fossil sources, and, even under optimistic growth assumptions, they will replace only a small part of the energy currently produced from fossil sources.

Faced with this conundrum, policymakers have responded with a mishmash of legislation—some actions designed to promote cheap energy, others to promote clean energy, and other legislation aimed at secure energy. The problem is that specific legislation to promote one goal often conflicts with other goals or has unintended consequences elsewhere in the economy. In many parts of the world, energy is heavily subsidized to make it cheap. The problem of course is that it only makes energy *appear* to be cheap; tax revenues must be used to pay the subsidies. An unintended consequence is that the subsidies encourage over-consumption, which leads to greater carbon emissions and greater dependence on insecure energy forms.

Another example of the unintended-consequence problem is the U.S. policy to promote corn-based ethanol in place of gasoline. Congress conducted a beauty pageant for alternative fuels and bought into the idea that domestically produced corn-based ethanol should displace conventional gasoline, thereby displacing foreign oil imports and at the same time reducing greenhouse-gas emissions (the theory is that the $CO_2$ absorbed when the corn is growing should offset the $CO_2$ emitted when the ethanol is consumed). Unfortunately, what sounded good in theory has turned out to be a fiasco. Research shows that total $CO_2$ emissions from ethanol are in fact almost twice as great as those from conventional gasoline. Furthermore, replacing just 3.1 percent of U.S. effective gasoline consumption[2] with ethanol in 2007 required 23.7 percent of the corn crop and 7 percent of the total cropland acreage.[3] Finally, there is yet another unintended consequence—with corn prices tripling since 2005, all grain and livestock prices have risen sharply, bringing food and energy into direct conflict. Sadly, the United States is now locked into command-and-control legislation that mandates a fourfold increase in biofuels production by 2022. Clearly, there must be a better way than the current mishmash of command-and-control legislation and congressional beauty pageants for alternative fuels.

### AN ECONOMIST'S PRESCRIPTION: TAXES AND A PRICE-BASED ENERGY POLICY

In this book I argue that the best energy policy for balancing the often-competing goals of cheap, clean, and secure energy would use the price system to fundamentally alter consumer behavior, business behavior, and the incentives to develop alternative-energy technologies. Currently, the price system fails to incorporate the true social cost of fossil fuels—the costs associated with climate change and oil security. Because these fossil fuels are artificially cheap, alternative clean and secure energy technologies are forced to compete on a very uneven playing field. By taxing fossil fuels to reflect their true environmental and security costs, we can level the playing field for these new technologies. Given a level playing field, new technologies will flourish, and energy conservation will restrain the overall growth of energy consumption. There will be no need for special subsidies, tax credits, and so forth for alternative technologies deemed winners of the congressional beauty pageant for alternative fuels. Instead, the marketplace will identify the winners and winnow out failed technologies. There is currently no way for policymakers to identify the ultimate winners and losers. We have no idea what technologies will dominate in thirty or fifty years. Instead of policymakers attempting to socially engineer the outcome, as in the case of corn-based ethanol, it is far better to create the market conditions under which unknown and unknowable technologies will flourish.

Using the price system to modify human behavior is not a novel idea. "Sin taxes" on alcohol and cigarettes, for example, have been shown to substantially reduce consumption of both. Particularly in the Scandinavian countries, high taxes on alcohol have proved to be an effective means of curtailing consumption, after experiments with a variety of command-and-control policies, such as prohibition, generated much public discontent. But in the case of fossil fuels, taxes would not only discourage the consumption of fossil fuels, but they would also provide a level playing field on which new energy technologies could compete and flourish. Specifically,

*Congress should enact a security tax per barrel of oil and a carbon tax per ton of emissions, thus raising the prices of all carbon-containing fossil fuels to reflect their true social cost.*

Such a strategy has several advantages over the policy of awarding subsidies and protective tariffs to industries represented by strong, entrenched lobbies such as the Renewable Fuels Association (corn-based ethanol producers) and subjecting consumers to various command-and-controls:

- *All* new technologies would enjoy a more level playing field.
- The market, not the government, would determine which of the new technologies are the winners.
- This approach is more transparent. It is extremely difficult to assess the costs (in terms of lost tax revenues) and the effectiveness of the current patchwork of subsidies and tax credits. In contrast, imposing carbon and security taxes would force us to ask how much we are willing to pay for cleaner air and added oil security.
- A focus on getting the prices right for fossil fuels would limit the opportunity for Congress to pass legislation designed to enrich particular private-interest groups.

### Oil Security Tax

Oil security is a worldwide problem, with a built-in incentive for countries to underinvest in security since any one country cannot capture all the benefits.

Oil security can be achieved either by reducing world oil consumption or by increasing the amount of secure oil in the mix. Investment in the storage of emergency oil supplies, such as the United States' Strategic Petroleum Reserve, is an example of a means to accomplish the latter. But the question remains whether the price of a barrel of oil in world markets reflects its true social cost if we must buy an insurance policy in the form of adding a barrel of oil to the Strategic Petroleum Reserve. Isn't the true social cost of the oil in this case its purchase price *plus* the cost of the insurance policy? In principle, then, an oil security tax should be set equal to the cost of the insurance policy, thereby incorporating into the price the full social cost of the oil.

A security tax on all oil consumed *domestically* would raise the price to the consumer, thereby reducing consumption. Although increased prices due to an oil security tax would *not* increase the flow of oil from conventional production, they would promote conservation and accelerate the development of substitutes for conventional oil, such as oil sands and renewable fuels from promising new technologies.

Most importantly, we can use our willingness to impose such a tax as a bargaining chip to encourage other industrialized nations to follow our lead and to encourage developing countries to stop misguided oil-subsidy policies aimed at making oil artificially cheap. These subsidy policies thwart the desired conservation effects of higher oil prices and weaken oil security by increasing the reliance on Middle East oil.

### Carbon Tax

For a number of reasons, economists generally favor a carbon tax that escalates over time in a predictable manner in place of the cap-and-trade system used in the European Union.[4] First, a carbon tax establishes an observable price that society is willing to pay for $CO_2$ abatement and creates a more level playing field for new technologies. Second, a carbon tax avoids the potential problem of uncertain and highly fluctuating prices of emissions rights. Investors in new plants know with certainty the current carbon tax and the rate at which it will escalate in the future and thus can formulate sensible investment plans. Third, a carbon tax offers flexibility, so emissions reductions can occur optimally over time. As new technologies are gradually developed and the existing stock of energy-consuming capital is replaced, carbon emitters have the option to pay the tax if, indeed, it becomes too costly to abate the $CO_2$. Under the proposal advanced here, the carbon tax would increase at 4 percent per annum plus the overall inflation rate. Consequently, in constant dollars, the tax would double in eighteen years and quadruple in thirty-six years. With prospects for steadily rising carbon taxes and future technological advances, new investments in power plants and other long-lived energy-using capital equipment like cars, trucks, and airplanes will begin today. But the primary impact will occur in the future with the complete turnover of the energy-consuming equipment. This flexibility is especially important as we make the transition to lower carbon emissions.

There are two additional properties that distinguish a carbon tax. One is that a carbon tax would be much more transparent than tradable emissions allowances and potentially less subject to manipulation. There would be no offsets, for example, for farmers and foresters earning "allowance credits" that could be sold; nor would there be the clean development mechanisms that have resulted in abuses abroad. It is hoped that, as with the gasoline tax in the United States, there would be no special exemptions. The tax would be assessed on the carbon content of the fuel, which is readily measurable. Credits for carbon-sequestration technologies would be allowed only on the basis of measured quantities of $CO_2$ sequestered.

Another unique advantage of a carbon tax is that its revenues can be used to reduce other taxes.[5] It has long been recognized that income and payroll taxes generate a loss in general welfare by creating a disincentive to work, but they have been needed to fund government expenditures. Environmental-tax revenues could be used to reduce income and payroll taxes, correcting two economic distortions at once and giving society a double dividend.[6] Even for those who view every federal tax dollar as an invitation for increased government expenditures, it would be a simple matter to couple carbon and oil security taxes with offsetting income- or payroll-tax reductions, producing a revenue-neutral effect.[7]

## SETTING THE TAX RATE

Assuming the political process could actually deliver a policy to impose taxes for oil security and $CO_2$ emissions, what should the tax rates be? Economic theory offers a straightforward policy prescription for setting optimal tax rates: set the rate where the marginal cost of controlling the externality equals the marginal benefit received from its abatement. In effect, to set the carbon-tax rate, create a supply and demand curve for $CO_2$ abatement; the price at which the two curves intersect reflects society's willingness to pay for carbon abatement and thus the optimal tax. The carbon and oil security taxes will raise the prices of fossil fuels to reflect the true social costs of such fuels. The higher prices will make alternative fuels more economically attractive and induce more energy conservation.

This book examines in detail how the suggested taxes for oil security and carbon emissions would affect the prices of the primary fossil fuels—coal, oil, and natural gas—today and in the future. Available research supports rather modest security and carbon taxes—a $5-per-barrel oil security tax and an initial carbon tax of $5 per ton of $CO_2$. With 2007 energy prices as a base, these taxes would increase oil prices by 11 percent, natural-gas prices by only 5 percent, and coal prices by 49 percent. For consumers, gasoline prices would rise by 7 percent, heating-oil prices by 6 percent, residential natural-gas prices by 2 percent, and electricity generated by coal-fired plants by 14 percent. Recent emissions prices in the European Union suggest that the price increases under a cap-and-trade system might be as much as five or six times as great.

The case for moderate initial taxes that rise substantially over time is compelling. The existing stock of power plants, autos, housing, and buildings was configured on the basis of past energy prices, and in the short run, there is little one can do other than drive less and adjust the thermostat. Large energy price increases, such as could occur under a cap-and-trade system, basically punish consumers for their past decisions and achieve only small reductions in $CO_2$ emissions. In effect, cheap energy would be sacrificed for only minimal gains toward clean energy.

## CHANGING ENERGY USE AND
## NEW INVESTMENT

A carbon tax that quintuples by 2050 could dramatically change our future energy infrastructure. Knowing that the carbon tax will increase dramatically over the next forty-plus years, consumers and producers would begin altering their investment decisions today. The decision to buy a more or less fuel-efficient car, air conditioner, refrigerator, or other appliance would surely be affected by the anticipation of the carbon-tax rate rising, as proposed here, by 48 percent in ten years and 119 percent in twenty years. Likewise, planners of a new power plant would take into account that the price of coal—which would increase initially by 49 percent with the imposition of the carbon tax—would more than double in twenty years. Surely, such expectations would completely change the types of future energy investments.

## THE REVENUE POTENTIAL OF THE
## PROPOSED ENERGY TAXES

Another important advantage of a carbon tax and an oil security tax is that such taxes would generate significant federal tax revenues. It is estimated that in the first year the carbon tax would produce $37 billion and the oil security tax would produce $36 billion, a combined total of $73 billion. Over time, this figure would likely rise substantially, if only because the carbon tax would be adjusted upward annually by the rate of inflation, plus 4 percent. Assuming recent emission rates and the implementation in 2009 of a $5 carbon tax that escalates at 4 percent plus inflation of 3 percent, carbon-tax revenues in the year 2050 would be about $590 billion. With the oil security tax rising with inflation, it could contribute an additional $120 billion by 2050. Clearly, the two taxes could be huge generators of future tax revenues at the same time that they steer the economy toward lower emissions and less dependence on insecure oil. Not only would such tax revenues be a boon for the U.S. Treasury, but revenue-starved developing countries would clearly find such taxes attractive revenue generators as well. Perhaps even India and China would find such a revenue source superior to their other sources of revenue.

## OVERCOMING OBJECTIONS TO TAXES

Despite the clear merits of the proposed energy taxes, many Americans are likely to oppose them on philosophical as well as macroeconomic grounds. To overcome objections to energy taxes, I propose that they be revenue neutral. Under any energy-tax legislation adopted, the tax revenues should be earmarked for offsetting reductions in income and payroll taxes and increases in the earned income tax credit. The net effect on consumers' pocketbooks would thus be offset by income-tax reductions. Again, this approach has an important advantage over cap-and-trade proposals because it allows for greater benefits to the public—through relief from income and other taxes—at the expense of carbon-emitting industries. It is no accident that large carbon emitters favor a cap-and-trade system—they see it as a means of obtaining valuable emissions permits for free and acquiring for themselves competitive advantages vis-à-vis new entrants that lack the benefit of free emissions permits.

As to objections about the macroeconomic effects of revenue-neutral energy taxes, the effects would likely be inconsequential for two reasons. First, although consumers as a group would pay more for energy, the income- and payroll-tax reductions would offset these increased energy costs. To be sure, more prodigious energy consumers might not be fully compensated, whereas low energy users could receive a windfall. But these distributional issues should not be dispositive, because of the magnitude of the taxes. Furthermore, because of the relatively moderate level of the initial tax rates, these taxes would not be likely to cause any substantial short-run macroeconomic disruption.

### REASONS TO READ ON

The preceding discussion is a synopsis of the book from 30,000 feet. Only the skyscrapers were identified. But there is much more that one must understand to grasp the complexity of balancing cheap, clean, and secure energy. Missing are the details of why we choose to focus on climate change, since fossil fuels contain other serious pollutants. Missing is the explanation of why until recently oil was no longer cheap and a discussion of the factors that will determine long-term oil prices. Missing is the discussion of why markets have historically done a reasonable job of providing cheap energy and why government policies should be circumscribed to certain areas. Missing is the discussion of the alarming rise of petro-nationalism[8] and the mistaken belief that countries like China can buy oil security by locking up oil reserves around the world. Missing is the discussion of why, even though past temperature changes have been relatively small, there is good reason to take climate change seriously. Missing are the discussions of how to bring the world's major carbon emitters together to cooperate and why the Kyoto Protocol has met with only limited success. Missing is the discussion of the critical importance of government funding of basic research in the energy area as well as the importance of limiting the role of government in conducting congressional beauty pageants for new energy sources. Missing is a discussion of the politics of energy policy and why ideas like limiting government's ability to dole out subsidies, tax credits, and benefits to special interests will meet great resistance. Missing too is a discussion of why the usual Washington approach is a prescription for failure. We can do much better! Read on!

# Chapter 1  The Three

# Conflicting Goals of

# Energy Policy

Energy policy has lately attained a prominent place on the nation's public-policy agenda. In mid-2008, U.S. consumers were outraged when the price of gasoline hit $4 per gallon. Vast resources, both human and military, are being spent on the war in Iraq—a country whose oil reserves are eclipsed only by those of Saudi Arabia and Iran. Many feel that our military commitment to the region could be scaled back dramatically were it not for our dependence on Middle East oil. On the other hand, both the United States and our European allies are now hesitant to take action against Iran, despite its nuclear threat, for fear of disrupting the country's oil exports of 2.5 million barrels per day and sending prices to $200 per barrel. China, now the world's second-largest oil consumer, is actively courting rogue oil-producing countries like Iran, Myanmar, and Sudan, seeking bilateral trade agreements aimed at locking up reserves to feed its voracious economy.

Meanwhile, the scientific community points to mounting evidence of global warming. Fossil fuels, which provide 87 percent of the world's energy, are the major culprit.[1] The Kyoto Protocol, which called for its signatories to meet certain greenhouse-gas-emissions targets by 2010, is losing credibility as a number of key countries fail to meet their targets. Denmark, for example, is expected to miss its target by 38 percent, Spain by 33 percent, Ireland by 27 percent, Austria by 25 percent, and France and Italy by 10 percent each.[2] Carbon emissions from nonsignatories such as the United States, China, India, and South Korea continue to grow, essentially unabated.

Critics of the George W. Bush and previous presidential administrations lament what they say is the lack of a U.S. energy policy, but most members of Congress who supported the Energy Policy Act of 2005 or the Energy Independence and Security Act of 2007 may take exception to such criticism. With the 2005 bill filling 550 pages in the *Congressional Record* and doling out $12.3 billion in subsidies, as well as $1.6 billion in new expenditures, the United States does, in a sense, have an energy policy; but it is based largely on pork-barrel politics and an absence of imagination. The *Washington Post* called the spending bill "a broad collection of subsidies for U.S. energy companies, in particular the nuclear and oil industries." The *Philadelphia Inquirer*'s editorial page described Congress's mentality as "Let's pass it and claim we did something." Senator John McCain, who voted against the 2005 bill, described an earlier version as the "No Lobbyist Left Behind Bill" and the final version as "the latest incarnation of special interest influence in policymaking."[3]

## A FLAWED PROCESS

A key premise of this book is that the situation is urgent, and that our energy policy is fatally flawed both in the *process* by which problems are identified and in the *solutions* that are chosen. The process is guided largely by whatever interest groups are most vocal. The solutions often feature either command-and-control mandates reminiscent of energy policy in the 1970s or a grab bag of congressional goodies in the form of subsidies, tax credits, and grants. The result is a mishmash of legislation that is inconsistent, ineffective, and ill conceived.

In identifying problems, the current process fails to first ask the essential question: What should the goals of energy policy be? Instead, various interest groups identify a list of perceived problems, pick discrete policies to respond to each, and then lobby policymakers to act on them. Although this ad hoc approach may seem logical, at least according to the peculiar logic of congressional policymaking, there are two problems with it.

First, without goals guiding the policymaking process, there is no way to determine whether an issue is a genuine problem worthy of government attention. Second, ad hoc fixes for one problem might exacerbate others. For example, actions to reduce dependency on imported oil by producing synthetic fuels from domestic coal may produce environmental consequences far more serious than the security concerns prompting the actions.

Besides using a failure-prone process to identify the problems that policy must address, policymakers all too often go about choosing solutions as though engaged in a beauty pageant of sorts, looking at a set of existing energy technologies, picking winners, and then showering them with massive government subsidies, tax credits, and other prizes. This approach does not actually develop completely new technologies; instead, Congress typically encourages the adoption of established technologies that aren't economically viable without special incentives. Most often, these decisions are based on politics and the political clout of senators and representatives rather than on scientific data.

A good example of a first-place winner of such a congressional beauty pageant is corn-based ethanol. Not to be outdone by President George W. Bush's proposal calling for mandatory production of 35 billion gallons of renewable and alternative fuels by 2017, Senator Tom Harkin (D-Iowa), joined by Senators Byron Dorgan (D-N.D.), Tim Johnson (D-S.D.), Ken Salazar (D-Colo.), Richard Lugar (R-Ind.), Joseph Biden (D-Del.), and Barack Obama (D-Ill.), introduced a bill requiring the production of 60 billion gallons of ethanol or biodiesel by 2030 and mandating that half of all service stations be retrofitted to offer E85 fuel within a decade.[4] Ultimately, the Energy Independence and Security Act of 2007 mandated 36 billion gallons of ethanol and biodiesel production by 2022. Given current technology, the most likely fuel to meet the interim requirements of the bill is domestically produced corn-based ethanol; and on the face of it, replacing, say, 15 billion gallons of gasoline (out of current annual consumption of 140 billion gallons) with domestically produced corn-based ethanol would seem to be eminently sensible, reducing both the consumption of imported oil and greenhouse-gas emissions.

But all that glitters is not gold, and Michael McElroy, a Harvard professor of environmental studies, describes such legislation as "hype and hot air."[5] There are at least five major problems with promoting corn-based ethanol:

- It takes one and a half gallons of ethanol to generate the same energy as one gallon of gasoline. This means that 15 billion gallons of ethanol would save only 10 billion gallons of gasoline—about 7 percent of current gasoline consumption.

- McElroy calculates that in July 2006, ethanol in California sold for $4 per gallon—California motorists were paying more than $6 for enough ethanol to obtain the energy equivalent of a gallon of gasoline. Unfortunately, since the ethanol content of California gasoline may be only 5–10 percent, its costs get hidden in the price of gasoline. Interestingly, cheaper sources of ethanol exist—such as sugarcane grown in Brazil—but ethanol imports carry a tariff of $0.54 per gallon.
- A big increase in the production of corn-based ethanol will only exacerbate an ongoing conflict between food and fuel. As it is, corn prices in the United States have more than trebled since 2005, causing economic havoc for livestock producers. Even more serious are the effects of rising corn prices on the very poor in Mexico and elsewhere who depend on corn tortillas. In 2006 alone, the price of tortillas rose by almost 20 percent. Economists Glenn Fox and Kenneth Shwedel report that the lowest decile of Mexican households devote almost 12 percent of their expenditures to corn products.[6] Furthermore, reliance on corn-based ethanol to meet even 15 billion gallons of the 36-billion-gallon target will require doubling the acreage devoted to corn— 93.6 acres in 2007. Considering that in 2006 there were only 330 million acres of agricultural land in cultivation, this is a staggering increase that could drive up prices even further, to the detriment of all individuals and sectors of the economy that depend on food products.[7]
- In terms of greenhouse gases, McElroy concludes that there is no net benefit to switching to ethanol; the production of corn-based ethanol generates the same amount of greenhouse-gas emissions as the use of ethanol saves by reducing gasoline consumption.
- The story gets even worse when one factors in the changes in land use that must accompany the large increases in corn-based ethanol production. In two February 2008 studies reported in *Science,* Timothy Searchinger and others, and Joseph Fargione and others, point to the enormous one-time release of carbon stored in pastureland and forests when they are converted to cropland.[8] Searchinger and others conclude that, counting land-use change, over a thirty-year-period greenhouse-gas emissions from corn-based ethanol would be nearly twice those of conventional gasoline.

Other congressional beauty-pageant winners have been biodiesel, nuclear power, hybrid automobiles, wind power, and cellulosic-ethanol technologies. Unfortunately, all these expenditures (except those for cellulosic ethanol) are for the diffusion of *existing* technologies.[9] In the absence of subsidies or tax credits, many of these existing technologies would remain economically unattractive with little prospect of becoming attractive. In contrast, new energy technologies that, with technological breakthroughs, could dramatically alter the energy mix get short shrift.

Congress supplements its beauty-pageant approach to energy policy with the use of command-and-control mandates for the use of certain fuels like ethanol. A command-and-control approach is distinguished by government requirements that certain *quantitative* targets be met, often with prescriptions for how they are to be achieved. American energy policy in the 1970s was typified by command-and-control measures, such as the imposition of price controls on all petroleum products, including domestically produced oil. When shortages developed as a result, consumers were forced to queue up in long gasoline lines and were limited to purchasing gas on alternating days depending on whether their license plates ended in an odd or even number. Today, command-and-control measures are still very much apparent, as evidenced by the ethanol fiasco and California's mandate that by 2004 one-tenth of the cars sold in California produce no direct emissions.[10] The latest example is the Energy Independence and Security Act of 2007, which also mandates increased fuel economy for cars and light trucks, the elimination of incandescent light bulbs, and massive increases in ethanol production to displace gasoline.

Fortunately, there are alternatives to command-and-control regulations and congressional beauty pageants. My prescription for a consistent, effective energy policy corrects the process by which policies are formulated and solutions are chosen. There is a better way, but it will require looking at energy policy through the lens of economic reasoning. Congress must be willing to abdicate its role of judge, jury, and executioner and accept the more circumscribed, yet critical, role of helping to get the prices right. The result will unleash the creative forces of the market to solve the energy dilemma.

## IDENTIFYING THE THREE GOALS OF ENERGY POLICY

If we are to wean ourselves from the conventional policy process of forming lists of problems as they arise, we must begin by doing what the process has so far failed to do, namely, identify the goals of energy policy. My premise is that there should be three goals: energy should be cheap, clean, and secure.

These goals are already implicit in issues that concern the American public. Outrage over $4-per-gallon gasoline reflects the desire for cheap energy. Worries about $CO_2$ emissions from fossil fuels reflect the desire for clean energy. And concerns about our heavy dependence on oil imported from the Middle East reflect the desire for secure energy. Although having such clear goals in mind does not ensure good choices, it prevents policymakers from wandering down myriad rabbit trails leading nowhere.

Let us explore why these three particular attributes should be the goals of U.S. energy policy.

### Cheap Energy: The Lifeblood of a Growing Economy

In the vernacular of the economist, cheap energy plays a vital role in raising the productivity of workers because it allows the substitution of inanimate energy (fuel) for animate energy (labor). Historically, the invention of the cotton gin, grain combines, and tractors allowed energy to be substituted for human labor in the agricultural sector, greatly expanding farmers' productivity. In industry, electric-powered robots and computers have replaced thousands of production workers on the modern assembly line. Computers now perform in seconds calculations that would take days to solve by hand. Such phenomenal productivity gains have yielded significant improvements in standards of living and in national gross domestic product (GDP). One reason that poor countries stay poor is that they are unable to substitute energy for labor to a sufficient degree.

From the consumer's perspective, cheap energy is an essential element of a high standard of living. Affordable appliances coupled with cheap electricity have fundamentally changed household activities. Likewise, the invention of the internal combustion engine and subsequent advances in automobile design have allowed consumers in developed nations to live a lifestyle that is the envy of most of the world.

Yet energy expenditures remain a substantial percentage of Americans' incomes, particularly for lower-income Americans. Households in the lowest income quintile spend close to 10 percent of their income on energy.[11] A doubling of energy prices would force poor families to make difficult choices among food, housing, and energy. Energy prices matter greatly to middle-income families as well, as evidenced by the extreme short-run price inelasticity of energy demand in the whole economy.[12] Even households in the top quintile spend 5 percent of their income on energy.[13]

Indeed, most empirical studies agree that in the short-run, demand for various energy forms is extremely inelastic (that is, the quantity demanded is relatively unresponsive to price increases).[14] In effect, consumers exhibit little willingness (or ability) to reduce their use of energy in the short run in response to price increases. People have to drive to get to work and run errands; it is not easy for them to drive less, move closer to work, or buy more fuel-efficient vehicles in the short run. Having invested in a set of household appliances, consumers are unwilling to stop using their dishwashers, washing machines, televisions, air conditioners, and so forth when the price of electricity rises.

In the long run, however, the response is quite different. Over time, consumers can replace their energy-consuming equipment with more efficient cars, air conditioners, and other appliances. In the short run, consumers are stuck with the existing equipment infrastructure, but in the long run, everything can change.

Cheap energy is even more vital to consumers in developing countries. Having electrical appliances like refrigerators, radios, televisions, and air conditioners or electric fans represents a relatively greater advance in the quality of life than it does in developed countries. Consequently, it is quite common to subsidize the price of petroleum products so that consumers do not see higher fuel prices. For example, from January 2004 to June 2008 the price of gasoline in Beijing increased only by 47 percent,[15] whereas U.S. prices rose from $1.50 to $4.00 per gallon, or 166 percent. The Chinese government has chosen to subsidize the price of petroleum products to restrain inflation and encourage continued economic growth. Indeed, the International Monetary Fund surveyed forty-six developing nations and found that in only thirteen are energy prices allowed to fluctuate with supply and demand.[16] In most of the developing countries, domestic prices are set by the government and subsidies make up the difference between the world price and the domestic price.

From an economist's perspective, subsidies are a contrivance because they only *appear* to make energy cheap. Since the government must raise taxes to pay subsidies, consumers end up paying anyway. Furthermore, by making energy seem cheaper, subsidies encourage overconsumption and waste, driving prices up further. Nevertheless, the pervasive nature of energy subsidies, even in a country as affluent as the United States, illustrates the public's desire for cheap energy. To satisfy that desire, the policy goal should be to make energy truly cheaper, not just *appear* cheaper.

### Clean Energy: A Public Good Highly Valued by Affluent Societies

Everything else being equal, cheap energy is strongly preferred to expensive energy—but everything else is not always equal. Given the choice between dirty energy and clean energy at a moderately higher price, clean energy wins hands down. The more affluent a society becomes, the more willing it is to pay for clean energy. Just as rising income levels cause us to demand nicer homes, more comfortable cars, more sophisticated electronics, and better meals, we also demand cleaner air to breathe. For the most part, cleaner air is not provided through the usual market mechanism in the same way that a gourmet meal would be. Nevertheless, throughout the developed world, clean-air laws have essentially decoupled growth in energy consumption from increased air pollution.

Some may think that concern for air quality in the United States began with the passage of the Clean Air Act of 1970 and the formation of the Environmental Protection Agency (EPA) that same year, but in fact it began many years earlier. In 1950, coal was commonly used for home heating, particularly in the Northeast, and it was also the dominant source of heat in the industrial sector. The dirtiest of fossil fuels, coal produces a range of air pollutants as well as proportionally more $CO_2$ than other fuels. Between 1950 and 1970, residential coal consumption fell from 51.6 million tons to only 9 million tons and industrial consumption fell from 224.6 million tons to 186.6 million tons. During that same period, diesel locomotives replaced coal-powered steam engines as railroads realized that their clientele would pay more to travel without black smoke billowing from the train. Clearly, homeowners preferred cleaner fuels such as oil or natural gas. To a lesser extent, so did industry and the railroads. Today, coal is used as a fuel only for electric power plants in developed countries.

Since these changes were the result of consumer choices, at first no regulatory action was needed. By 1970, however, it was clear that measures were necessary to continue the drive toward cleaner energy. Following the Clean Air Act of 1970, additional legislation strengthened environmental standards. Especially noteworthy was the Clean Air Act Amendments of 1990, which added emissions trading and other provisions to reduce acid rain and ozone depletion.

Figure 1.1 shows trends in various forms of air pollution and total energy consumption during this period. Unsurprisingly, energy consumption grew steadily with the overall economy, increasing by almost 50 percent between 1970 and 2006. Meanwhile, emissions of sulfur dioxide and volatile organic (hydrocarbon) compounds fell by 56 percent and emissions of carbon monoxide fell by 51 percent. Particulates fell by 70 percent. Nitrogen oxides showed the smallest reduction—32 percent—because more complete combustion of hydrocarbons has led to offsetting increases in nitrogen oxides. If the public did

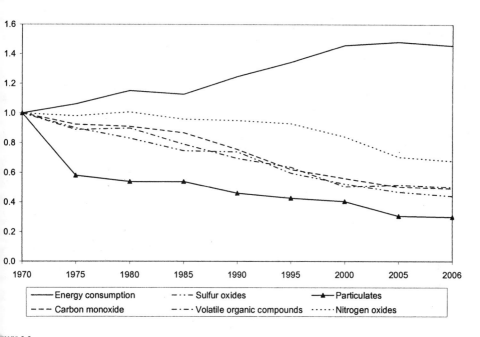

ﬁure 1.1

iteria pollutants and energy consumption, 1970–2006

ta from EPA (2008).

not care about clean energy, one would expect to see the various types of air pollution growing in lockstep with energy consumption. Instead, this very different picture emerges.

America's impressive progress in dealing with air pollution might leave you with the mistaken notion that the problem of clean energy has been solved. With most conventional pollutants, as shown in figure 1.1, that is largely the case—but not with greenhouse gases. Fossil fuels produce $CO_2$, the major greenhouse gas that contributes to global warming. The Intergovernmental Panel on Climate Change has concluded that anthropogenic emissions of greenhouse gases have been a major contributing factor to the warming we have seen over the last century.[17] Unfortunately, fossil fuels provide 87 percent of the world's energy, and use of these fuels tends to grow proportionally with the size of the economy. Consequently, the question is not whether additional global warming will occur but how much and how fast warming will occur.

To complicate the problem further, it is worldwide $CO_2$ emissions that matter, not just those of the United States. Indeed, China is poised to overtake the United States as the leading emitter of greenhouse gases. For many such developing countries, clean energy is a luxury they cannot yet afford; their priority is cheap energy. China and India, for instance, tend to rely extensively on their large indigenous supplies of coal for energy, despite the heavy emissions.

China is an interesting case in point because, as income rises, so does the demand for clean energy. Even with its enormous reserves of low-cost coal, coal as a fraction of total energy consumption has already begun declining, from 73.3 percent in 1980 to 70.4 percent in 2007.[18] Coal remains the most common fuel source for home heat and industrial-process heat, but further reductions will no doubt occur as the country develops. What we see is not that China and other developing countries are unwilling to pay for clean energy, but rather that they are not willing to pay much. Presumably, as incomes rise, these countries will increasingly be concerned with air pollution and will demand cleaner fuels. Unfortunately, it may be many years before per capita incomes in India and China approach the levels in developed countries. In the interim, rapidly rising greenhouse-gas emissions pose a worldwide problem.

### Secure Energy: Critical to National Security

Energy security is our third goal because energy is a critical ingredient for a high living standard and has few substitutes in the short run. Imagine what would happen to the U.S. economy if all energy sources were shut off tomorrow. The lights would go out, factories would shut down, and transportation would come to a grinding halt. If it was summer, we would swelter in the heat; if it was winter, we would freeze. So although we want cheap and clean energy, we must also have reliable sources of energy that are available on a continuous basis.

Fortunately, the market does a remarkably good job of keeping the lights on, as providers proved unreliable are punished by customers' moving to more reliable ones. Despite episodes like the great East Coast power failure in August 2003, which resulted in lost power for up to two days in many areas,[19] the United States enjoys great reliability in the provision of electricity and most energy sources. Although gasoline prices vary, supplies are always available. Just as with clean energy, the more affluent a society is, the greater importance it will attach to secure energy.

When Americans talk about energy security, they really mean oil security because of the political instability of the Middle East and its key role in the world oil market. Europeans share similar security concerns regarding Middle East oil, but they also have serious concerns about their dependence on Russian natural gas, which accounts for almost 50 percent of European supplies.[20] It is often noted that the Middle East accounts for only about 30 percent of world oil

Table 1.1  Ten countries with largest oil reserves, 2007 (billions of barrels)

| Country | Reserves | USGS estimated undiscovered reserves | Reserves + undiscovered reserves |
|---|---|---|---|
| Saudi Arabia | 264.2 | 87.1 | 351.3 |
| Iran | 138.4 | 53.1 | 191.5 |
| Iraq | 115.0 | 45.1 | 160.1 |
| Kuwait | 101.5 | 38.4 | 139.9 |
| United Arab Emirates | 97.8 | 77.0 | 174.8 |
| Venezuela | 87.0 | 19.7 | 106.7 |
| Russia | 79.4 | 77.4 | 156.8 |
| Kazakhstan | 39.8 | 21.1 | 60.9 |
| Libya | 41.5 | 82.7 | 124.2 |
| Nigeria | 36.2 | 37.6 | 73.8 |

*Sources:* Data on reserves are from BP (2008), and data on estimated undiscovered reserves are from USGS (2000).

supplies. That observation, although true, is misleading because reserves in the United States and the North Sea, which account for 15 percent of current production, are being rapidly depleted.[21] Furthermore, political instability that can disrupt oil supplies is not limited to the Middle East, as evidenced by events in Venezuela and Nigeria.

As table 1.1 suggests, the world's oil reserves are not proportional to land mass; if they were, the Middle East would have only about 1 percent of reserves. In fact, it accounts for 62 percent. The ten countries listed in the table are the largest in terms of oil reserves; of these, the five largest are all in the Middle East. The second column presents the U.S. Geological Survey's estimate of undiscovered reserves, which suggests that significant portions of undiscovered reserves are likely to be in these same areas.[22]

It is clear that by whatever metric one adopts, the Middle East will always play a vital role in the world oil market. At the same time, the major oil-consuming countries are generally not major reserve holders. Table 1.2 ranks the top nine oil-consuming nations (treating the European Union as a single nation) and shows the fraction of world oil reserves and production located in each, as well as its GDP and percentage of world GDP.

Note that the ranking of countries by oil consumption closely matches the ranking by GDP. Clearly, oil consumption and economic activity are related.

Table 1.2 Nine largest oil-consuming nations, 2007

| Country | Annual oil consumption ($10^6$ barrels per day) | % of world oil consumption | % of world oil production | % of world oil reserves | GDP$^a$ ($ trillions) | % of world GDP |
|---|---|---|---|---|---|---|
| United States | 20.7 | 23.9 | 8.0 | 2.4 | 13.84 | 21.1 |
| EU-27 | 14.9 | 17.8 | 2.9 | 0.5 | 14.38 | 21.9 |
| China | 7.9 | 9.3 | 4.8 | 1.3 | 6.99 | 10.7 |
| Japan | 5.1 | 5.8 | <1 | <1 | 4.29 | 6.5 |
| Russia | 2.7 | 3.2 | 12.6 | 6.4 | 2.09 | 3.2 |
| India | 2.7 | 3.2 | 1.0 | 0.4 | 2.99 | 4.6 |
| South Korea | 2.4 | 2.7 | 0 | 0 | 1.20 | 1.8 |
| Canada | 2.3 | 2.6 | 4.1 | 2.2 | 1.27 | 1.9 |
| Mexico | 2.0 | 2.3 | 4.4 | 1.0 | 1.35 | 2.1 |

*Sources:* BP (2008) and CIA (2008).
$^a$GDP is adjusted to reflect purchasing power parity.

The United States currently accounts for 23.9 percent of total world consumption and 21.1 percent of world GDP. In contrast, U.S. oil production accounts for only 8.0 percent of global production, and the U.S. reserve base represents only 2.4 percent of world oil reserves. Next come the 27 countries of the European Union, which account for 17.8 percent of world oil consumption and 21.9 percent of world GDP. Their shares of world oil production (2.9 percent) and reserves (0.5 percent) are trivial compared with their share of oil consumption. China accounts for 9.3 percent of world oil consumption and produces 4.8 percent of the world's supply. But with stable domestic production and rapidly growing consumption, it is easy to see why China is looking for foreign sources of oil. Japan, India, and South Korea are all highly dependent on imported oil. The exceptions appear to be Russia, Canada, and Mexico. Russia, the fifth-largest oil consumer, has a greater percentage of production (12.6 percent) than consumption (3.2 percent). The mismatch between consuming nations and producing nations would not in itself be a great concern for security if not for the political instability of the Middle East and other oil-producing areas such as Venezuela and Nigeria.

Another strategic consideration is that oil production in the Middle East is strictly controlled by the state-owned oil companies. Consequently, these companies' production decisions are not based on the standard calculus of profit maximization. A profit-maximizing oil producer in the region would never choose to embargo its best customers. In a state-owned enterprise, actions that constitute economic suicide can be justified on political grounds. Middle Eastern leaders are well aware that oil can be used as a very powerful weapon to achieve political objectives. The Arab oil embargo that began in the fall of 1973 quadrupled world oil prices and wreaked havoc on the economies of developed countries.[23]

Unfortunately, conditions in the Middle East do not appear appreciably better today than they were in 1973. Terrorist activities linked to al-Qaeda have replaced intercountry rivalries, and many Middle Eastern countries cannot control the terrorist minorities living within their boundaries. Among Muslims, the schism between the more radical Shiites and the more conservative Sunnis has widened. Even within the relatively moderate Sunni sect, militant groups calling for the overthrow of Sunni-led monarchies have emerged.

Particularly prescient are the dire warnings of Samuel Huntington in *The Clash of Civilizations and the Remaking of World Order.*[24] Huntington argues that religious and cultural differences between Western industrialized countries and Islamic countries are so deep that conflict is inevitable. In Huntington's framework, countries that pursue a fundamentalist agenda are naturally driven to conflict with the more secular Western nations.

## THE INHERENT CONFLICTS BETWEEN CHEAP, CLEAN, AND SECURE ENERGY

Ideally, the cheapest energy sources would also be the cleanest and the most secure; unfortunately, that is not the case. Figure 1.2 shows why. Of the energy sources used by the world in 2005, fossil fuels dominated, accounting for 87 percent of the total. Other sources included hydropower (6 percent), nuclear power (6 percent), and other forms of renewable energy, such as firewood, biomass, and solar power (1 percent). Among fossil fuels, petroleum accounts for the lion's share, with 38 percent of consumption, and coal and natural gas account for 26 percent and 23 percent, respectively.

Figure 1.3 shows the mix of energy chosen by the United States in 2007. The U.S. energy mix is not significantly different from the global mix, even though, as noted, the United States accounts for about one-fourth of world consumption. For example, fossil fuels accounted for 86 percent of U.S. consumption: oil accounted for 40 percent, natural gas 24 percent, and coal 22 percent.

Is the dominant fuel—petroleum—the cheapest, cleanest, and most secure source of energy? No. Petroleum-based fuels have until recently been quite ex-

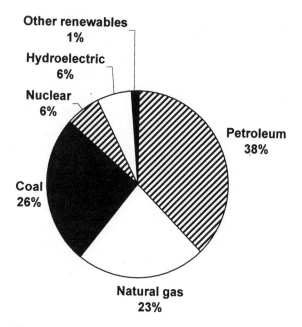

Figure 1.2
World primary energy consumption by source, 2005
Data from DOE (2007b, table 1.1).
*Note:* Other renewables includes biomass, geothermal power,
solar power, and wind power.

pensive, and they could hardly be described as secure; the regions that produce the largest share of oil are politically unstable. Nor are they clean; petroleum use accounts for 43 percent of world $CO_2$ emissions. Until recently, these fuels were no longer cheap. Retail prices of gasoline in the United States rose from $1.50 per gallon in January 2004 to over $4.00 per gallon in June 2008.

The next most important fuel, coal, is cheap and secure but extremely dirty. Today, coal is used extensively as a source for electricity generation. On a price-per-million-Btu basis, coal costs one-sixth as much as oil and one-fourth as much as natural gas. Unfortunately, coal emits a variety of air pollutants, such as sulfur and nitrogen oxides, as well as particulates. Although advances in combustion technology have dramatically lowered emissions of these pollutants, $CO_2$ emissions remain unabated. In contrast, a natural-gas combined-cycle generator emits 62 percent less $CO_2$ than a typical pulverized-coal plant.[25] Although coal scores badly on a cleanliness basis, large domestic supplies make it an extremely secure fuel. Indeed, as a means of displacing petro-

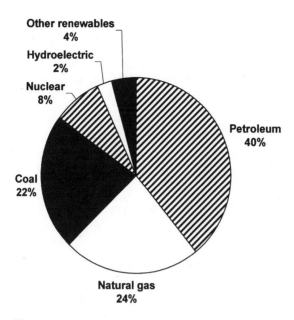

Figure 1.3
U.S. primary energy consumption by source, 2007
Data from DOE (2008a, table 1.3).
*Note:* Other renewables includes biomass, geothermal
power, solar power, and wind power.

leum, some favor coal-liquefaction technologies, which involve the conversion
of coal into liquid petroleum products like gasoline.

Natural gas is the cleanest of the fossil fuels and produces far lower $CO_2$
emissions (117 pounds per million Btu) than petroleum (160 pounds per million Btu) and coal (205 pounds per million Btu). Furthermore, U.S. supplies
come from secure domestic and Canadian sources. Once thought to be cheap,
recent U.S. price escalations from $2.50 per million Btu in January 2002 to
$6.50 per million Btu in December 2007 suggest that, at least by historical
standards, natural gas is no longer a cheap energy source.

Hydropower, which accounts for 6 percent of world energy supplies, is probably the least objectionable fuel source, since it is generally cheap, clean, and secure. The problem is that virtually all the major hydro sites have already been
developed.

Nuclear fuel, which accounts for 6 percent of world energy supplies and 8
percent of U.S. supplies, emits no $CO_2$ or any other air pollutants, but it is not
cheap, at least when compared with coal-fired power plants; nor is it free of en-

vironmental problems. Because of security concerns with waste disposal, as well as the high cost of nuclear plants, no new nuclear plants have been built in the United States for more than twenty-five years. Nonetheless, with the emergence of concerns about global warming, nuclear power may again become a viable choice.

Renewable sources of energy offer intriguing possibilities because of their reduced carbon emissions and local supplies, but they are not cheap. The most successful have been wind farms, which grew tenfold in number between 2001 and 2005,[26] but their usefulness depends on continuous high wind speeds. Biofuels, particularly corn-based ethanol, appear to be emerging as important transportation fuels to replace petroleum. However, as noted earlier, their economic viability has depended more on their popularity in Washington than on their popularity in the marketplace.

Fossil fuels historically have been the cheapest energy sources and probably will continue to be the cheapest energy sources for the foreseeable future, but they are hardly the cleanest or the most secure. Obviously, there are trade-offs between cheap, clean, and secure energy, and getting the balance right is the true test of a successful energy policy. But how do we go about balancing the three goals?

## BALANCING THE CONFLICTING GOALS OF
## CHEAP, CLEAN, AND SECURE ENERGY

Having identified the goals of energy policy—cheap, clean, and secure energy—we must ask how much we, as a society, are willing to pay for clean and secure energy. Indeed, the failure of existing policy is its inability to come to grips with this fundamental question. Instead, we jump immediately to consider various proposals for achieving one of these goals without considering their impacts on the other goals. To illustrate the dilemma, Robert Socolow and Stephen Pacala of Princeton University have outlined the following fifteen possible actions—some of them draconian—that would help stabilize worldwide greenhouse-gas emissions:[27]

1. Cutting world electricity use by 25 percent
2. Raising the fuel efficiency of coal-fired plants from 40 percent to 60 percent
3. Replacing coal-fired plants with gas-fired plants
4. Installing carbon capture-and-sequestration technologies in half of all coal plants

5. Doubling existing nuclear capacity, thereby displacing coal plants
6. Increasing wind power by a factor of forty to displace coal plants
7. Increasing solar power by a factor of seven hundred to displace coal plants
8. Doubling the efficiency of the automobile fleet
9. Cutting miles driven per auto by 50 percent
10. Converting all autos to ethanol[28]
11. Implementing carbon sequestration for plants using coal to produce synthetic gas
12. Implementing carbon sequestration on additional coal-fired power plants that would produce enough hydrogen to supply 75 percent of the auto fleet
13. Increasing wind power by a factor of eighty to produce hydrogen for the auto fleet
14. Stopping all deforestation
15. Mandating conservation tillage of all farms

Socolow and Pacala estimate that to stabilize greenhouse-gas emissions at current rates, seven of these fifteen actions would be necessary. Imagine the difficulty Congress would have deciding which seven to adopt. Which ones would strike the proper balance between cheap, clean, and secure energy? The choices are bewildering and contingent on many considerations. For instance, a key to reducing carbon emissions is reducing the use of conventional coal-fired power plants because, even though coal accounts for 26 percent of world energy consumption, it accounts for 37 percent of worldwide carbon emissions. Of the fifteen options, seven involve reducing the use of coal in power plants. Which of these seven are superior to the others? Should we choose all seven? What are the current costs of these options? What is the likelihood of future cost-reducing technological advances?

Attractive for security reasons is reducing petroleum use, which would also bear upon cleanliness, since petroleum use accounts for 43 percent of world $CO_2$ emissions. Five of the options, items 8 through 13, would reduce petroleum use and auto emissions, but here again the question is, at what cost?

Items 14 and 15 are aimed at stopping deforestation and altering farming practices so as to increase the earth's capacity to absorb $CO_2$ and thereby prevent emissions from being released to the atmosphere. Without command-and-control edicts to affect land use, compliance would be a serious issue, but forcing landowners to use their land in certain ways poses serious property-rights problems.

Choosing which seven of the fifteen options would be most appropriate requires current and future information that even the best engineers and government planners do not have. Making the choice rationally without such information is difficult enough; certainly, Congress cannot make it using its standard beauty-pageant approach with a few command-and-control requirements thrown into the mix.

Although the current approach to selecting the best options is hopelessly flawed, there is a novel alternative approach that would let the market decide which of these options is best. It involves getting the prices right and then letting the market determine which of the fifteen options make economic sense.

## WHAT IS MEANT BY GETTING THE PRICES RIGHT?

Getting the prices right means including in the market price the premiums that we as a society should be willing to pay for clean and secure energy. It also means eliminating the need for ad hoc command-and-control solutions, congressional beauty pageants, and indiscriminate choices among a range of policy options put forward by special-interest groups.

Currently, the market remains focused on providing the cheapest energy possible. Although we are willing to pay more for cleaner and more secure energy, that willingness is not being incorporated into market prices. And since we're not paying for it, we're not getting it.

Consumers pay more for higher-quality food products at the supermarket; this creates incentives for their production. Unfortunately, energy markets do not work like supermarkets. The purchaser of clean energy is not able to internalize or capture its benefits. Likewise, oil markets do not distinguish between secure and insecure oil. The marketplace on its own will not reflect the willingness to pay for clean and secure energy, so consumers revert to choosing the lowest-cost energy source.

The problem is that there are significant costs to society that are not incorporated into the prices we pay for oil and other fossil fuels. If we as consumers were forced to pay an additional amount equal to the environmental and security costs imposed on ourselves and others, the price of dirty and insecure energy would rise significantly. Consequently, consumers would demand alternatives that offered cleaner and more secure energy. Raising the prices of conventional fuels to reflect their true and complete cost to society—their true social cost—would level the playing field on which cleaner and more secure energy sources compete with conventional fuels. And once cleaner, more secure energy sources were rewarded in the marketplace, producers would be more than happy to produce them.

The key is getting the prices right—and in that, government must get involved. How and why this would work is the subject of this study.

## A ROAD MAP OF THIS BOOK

A key premise is that markets generally do a reasonable job of providing cheap, but not necessarily clean or secure, energy. But is this true? The next chapter begins with an examination of the world's preeminent fuel—oil—and the workings of the world oil market. Focusing on the world oil market, I ask three questions: Why until recently were oil prices no longer cheap? Can markets be relied upon to provide cheap energy? and What are the prospects for future oil prices?

In chapter 3 I turn to the question of security, focusing specifically on oil security. There has been a curious resurgence of petro-nationalism, with key consuming countries like China attempting to forge bilateral trade agreements to be assured of future oil supplies. Like climate change from carbon emissions, oil security is a worldwide problem, not a national one. To complicate matters further, oil security policy is plagued by a number of misconceptions. In chapter 3 I attempt to dispel such misconceptions while outlining the breadth of the security problem.

Chapters 4 and 5 take up a specific problem facing clean energy: global climate change caused by $CO_2$ emissions. Whereas most conventional air pollutants, such as sulfur and nitrogen oxides, are essentially national problems that are being addressed by individual countries, the most significant greenhouse gas, $CO_2$, is a worldwide problem requiring international cooperation. Chapter 4 focuses on the science, economics, and engineering aspects of reducing $CO_2$ emissions. Chapter 5 examines the political constraints to achieving international cooperation, the best institutional framework for achieving cooperation, and the policy options available, including the trading of carbon allowances.

Chapter 6 outlines from an economist's perspective a smart energy policy. Major technological advances are going to be necessary if we are to substantially alter the current energy mix. To achieve these advances, we must get the right prices for energy, which means adopting an oil security tax and a carbon tax. This alternative offers a radical departure from current policies.

# Chapter 2 The End of
# Cheap Oil?

As indicated in figure 1.2, petroleum is our dominant fuel source, so it is not inconsequential that oil prices quadrupled between January 2004 and June 2008. Over the same period, U.S. gasoline prices sky-rocketed from $1.50 per gallon to more than $4.00 per gallon. Diesel prices rose even more sharply. Figure 2.1 reports the price per barrel of oil in both current and constant (inflation-adjusted 2007) dollars going back to 1950. Oil prices (measured in constant 2007 dollars) were even higher in June 2008 than during the energy crisis of the 1970s and early 1980s. Over this period, oil could no longer be considered cheap. Therefore, the first question that this chapter addresses is what caused this price spike.

Since a major theme of this book is that over the long haul energy markets do a reasonable job of providing cheap energy (freeing up government policymakers to concern themselves with clean and secure energy), the burden of proof is on me to explain the causes of the recent price spike and to evaluate the performance of the oil market from a historical perspective.

It is also imperative that we look into the future and contemplate

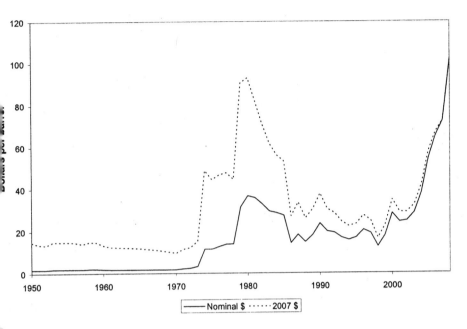

Figure 2.1
World oil prices, 1950–2008
Data from BP (2008).

the prospects for future prices of oil. After recovery from the current recession, will they resume their meteoric rise, or stabilize at 2004 levels? The outcome will greatly influence the trade-offs between cheap, clean, and secure energy. But before we can look into the future, we need to look back at the history of the world oil market going back to the 1950s. For many of us that lived through the energy crisis of the 1970s, there is a feeling of déjà vu. At the end of the chapter, I evaluate the key determinants of future prices and their implications for oil security and climate change.

## NINE POPULAR EXPLANATIONS FOR THE OIL PRICE SPIKE: 2004 TO SUMMER 2008

Figure 2.1 shows that for long periods, consumers have enjoyed relatively cheap oil—from 1950 to 1973 and then from the mid-1980s to 2004. But the oil price spikes of the 1970s and from 2004 to summer 2008 are painful reminders that oil prices can be quite volatile and that oil has not always been cheap.

The approach here is to look carefully at nine popular explanations for the oil price increases since 2004 and attempt to weight their relative importance. Specifically, I consider the following popular explanations:

1. China's oil demand has mushroomed.
2. The Organization of the Petroleum Exporting Countries' (OPEC's) capacity limits have prevented increased production.
3. Worldwide refining capacity is the bottleneck.
4. The shortage of low-sulfur diesel fuel is driving up oil prices.
5. The declining value of the dollar is the cause of high oil prices.
6. The real culprits are the international oil companies.
7. No, Wall Street speculators are the culprits.
8. World oil production has peaked.
9. The OPEC cartel is propping up prices.

It is no wonder that the average citizen is totally confused and simply seizes on the explanation that best meets with his or her own prior ideological viewpoints. But put aside your preconceptions, and let's take a hard look at the theory underlying each explanation and the data to support it. Remember, there can be more than one explanation. The key is first to separate the wheat from the chaff and to weight the relative importance of the valid factors.

### Explanation 1: China's Oil Demand Has Mushroomed

Probably the most popular explanation is an old-fashioned supply-and-demand story. In a nutshell, oil demand, primarily in China and other Asian countries, has grown at an *unexpectedly* rapid rate, a rate that suppliers did not anticipate.[1] Figure 2.2 shows the annual *increases* in oil consumption over the 2001–2007 period and how key groups of oil-consuming countries have contributed to that growth.

During the 1990s and for the three-year period 2000–2002, worldwide demand growth was well below 1 million barrels per day. As figure 2.2 indicates, the annual growth in consumption accelerated sharply in 2003 by 1.6 million barrels per day and then by an additional 2.9 million barrels per day in 2004. In response to the higher prices, the annual growth rates have slowed since 2004, but worldwide consumption continued to increase through 2007. Shown for each period is the country contribution to this growth broken into five groups: China, other Asia, the Middle East, the member countries of the Organization for Economic Cooperation and Development (OECD), and the rest of world.[2]

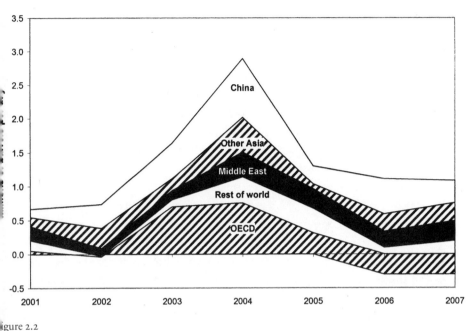

Figure 2.2
Annual increase in oil consumption by area, 2001–2007
Data from BP (2008).

The "rest of the world" grouping consists of Latin America, Africa, and the former republics of the Soviet Union.

China has, of course, been the big surprise. Over the period 2000–2002, growth in Chinese oil consumption averaged only 0.2 million barrels per day. But in 2003, consumption grew by 0.5 million barrels per day, and in 2004 increased by an additional 0.9 million barrels per day. The Chinese economy grew at the prodigious rate of about 9.2 percent annually over the period 1995–2005, so it is not surprising to learn that China is now the world's second-largest oil-consuming nation. Since 2004, the growth in Chinese oil consumption has slowed, averaging about 0.4 million barrels per day. But China is not the sole source of demand growth. Other Asian countries (excluding Japan) have shown steady growth over the whole period, adding on average another 0.24 million barrels per day. India has been a strong contributor and is now the world's fifth-largest oil consumer.

One does not normally think of the Middle East as a source of indigenous demand growth, but this region matches the growth of other Asian countries over this period. Likewise, the rest of the world, consisting of the former Soviet Union, Latin America, and Africa, has experienced impressive demand growth. Proponents of globalization point with pride to the way in which living standards are being dramatically improved in major population centers of the world, but it has come at the cost of rising oil prices.

Interestingly, the OECD countries, consisting of the developed countries in North America, Europe, and the Far East, showed substantial demand growth in 2003 and 2004, but since 2005 consumption has actually declined, as one would expect in response to the rising price of oil. This explains why the bottom line in figure 2.2 becomes negative in 2006 and 2007.

Before we leave figure 2.2, a possible misconception needs to be addressed. How is it that oil consumption continued to increase over the years 2005–2007 in China, other Asia, the Middle East, and the rest of the world while the price of oil trebled? Of course, the OECD countries' oil consumption did decrease, but for the developing countries, the growth rate slowed but did not actually decrease. Some might argue that this refutes the famous law of demand that holds that when price increases, consumption decreases. The explanation is twofold. First, the law of demand is conditioned on "everything else being equal," or in this case, a constant world GDP, and consumers actually experiencing higher prices. Robust economic growth in developing countries over this period pushed oil consumption upward. Second, China and other developing countries tend to cap retail petroleum prices, thereby preventing higher oil prices from inducing conservation.[3] For example, over the same period that U.S. gasoline prices increased 166 percent, gasoline prices in China increased by only 47 percent, and gas remains heavily subsidized in China, costing about $2.65 per gallon as of May 2008.[4] Given that Chinese and other consumers in developing nations do not feel the full pinch of rising oil prices, it is not surprising that oil consumption continues to increase in these countries.

### Explanation 2: OPEC's Capacity Limits
### Prevented Increased Production

Because oil prices began to rise sharply in 2004, production must not have expanded sufficiently to meet the unexpected surge in oil demand. But the question is why? A popular explanation, particularly in 2004 and 2005, was that OPEC and non-OPEC oil producers faced a short-term capacity constraint and that non-OPEC countries were producing all they could.[5]

To test this theory, let us look at figure 2.3, which plots oil prices on the right axis and OPEC's spare production capacity on the left axis for the period 2001–

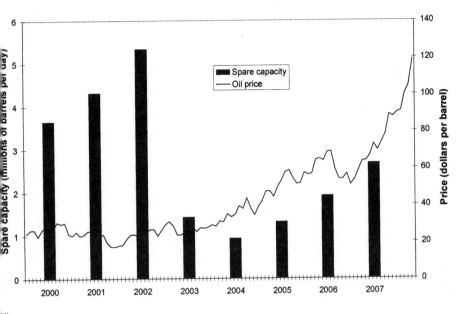

Figure 2.3
Spare capacity in OPEC versus oil prices
Data from DOE (2008c) (oil prices) and IEA (2008) (spare capacity).

2007. We should note that non-OPEC countries tend to produce at full capacity, so if there is spare capacity, OPEC has it. As OPEC expanded production in
2003 and 2004 to meet demand, OPEC's spare capacity declined dramatically
from 5.3 million barrels per day in 2002 to less than 1 million barrels per day by
2004. In effect, we observe a very "tight" market—surging demand (explanation 1) combined with a limited supply (explanation 2). Given a tight oil market, prices would have been expected to rise substantially in 2004 and 2005.

But the "tight market" explanation, combining explanations 1 and 2, does
not fare as well in explaining oil price increases in 2006 and 2007. By 2006,
OPEC's spare capacity had reached 1.9 million barrels per day and by 2007, 2.7
million barrels per day. By summer 2008, spare capacity stood at over 3 million
barrels per day. How could prices continue to rise as spare capacity expanded?
It appears that the "tight market" explanation is insufficient to explain price increases after 2005, when oil prices continued their spectacular rise.

### Explanation 3: No, Worldwide Refining
### Capacity Is the Bottleneck

Oil refineries transform crude oil into petroleum products such as gasoline, jet fuel, diesel fuel, heating oil, residual fuel oil, petrochemical feedstocks, and a host of specialty products. The previous two explanations basically argue that it was the "tight" crude-oil market that precipitated the oil price increases, but there is an alternative explanation based on the ability of refineries to convert crude oil into petroleum products. Specifically, the refinery bottleneck was the inability to process sufficient amounts of heavy high-sulfur crude oils into the lighter, more highly valued petroleum products such as gasoline, kerosene jet fuel, and diesel fuel.[6] Adequate refining capacity was available to process light sweet (low-sulfur) crude oils because they can be processed in simple refineries. However, complex refineries lacked spare capacity in the downstream processing units needed to process heavy sour (high-sulfur) crude oils.

To understand this argument, let's take a brief detour into crude-oil qualities and petroleum refining. Crude oils can differ significantly depending on the geologic formation from which they are produced. The two most important determinants of crude-oil quality are American Petroleum Institute (API) gravity, which can range from 10 degrees (for a very heavy viscous crude oil) to 50 degrees (for a very light crude oil), and the sulfur content, which can range from 0.1 percent to 5 percent. Light high-gravity crude oils are more valuable because in the first step of the refining process, atmospheric distillation, these crude oils yield a much larger fraction of high-value products like naphtha (for gasoline), kerosene (for jet fuel), and distillates (for diesel fuel) and a smaller fraction of low-value residual fuel oil, which is used in power plants and ship bunkers. In addition, sulfur content is inversely correlated with gravity. For example, one grade of Nigerian crude oil has an API gravity of 34 degrees and a sulfur content of 0.2 percent, whereas Mexican Mayan crude oil has an API gravity of 22 degrees and a sulfur content of 3.3 percent. The 34-degree-gravity Nigerian crude oil provides a double bonus—a greater fraction of lighter products (74 percent) and very low sulfur content. In contrast, the light-product yield of the Mexican Mayan crude oil is only 45.3 percent from the atmospheric distillation process, and the remaining 54.7 percent requires substantial processing in a variety of expensive, complex processing units.[7] In addition, hydrotreaters are required to reduce the high levels of sulfur in order to meet environmental specifications for the various petroleum products.

In principle, even though crude-oil qualities differ significantly, a complex refinery processing heavy sour crude oils can produce the same product yields as a simple refinery processing the light sweet crude oils. In effect, *given adequate capacity* of complex refineries, virtually all crude oils become fungible. During normal conditions with spare complex-refinery capacity, heavy sour crude oils will sell at only a small discount that reflects their added refining costs.

If the refinery-shortage theory is correct, the real bottleneck is complex-refining capacity, not crude-oil production, so we should expect to see a rising price premium for light sweet crude oils. Evidence to support this theory is readily available in figure 2.4, which plots the price premium that light sweet crude oils enjoyed over their heavy sour counterparts (the price difference between West Texas Intermediate crude oil—37 degrees gravity and 0.5 percent sulfur—and Mexican Mayan crude oil). Note that between January 2000 and July 2004, the price differential fluctuated primarily between $4 and $7 per barrel. Thereafter, the price premium jumped to $10 to $15 per barrel. In May 2008, there were reports of Iranian tankers full of heavy sour crude without a market.[8]

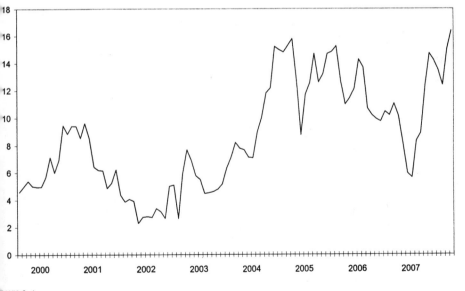

ϝure 2.4
ice premium for light sweet crude oil (price difference between West Texas Intermediate crude and exican Mayan crude)
ta from DOE (2008c).

Fortunately, help is on the way in the form of substantial increases in refining capacity. The International Energy Agency's analysis of planned capacity additions predicts that 10.6 million barrels per day in added distillation capacity will be onstream by 2012. In addition, complex-refining capacity is projected to increase substantially over the period, with an additional 11.3 million barrels per day in coking capacity and 1.5 million barrels per day in added hydrocracking capacity.[9] The latter will be particularly useful in processing heavy sour crude oils into lighter high-value petroleum products. In 2009, a number of these projects will come onstream.

The advantage of explanation 3 (the shortage of complex-refinery capacity) is that it helps explain the crude-oil price increases in 2006 and 2007, which explanations 1 and 2 cannot explain. Recall from figure 2.3 that by 2006, OPEC had significantly increased its spare production capacity. But refinery construction and the installation of complex processing equipment requires a much longer lead time.[10]

### Explanation 4: The Shortage of Low-Sulfur Diesel Fuel Is Driving Up Oil Prices

This explanation, advanced by Philip Verleger, shares many similarities with explanation 3, but it specifically focuses on diesel fuel, tightened sulfur regulations, and the shortage of low-sulfur crude oils with a high diesel-fuel yield.[11] Verleger's explanation appears most applicable to the period 2006–2008, when the United States and many E.U. countries implemented increasingly stringent sulfur regulations for diesel fuels. For example, the EPA mandated dramatic reductions in sulfur content, from 500 parts per million (ppm) to 15 ppm in most oil refineries.

The supplies of Nigerian crudes, which are ideally suited for producing high yields of diesel fuel with minimal sulfur, were cut by between 500,000 and 1 million barrels per day in 2007 and 2008. Rebel activities in the Niger Delta have caused production to cease in a number of fields. Without any further processing, Nigeria's Bonny Light crude oil produces a diesel yield of 38.4 percent, and the overall sulfur content of the crude oil is only 0.14 percent. In contrast, Mexican Mayan crude oil refined along the Texas coast has a diesel yield of only 7 percent.[12] Of course, complex refineries are able to boost the yield of diesel fuel and reduce its high sulfur content with additional refining processes such as cokers, catalytic crackers, and hydrotreaters. But if these units are operating at capacity, the supply of diesel becomes fixed, and with rising worldwide demand for diesel fuel, its price must rise.

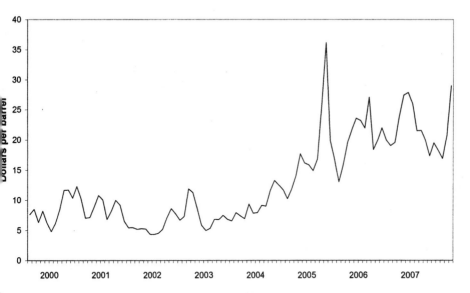

Figure 2.5
Price premium for diesel fuel over crude oil (price difference between diesel fuel and West Texas Intermediate crude)
Data from DOE (2008c).

The worldwide demand for diesel fuel has increased far more rapidly than even the demand for gasoline. From 2000 to 2007, worldwide demand for distillate (diesel fuel plus heating oil) grew by 5.2 million barrels per day, whereas the demand for gasoline grew by only 2 million barrels per day. Furthermore, it is estimated that over this period, refiners added only 700,000 barrels per day of process units to produce distillates, resulting in a mismatch between demand and refining capacity.[13]

Verleger argues that rising prices for diesel fuel directly caused the price increase for light sweet crude oils. Since all crude oils are substitutes to varying degrees, the increased price for light sweet crude oils has caused all oil prices to increase. If Verleger's theory that higher diesel prices are driving up oil prices is correct, we would expect to see diesel fuels selling at an increased premium even vis-à-vis light sweet crude oils. Figure 2.5 shows the price difference between diesel fuel and West Texas Intermediate crude oil. Note that beginning in 2005, the premium began to rise steadily and increased even more in 2006 with the implementation of the ultra-low-sulfur regulations. The data thus seem to support Verleger's explanation, particularly for the period 2006–2007.

### Explanation 5: The Declining Value of the
### Dollar Is the Cause of High Oil Prices

Investors watching daily oil price fluctuations and exchange-rate fluctuations are all too familiar with a common phenomenon—rising oil prices and the falling value of the dollar.[14] Observers of this phenomenon wonder about the direction of causation. Do higher oil prices cause a drop in the value of the dollar, or is it that the decline in the value of the dollar causes oil prices to be bid upward? Which is cause and which is effect? Or is it possible that causation runs both ways, causing feedback effects that exacerbate swings in both oil prices and the dollar?

First, let us test the simple hypothesis that the falling value of the dollar can *fully* explain the rise in oil prices. If this hypothesis were true, Europeans paying for crude oil in euros would pay no more in 2008 than they did in 2004. Crude oil is, of course, traded in world markets and its price is denominated in U.S. dollars. Suppose instead that crude oil were traded in euros. Has the price of oil in euros remained constant? In January 2004, a mixture of crude oils sold for $28 per barrel. At the time, one dollar bought 0.795 euros, meaning that Europeans paid EUR 22.26 per barrel. By June 2008, the blend of crude oils traded at $121.36 per barrel (a 333 percent increase), and the dollar had fallen to 0.643 euros, implying a euro-denominated price of EUR 78.03 per barrel (a 250 percent increase). Clearly, Europeans have experienced a significant increase in oil prices, disproving the notion that the price spike was just an American phenomenon attributable to its weak dollar.

Having disposed of the simplistic view that the weakening dollar was totally responsible for the spike in oil prices, let us explore how oil prices and exchange rates are causally related. There is a clear causal link running from high oil prices to a weaker U.S. dollar. Because the United States imports large volumes of crude oil and has a large trade deficit, higher oil prices should result in a weaker dollar. To entice foreign entities to hold dollar-denominated assets (bonds, stocks, real estate, and the like), the value of the dollar must fall vis-à-vis other currencies such as the euro.

But the more important question is whether a declining dollar also leads to higher oil prices. A weakening dollar means that Europeans and other foreigners do not experience the same magnitude of an oil price increase as Americans, because exchange-rate changes cushion the price increase in euros. With a smaller price increase, European consumption will not decrease as much as U.S. consumption. Consequently, to achieve a given reduction in worldwide oil consumption, the price of oil in dollars must rise more than it would have had to if euro-denominated oil prices had risen to the same extent as dollar-denominated prices. The magnitude of this price increase varies directly with the "cushioning" European consumers receive from the weakening dollar. Europeans experienced a 250 percent increase in oil prices compared with the 333 percent increase faced by Americans for the period January 2004 to June 2008. The Federal Reserve Bank of Dallas estimates that in the absence of the declining dollar, oil prices in early 2008 would have been about $21 per barrel lower.[15]

### Explanation 6: The Real Culprits
### Are the International Oil Companies

In the May 2007 and 2008 Gallup Polls, the most popular explanation for the rising price of gasoline was price gouging by the oil companies, with between 20 and 34 percent of respondents choosing this explanation.[16] During this period, routine news clips showed oil-company executives testifying before Congress and being berated for surging oil and gasoline prices.

Despite its popularity in polls and the halls of Congress, this explanation is the least credible. How is it that the international oil companies, which account for only 20.9 percent of world oil production,[17] can manipulate the world price of oil? If they had such power, why would they have waited until 2004 to raise prices? To be sure, the international oil companies have benefited immensely from the spike in oil prices, but the existence of these profits provides the incentives to find new oil reserves. Curiously, talk of singling them out for special taxes on their "windfall profits," as was done in the Crude Oil Windfall Profit Tax Act in 1980, suggests that public officials have forgotten some valuable lessons. Besides being hopelessly complex to administer, the tax reduced incentives for new exploration and caused the premature abandonment of old oil fields with declining production.[18] Blaming and penalizing the international oil companies shows a complete misunderstanding of the situation.

### Explanation 7: No, Wall Street
### Speculators Are the Culprits

In 2008, a new explanation given for the price run-up from $70 in August 2007 to more than $130 in June 2008 was commodity index funds traded by Wall Street speculators. Vast sums of money poured into commodity index funds, of which oil futures contracts[19] were a large component. These funds typically buy futures contracts, which create an obligation to purchase oil at some future date at a predetermined price. If by the time the futures contract expires, oil prices have risen significantly, investors in such commodity index funds will profit handsomely. Over this time period, with oil prices rising sharply, investors in such commodity index funds made huge returns while investors in U.S. real-estate and stock funds did poorly. So Wall Street financial institutions saw these commodity index funds as a new and exciting alternative and touted them as a worthy component of any well-diversified portfolio of assets. Steven Heston and K. Geert Rouwenhorst's 1994 paper became widely cited for its finding that such index funds had historically provided returns commensurate with common stocks. In addition, their inclusion in a portfolio of assets lowered overall risk because commodity index returns tended to be negatively correlated with common-stock returns.[20]

But how could "paper" barrels, obligating one party to buy and another party to sell a hypothetical barrel of West Texas Intermediate crude oil at Cushing, Oklahoma, at some date in the *future,* have any effect on the present price of "wet" barrels of oil flowing to refineries all over the world? After all, for any buyer of a paper barrel, there was a seller. It would seem that the market for "paper" barrels of oil is totally divorced from the market for "wet" barrels of oil traded between oil producers and refiners.

Not so! The market for "paper" barrels cannot get too far out of line with the market for "wet" barrels, because sellers of wet barrels can choose to put their barrels in inventory and sell them in the future, when the futures contracts expire. Here again, we have a causation question. Can price fluctuations in the futures market for "paper" barrels drive prices upward in the spot market for "wet" barrels? The answer is yes. The mechanism of adjustment is the level of inventories held in the system. If investors are convinced that future oil prices will rise for whatever reason, the futures price will be bid up. In anticipation of higher prices in the future, holders of oil inventories will increase inventory levels so that they have more oil to sell at the higher price likely to prevail in the future. But holding oil as inventory decreases the supply of oil, and thus the price of "wet" barrels today will rise. In effect, "paper" barrels—futures contracts—are close substitutes for "wet" barrels refined today.

Many observers believe that the price increase from $70 per barrel in August 2007 to more than $130 per barrel in June 2008 was caused by massive funds flowing into commodity index funds. The expectation of higher future prices became self-fulfilling as holders of crude oil inventories increased their inventory levels in anticipation of higher prices in the future. With more oil flowing into inventories and less to refineries, the market price of oil rose spectacularly along with futures prices. Indeed, OPEC's *Monthly Oil Market Report* for May

2008 reported that oil prices were far above the level justified by market funda-mentals.[21] Congressional hearings led to numerous statements blaming oil speculators for the rise in oil prices.

Can commodity markets produce prices that are out of line with market fun-damentals of supply and demand? Over the long run, we know that the answer is no, because such speculators will lose vast sums as prices return to funda-mentals. But for shorter periods of a few years or less, speculation can be desta-bilizing, as explained in a famous paper by J. Bradford de Long and others.[22] They argued that rational informed investors can profit from the herding ten-dencies of uninformed investors. Uninformed investors will herd to invest-ments that have recently generated large returns. Even though the informed in-vestors may know that such securities are overpriced, it is rational for them to continue to buy them because uninformed investors will herd to those invest-ments that are going up. This behavior produces bubbles in security prices, and the key strategy for the informed investor is to liquidate his or her position at the top of the bubble.

In effect, many believe that commodity index funds produced a bubble in oil markets and that irrational speculation severely damaged the economy.[23] Surely, the explanation offered by de Long and others makes a lot of economic sense. We have witnessed many bubbles—in hi-tech stocks, California real es-tate, and so on. But it is not clear whether the bubble story applies to oil and, if it does, whether Congress can legislate away speculative bubbles. Could it be that investors in commodity index funds are correct that the long-run trend of oil prices calls for steadily rising prices with an occasional Middle East supply disruption thrown into the mix? In retrospect, these investors did not factor in the international credit collapse, which precipitated the sharp decline in oil prices in the fall of 2008. But even in the absence of the deteriorating world economy, it seems clear that speculation contributed to the price spike.

## Explanation 8: World Oil Production Has Peaked

A relatively small group of scholars and oil-industry analysts believe that world oil production either has peaked or will peak soon.[24] This theory, relying on a logistic curve, goes back to M. King Hubbert, who correctly predicted that U.S. oil production would peak in the early 1970s.[25] Modern-day followers of Hubbert include Colin J. Campbell and Jean H. Laherrere.[26] They conclude that for most non-OPEC countries, oil production has already peaked or will peak soon. Surely, we can all agree that since there is a finite amount of hydrocarbon fuels within a country's boundaries, production must peak at some point and then decline as reservoir pressures decline. At issue is whether the date of peak production is imminent and whether it can be deferred by new enhanced oil-recovery technologies and higher oil prices. Michael Lynch has shown that this simple curve-fitting methodology tends to bias the predicted production rates and peak date substantially downward and points out that this methodology does not account for technology improvements or higher oil prices.[27] In any event, as shown in figure 2.6, non-OPEC supplies continue to increase.

But even if non-OPEC production were to peak soon, the conventional wisdom is that key OPEC countries like Saudi Arabia, Iraq, Iran, Kuwait, the United Arab Emirates, and Venezuela are sitting on enormous reserves sufficient to expand oil production for many years. Concerns about the adequacy of the underlying resource bases of the OPEC countries are relatively new and best illustrated by Matthew Simmons's recent book, *Twilight in the Desert.* Simmons argues that the production capacity of Saudi Arabia's giant Ghawar oil field will soon decline and that Saudi reserves may well be considerably overstated.[28] Even if Simmons is correct about Saudi Arabia, notions of physical limitations on production seem implausible for other key OPEC countries. To date, the peak-oil alarmists have yet to present a very convincing story.

### Explanation 9: The OPEC Cartel Is Propping Up Prices

Perhaps the least popular explanation is that the OPEC cartel is willingly limiting production in order to raise prices.[29] Interestingly, designers of the May 2008 Gallup Poll—in which 20 percent of respondents blamed the oil companies—did not even include OPEC as a possible cause. Nevertheless, although it is not a popular explanation, Javier Blas, writing in the *Financial Times,* explained that OPEC caused the price spike in spring 2008 when it decided to cut production.[30] Figure 2.6 shows the contribution of OPEC and non-OPEC oil producers to meet the growth in demand shown in figure 2.2,[31] as well as oil prices for the period 2001–2007.

Even if OPEC is behaving as a cartel, it meets the demand not satisfied by the non-OPEC countries (which are assumed to behave competitively). Interestingly, in 2001 and 2002, non-OPEC production was more than enough to satisfy demand at existing prices, so to prevent prices from falling, OPEC reduced production significantly—by 0.9 million barrels per day in 2001 and by

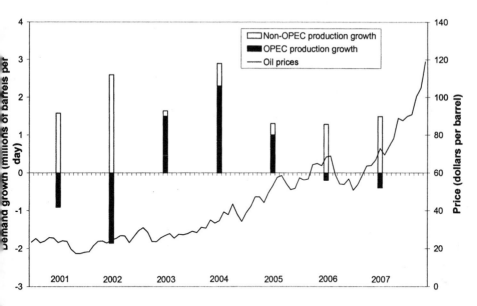

Figure 2.6
Annual growth in OPEC and non-OPEC production, 2001–2007
Data from DOE (2008c) and IEA (2007).

an additional 1.9 million barrels per day in 2002. Then in 2003 and 2004, as world demand accelerated and non-OPEC crude-oil production showed only modest increases, OPEC stepped in to meet the demand growth at similar price levels. Recall from figure 2.3 that the production increases in 2003 and 2004 caused OPEC spare production capacity to fall from 5.3 million barrels per day in 2002 to less than 1 million barrels per day by 2004. Even in 2005, with OPEC production meeting the bulk of demand growth, OPEC was able to expand its spare production capacity to 1.3 million barrels per day. Even though prices were increasing in 2004 and 2005, there is little evidence that OPEC was restraining output in order to raise prices.

The more interesting behavior occurred during the period 2006–2008. OPEC succeeded in expanding its spare capacity to 1.9 million barrels per day in 2006 and 2.7 million barrels per day in 2007 and actually cut production by 200,000 barrels per day in 2006 and by 400,000 barrels per day in 2007. Non-OPEC production more than satisfied demand growth in 2006, and in the absence of production cuts by OPEC, oil prices would have fallen. A similar story appears true for 2007. Likewise, in early 2008, OPEC production was reduced again by about 350,000 barrels per day in the face of increasing world demand. This behavior suggests that OPEC played a contributory role in price increases over the 2006–2008 period.

### Summing Things Up

No single explanation seems sufficient to explain the increases in oil prices from January 2004 to June 2008. The analogy of the perfect storm seems to best describe the price increases of 2004 and 2005. Unanticipated robust demand growth, particularly in China and other developing countries (explanation 1), combined with anemic production increases by non-OPEC sources and OPEC's limited spare capacity (explanation 2) resulted in a very tight crude-oil market. Couple this with a shortage of complex-refining capacity capable of transforming heavy sour crude oils into transportation fuels (explanation 3), and we have the perfect storm—rising prices for oil and petroleum products.

The nice thing about perfect storms is that after they abate, conditions return to normal. But the price increases of 2006 to June 2008 were certainly not a return to normal. Instead, they raise a number of unanswered questions. Over this period, oil demand growth slowed, but demand still continued to grow despite higher prices. Much of this demand was for diesel fuel, which during this period became subject to new ultra-low-sulfur restrictions in the United States and the European Union. The difficulties facing refineries in meeting these specifications was exacerbated by the loss of up to 1 million barrels per day of the most desirable Nigerian crude oils for producing ultra-low-sulfur diesel (explanation 4). But the story is not complete without three other factors—the declining dollar (explanation 5), Wall Street's craze for commodity index funds (explanation 7), and production cuts by the OPEC cartel (explanation 9).

The long-term trend of oil prices will not be dominated by Wall Street speculation, imbalances in refining capacity to process heavy sour crude oil, rebel activity in Nigeria, the declining value of the dollar, or even unexpected surges in demand. All these explanations may produce significant short-term fluctuations that are largely unpredictable. But in the long run, market fundamentals will prevail. Wall Street's speculative bubbles will be deflated by market realities. Massive refinery capacity additions are already underway and adapting to the types of crude oils available and the environmental constraints on petroleum products. We must now turn our focus to those market fundamentals that govern the long-term path of crude oil prices. To do so, we must look at the world oil market since the 1950s.

## LESSONS FROM THE PAST: A BRIEF HISTORY
## OF THE WORLD OIL MARKET SINCE 1950

Before we attempt to look into the future, it is useful to review how market forces have performed since 1950. As we shall see, the world oil market can hardly be described as a competitive market, yet market forces were at work, placing limits on the market power first of the Seven Sisters and then of the OPEC cartel.

### 1950–1960: The Seven Sisters Joined by
### Too Many Stepsisters

In 1950, the primary source of oil traded in the world market was centered in the Middle East, where the Seven Sisters—British Petroleum (BP), Royal Dutch Shell (Shell), Standard Oil of New Jersey (Exxon), Mobil, Texaco, Gulf Oil, and Standard Oil of California (Chevron)—controlled the key concessions (the exclusive rights to explore for oil). Together, the Seven Sisters exported almost all of the oil produced in the Middle East following World War II. Normally, rivalries among seven firms would rapidly evolve into a competitive situation with prices being driven down to marginal costs. However, the Seven Sisters were tied together with overlapping and joint interests in the key concessions. Production decisions were made jointly, so the incentives for excessive crude-oil production by any one company were severely curtailed. The effects on price were predictable.

Long before the formation of the OPEC cartel, the Seven Sisters figured out how to exercise monopoly power in the world oil industry. They had access to the lowest-cost production, so they set a price to match higher-cost oil elsewhere in the world, such as in the United States. The difference was a nice profit. In 1950, Saudi crude oil sold for about $1.75 per barrel, yet the concessionaires paid far less for it, with royalties of about $0.50 per barrel and incredibly low production costs of about $0.10 per barrel. Pretax profits of $1.15 per barrel seemed quite impressive at the time.[32] In constant 2007 dollars, however, the price of oil was just $12.30 per barrel. In terms of today's oil prices, the Seven Sisters thus appear to have been rather ineffectual as a cartel. To a considerable extent, market forces tied their hands. They knew that if they raised the price above that of oil produced in the United States, American exports would become a strong competitive force. In short, the Seven Sisters were happy to get what they could.

Over time, the Seven Sisters saw their monopoly power eroded not by U.S.

exports but rather by new oil discoveries outside their concessions, both in the Middle East and elsewhere around the world. Recall figure 2.1, which shows oil prices expressed in both constant 2007 dollars and nominal dollars. New entrants to the international oil market found significant reserves in areas adjacent to the concessions. The Seven Sisters' production from the Middle East declined from 98 percent in 1950 to 89 percent by 1957.[33] Consistent with economic theory, the added production decreased prices. Measured in constant dollars, the price of oil had decreased by about 15 percent by 1960.

### 1960–1973: The Birth and Childhood of OPEC

This price decline created great consternation not only among the Seven Sisters but also among the host governments whose royalty receipts were tied to the Seven Sisters' profits. Paradoxically, it was the failure of the Seven Sisters to maintain their monopoly power that led to the creation of OPEC. The original OPEC wedding took place on September 14, 1960, uniting Iran, Iraq, Kuwait, Saudi Arabia, and Venezuela in the unholy bonds of the pursuit of monopoly power. At the time, significant spare production capacity limited what the nascent cartel could do to raise oil prices.

Market forces continued to take their toll on the Seven Sisters and on oil prices generally during the 1960s, as shown in figure 2.1. To add insult to injury, new entrants made important discoveries outside the original concessions held by the Seven Sisters; Occidental and Conoco found large reserves in Libya in areas previously controlled by Shell and relinquished as "nonproductive." By 1969, the share of Middle East production controlled by the Seven Sisters had further decreased to 76 percent. The international oil companies found themselves caught in a squeeze between declining prices and rising taxes paid to the host countries, and by the end of the decade, monopoly profits had, for all intents and purposes, evaporated.[34]

Although the 1960s signaled the end of any excess profits for the Seven Sisters, the decade was highly favorable to OPEC. Internally, the cartel proceeded cautiously, achieving moderate gains by raising taxes on the oil companies, making no real mistakes, and avoiding temptations to overreach. OPEC countries had wisely found ways to base their tax collections from the oil companies on an excise tax (a flat levy based on the amount of oil extracted) in place of a profits tax, resulting in higher tax collections per barrel despite declining oil prices. Furthermore, events outside OPEC borders greatly strengthened the cartel's hand. Most significantly, world oil demand grew rapidly at the same time as production in the United States and Canada peaked in the late 1960s. The result was a huge increase in the demand for OPEC oil. By 1973, even though the OPEC nations possessed immense untapped reserves, actual installed productive capacity was barely adequate to meet the surging demand. If OPEC members were to unite in restricting supplies, there would be no alternative source.

## 1973: The Genie Is out of the Bottle

Not surprisingly, political events leading up to and including the Yom Kippur War of October 1973 provided a unifying force for the Arab member countries of OPEC. These countries—Saudi Arabia, Kuwait, Libya, Algeria, Iraq, Qatar, and the United Arab Emirates—announced an embargo against the Netherlands and the United States because of their support of Israel. Although Arab oil destined for the Netherlands and the United States was simply diverted elsewhere and crude oil from non-Arab sources was redirected to those countries, panic buying pushed oil prices to around $10 per barrel—a quadrupling of prices in less than a year. Through coordinated action, the OPEC cartel had suddenly achieved what the Seven Sisters could only have dreamed about. The genie was out of the bottle; a cohesive cartel could achieve untold riches.

But a unified cartel is not immune to market forces limiting the price it can charge. Admittedly, in the short run, with a "tight" market (characterized by little or no spare productive capacity), OPEC could seemingly charge any price it chose, thanks to the extreme price inelasticity of demand in the short run. OPEC ministers, however, recognized a fundamental market principle: what is true in the short run is not necessarily true in the long run. If the market were given time to adjust to high prices, consumers would surely choose more energy-efficient autos and appliances. Homes would become better insulated, and factories would find ways to conserve energy. Likewise, non-OPEC oil producers, benefiting from the higher prices, could justify exploration in high-cost offshore and remote areas. The critical questions facing the cartel were (1) What is the magnitude of the long-run non-OPEC supply response (supply elasticity) to these high prices? and (2) What is the magnitude of the long-run demand response (demand elasticity) to these high prices?

Besides addressing these questions, the cartel had to face two other powerful market-induced forces. The first was the incentive of cartel members to cheat by producing more than their assigned output quotas. Especially in a "loose" market, characterized by excess production capacity, each additional barrel of oil cost a few dollars at most to produce but could be sold at the much higher

market price. The instruments to punish cheaters were blunt, making it difficult to punish one cheater without punishing all producers. For example, in
1986, when Saudi Arabia chose to discipline rampant cheating in the cartel, its
increased production drove down worldwide oil prices, punishing cheaters and
noncheaters alike.

The second market-induced factor limiting the cartel's ability to set high
prices was the incentive to expand production. The more successful a cartel is at
earning monopoly profits in the short run, the less successful it will be in the
long run. The economic principles are clear: higher initial prices lead to a
slower growth rate of oil consumption, leaving more oil in the ground for the
distant future; but more oil available for a very distant future only increases the
incentive to expand current production, bringing prices down.

OPEC discovered in 1973 that the genie was out of the bottle. Consuming
nations quickly discovered that putting the genie back in the bottle was not an
option. Yet OPEC was still not immune to powerful market forces. It had to set
a long-run price that would minimize cheating within the cartel and ensure robust demand for OPEC crude oil.

### 1974–1981: OPEC's Seemingly
### Invincible Cartel

If the 1960s and early 1970s were very good to OPEC, the period 1974–1981 left
the cartel feeling invincible. Consider OPEC's position in 1974: it enjoyed un-
precedented windfalls yet wondered if it was leaving money on the table by failing to exploit its monopoly power fully. Following a fourfold price increase in
the period 1973–1974, OPEC carefully watched to see what would happen to
world oil consumption, non-OPEC production, and thus demand for OPEC
crude oil. The period 1974–1978 was essentially one of wait and see. OPEC
chose to consolidate its gains and allow oil prices to match worldwide inflation.

The worldwide recession of 1974–1975 led to a flattening of world oil consumption, as shown in figure 2.7. Then, as growth in GDP resumed, oil consumption increased from 56.4 million barrels per day in 1973 to 63.2 million
barrels per day in 1978. At the same time, non-OPEC supply, shown in figure
2.8, responded, increasing from 27.6 million barrels per day in 1973 to 33.4
million barrels per day in 1978. Basically, the growth in non-OPEC supply
matched the growth in world demand, and OPEC production did not change,
as shown in figure 2.9. As predicted, market forces were working.

What should OPEC have concluded from this? Obviously, had it not quadrupled prices in 1973–1974, the demand for OPEC crude would have contin-

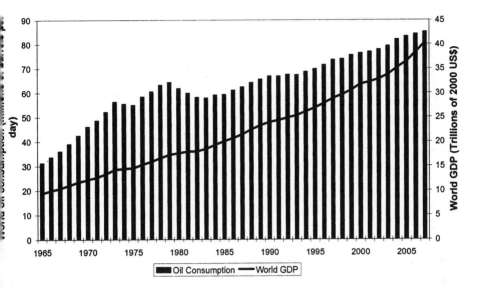

Figure 2.7

World oil consumption and world GDP, 1965–2007

Data from DOE (2008b) (oil consumption) and World Bank (2008) (GDP).

ued to increase along the path shown for the period 1970–1973 in figure 2.9. By 1978, the cartel knew it was much better off selling the same amount of crude oil at the fourfold price than charging the pre-1973 price and selling one-third more oil at the lower price. Yet, even if quadrupling prices was a wise move, OPEC members still had to ask if they were leaving vast sums on the table in 1978, just as they had before the 1973 embargo.

Even though the popular press characterized the second oil crisis in 1978–1980 as resulting from supply disruptions caused by the Iranian revolution, the doubling of prices was, in fact, triggered by Saudi Arabia. Political unrest surfaced in Iran in September 1978, when Iranian production was at 6 million barrels per day. The upheaval soon affected the oil sector, causing production in Iran to fall to 2.4 million barrels per day by December and leaving a shortfall of 3.6 million barrels per day. Saudi Arabia had spare capacity and raised production by 2 million barrels per day, from 8.4 to 10.4 million barrels per day. Over the same period, Nigeria, Venezuela, and Iraq added another 0.5 million barrels per day, leaving a net shortfall of only about 1 million barrels per day.

Initially, the Saudis had moved to offset the loss of Iranian production, but they changed their minds on January 20, 1979, and retroactively imposed a pro-

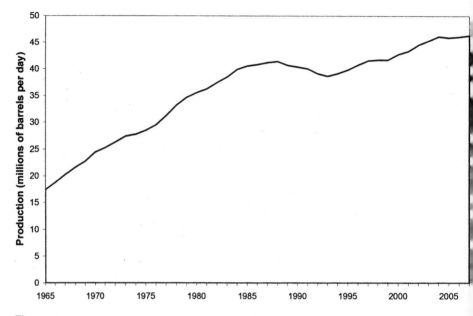

Figure 2.8
Non-OPEC oil production, 1965–2007
Data from BP (2008).

duction ceiling of 9.5 million barrels per day for the month of January. To meet
that ceiling, Saudi Arabia cut production from 10.4 to 8.0 million barrels per
day for the remaining ten days of the month. The effect was predictable. Spot
prices for crude oil jumped from $18.50 per barrel in January to $27.38 per barrel in February.[35] Prices continued to rise in March as Saudi Arabia further reduced its production ceiling from 9.5 to 8.5 million barrels per day. By July
1979, when the Saudis raised their production back to 9.5 million barrels per
day, the spot price of crude oil had doubled.[36] Figure 2.9 shows OPEC production and production capacity. In 1978, the gap between production capacity and actual production was about 6.0 million barrels per day, but with the
loss of Iranian production, a loose market suddenly became a tight one, with
little spare capacity. It is precisely in these situations that production shocks
such as the Saudi production cutbacks can result in large price increases.

   The remainder of 1979 and 1980 were characterized by rising spot prices, followed by increases in the official sales prices of the various OPEC crude oils.
When war broke out between Iran and Iraq in the fall of 1980, spot prices again
shot up with the prospect of losses of both Iraqi and Iranian production. Curi-

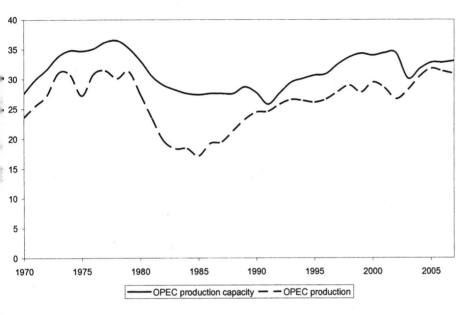

igure 2.9
●PEC oil production and production capacity, 1970–2007
●ata from DOE (2008a).

ously, rather than raising their official sales price to the lofty spot prices of $43 per barrel, the Saudis raised their official price by only $2 per barrel—from $32 to $34 per barrel. What prompted the Saudis' newfound caution?

### 1981–1986: OPEC Fights for Survival

Just as the 1973–1974 oil price spike had induced a worldwide recession in 1974–1975, the oil price spike of 1979–1980 started one as well. With the re-duction in economic activity, oil consumption fell in 1980, just as it had in 1975. However, even though economic growth resumed in 1981, as shown in figure 2.7, world oil consumption did not rebound as it had in 1976. In fact, con-sumption remained relatively flat through 1985, even though the world econ-omy was growing. What could account for this anomaly?

Recall the distinction we made between the short-run and the long-run price elasticity of demand.[37] Given time to modify the stock of equipment that relies on petroleum, users can find substitutes—that is, they can engage in a variety of activities that economists call "substitution responses." The changes between the mid-1970s and early 1980s were sweeping. By 1981, the gas guzzlers that had

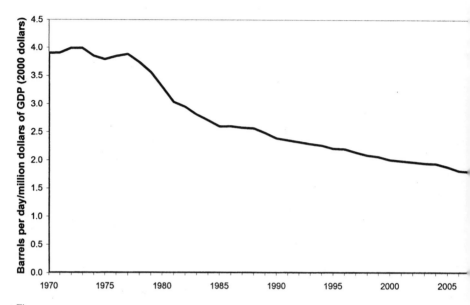

Figure 2.10
Ratio of U.S. oil consumption to U.S. GDP, 1970–2007
Based on author calculations using information from DOE (2008c) and DOC (2008).

existed in 1973 had been largely replaced by a far more efficient fleet of automobiles. Industrial equipment had been redesigned to achieve much greater thermal efficiencies. Even commercial jet engines could now carry much heavier payloads with less kerosene jet fuel, though these changes were slower to occur.

Figure 2.10, which shows the ratio of oil consumption to U.S. GDP between 1970 and 2007, illustrates how powerful market forces are in altering the relationship between oil consumption and GDP. If there were no substitution responses, we would expect this ratio to be constant over time.[38] Note, instead, that the ratio began to fall slowly after 1973, reflecting short-run substitution responses. By the 1980s, dramatic efficiency gains were occurring, as these long-run delayed responses to the past oil price increases began to kick in. It is interesting to note that like Chinese energy policy today, U.S. energy policy up until 1983 aimed at providing artificially cheap prices for oil products through an elaborate system of price controls. No doubt, this system encouraged overconsumption and slowed the rate at which efficiency gains were realized.[39] Without such policies, the efficiency gains reported in figure 2.10 would have been even more impressive in the late 1970s and early 1980s.

OPEC had discovered another fundamental market principle: not only was the long-run price elasticity of oil demand much greater than its short-run elasticity, but so too was the long-run supply elasticity from non-OPEC oil-producing areas. Despite a peaking of U.S. production, as shown in figure 2.8, worldwide production from non-OPEC areas continued to rise steadily following the first price spike. The process continued following the second price spike in 1978–1979. Suddenly, OPEC was caught in a vise, squeezed by declining worldwide oil demand on one side and increasing non-OPEC supply on the other; the result was falling production after 1980, as shown in figure 2.9. Market forces were exacting their revenge for OPEC's excesses of the 1970s.

By 1982, OPEC production had plummeted to 19.7 million barrels per day. The cartel faced two problems. First, prices had to come down from their 1981 high, but how much to cut them wasn't clear. Second, members needed to cut production to match the reduced demand for their product, but they were reluctant to do so. The "loose" market, with its considerable excess capacity, was being flooded with cheap oil, which drove prices down even further.

In circumstances like these, many cartels have failed.[40] Would OPEC share a similar fate? To deal with the first problem, the Saudis gradually reduced the nominal price of oil from $34 per barrel in 1982 to $28 per barrel in 1985. As shown in figure 2.1, the real price of oil (in 2007 dollars) had been reduced even more significantly—falling by about 35 percent.

The second problem, coercing members to reduce their oil production to match the plummeting demand for OPEC crude, was more difficult. Before 1983, these adjustments were informal and only partially successful, so OPEC had, in response, instituted a formal quota system, with each member country assigned a daily production quota. Saudi Arabia would meet any unfilled demand at the official agreed-upon price. In principle, this would solve the problem of coordinating the output decision of OPEC's twelve member countries. OPEC would periodically meet to estimate market demand and then assign production quotas for each country except Saudi Arabia, which was to act as the "swing" producer.

This system, however, was severely flawed. There was no penalty for cheating, and the incentives to cheat were overwhelming. Oil revenues were critical to the economies of virtually all the OPEC countries; declining prices coupled with declining production created huge financial hardships. At the same time, selling additional oil that cost only a few dollars to produce at the price supported by Saudi Arabia was irresistible. Cheating by one country provided justification for others to cheat, and Saudi Arabia bore the full brunt of the cheating, since every barrel sold in excess of OPEC quotas resulted in a one-barrel reduction in Saudi sales. Moreover, the cheaters did not even have to reduce their price to sell more oil. The result was predictable. As the demand for OPEC crude fell to 14.2 million barrels per day in 1986, Saudi production fell even faster, reaching 2.3 million barrels per day in August 1985. Clearly, this system was not sustainable.

### 1986–2003: Learning to Live with Cheating

In the fall of 1985, Saudi Arabia suddenly abandoned the role of swing producer and began ramping up production, reaching 9.3 million barrels per day by August 1986. Again, given the short-run inelasticity of oil demand and non-OPEC supply, the effect on price was predictable. Oil prices plunged to as low as $10 per barrel by July 1986. In return for promises by OPEC members that they would abide by their quotas, the Saudis cut production, and prices promptly rose to around $18 per barrel. For the first time, cartel members realized that Saudi Arabia had a powerful tool to use against cheaters.

Flooding the market with oil, however, was a blunt instrument for deterring cheating. The plummeting price punished all cartel members—both the cheaters and the "law-abiding" members. And, short of military invasion by the Saudis, a sharp instrument to punish only the cheaters did not exist. So the question for the Saudis became when to punish and by how much. Should they respond to every instance of cheating by doubling or tripling production? Imagine a situation in which one small OPEC producer exceeded its quota by 100,000 barrels per day. Would it be wise to bring down the whole price structure of crude oil to punish just this one cheater, especially since that country could simply leave the cartel and not be bound by any quota?

Clearly, the swing-producer model was fundamentally flawed, but what could replace it? The Saudis appear to have chosen the best of a not-so-good list of alternatives, which included dismantling the cartel. They ended up with a type of "tit-for-tat" punishment strategy, whereby they would match cheating with a proportional increase in their own production.[41] For example, if the extent of the cheating were 2 million barrels per day, the Saudis would increase production by 2 million barrels per day. This approach had two advantages. First, it meant that cheaters would receive a lower price for their oil, not just as the result of their own cheating (2 million barrels per day), but from the price decline resulting from a total increase in production of 4 million barrels per day. In effect, there was a significant price penalty for cheating. Although it was still profitable to cheat, hidden behind the tit-for-tat strategy was the veiled threat that if cheating became too rampant, the cartel might simply dissolve, with key OPEC producers flooding the market.

A second advantage of the tit-for-tat approach was that Saudi Arabia's market share could never plummet as it had in 1986. Rather, it would adjust incrementally. Interestingly, the Saudis ignored minor cheating, as they apparently did not react to small amounts of cheating, but levels above a given threshold were punished disproportionately.

The tit-for-tat strategy to deter cheating was moderately successful, in that cheating was reduced but by no means eliminated. During the period 1990–2000, cheating under tit-for-tat averaged 13 percent above quotas, as compared with 20 percent in late 1985. Particularly among small producers with rapidly expandable production capabilities, cheating remained endemic. Curiously, when Saddam Hussein invaded Kuwait in August 1990, he offered as a justification Kuwait's violation of its OPEC quota. Yet Iraq's own record was even worse. During the fourth quarter of 1987, Iraq exceeded its quota by 65 percent, ultimately forcing OPEC to increase Iraq's quota.

During the period 1986–2003, oil prices fluctuated between $12 and $30 per barrel in constant 2007 dollars—prices well below those recorded during the period of OPEC's supposed invincibility (1974–1981). Market forces had, indeed, exacted their revenge. As shown in figure 2.10, on the demand side of the market, the ratio of oil use to GDP in the United States—and in other consuming countries—had declined significantly. Even though world oil consumption resumed its growth after 1986, continued efficiency improvements in consumption vis-à-vis GDP persisted well into the 1990s. The net effect was that, over the course of the decade, world consumption increased by only 9.4 million barrels per day—less than 1 million barrels per day per year. With non-OPEC production growing by only 2.7 million barrels per day, this left a residual demand of only 6.7 million barrels per day to be met by OPEC. OPEC was quietly recovering from its pricing binge of the early 1980s.

With prices fluctuating at levels well below those reached during the period 1979–1981 and with no apparent trend in prices, many observers questioned whether OPEC had become completely ineffectual. Had crude-oil markets finally decided to approximate the strictures of the competitive model? Academic opinions on this subject are mixed, but there is agreement that oil prices were well below the level that a monolithic wealth-maximizing cartel would have been able to charge.[42] At the same time, they were likely still above the levels that would have existed if OPEC had been disbanded. OPEC was still in business, but on a much smaller scale.

### 2004–2008: A Perfect Storm plus Déjà Vu?

As explained earlier, the perfect-storm analogy seems to explain price increases in 2004 and 2005. But after the storm, oil prices should have returned to their previous levels. They did not. Likewise, following the Arab oil embargo of 1973–1974 and the restoration of peace in the Middle East in 1974, oil prices should have returned to their earlier levels, but they did not. There is a definite feeling of déjà vu. As in the earlier period, conditions since 2004 have greatly increased OPEC's market power. With total oil consumption continuing to increase and most OPEC countries producing at capacity, cheating by cartel members is no longer a problem. OPEC countries are flush with cash. It is noteworthy that OPEC chose to ratify the price increases from 2006 to the summer of 2008 by cutting production rather than to increase production and restrain prices. Again, there is a feeling of déjà vu. Although history never exactly repeats itself, market fundamentals observed in the past are often guidelines for the future.

### FOUR KEYS TO THE LONG-TERM TREND OF FUTURE OIL PRICES

Certainly, day-to-day or even year-to-year fluctuations in oil prices hinge on a number of largely unpredictable factors such as bubbles in commodity index funds, exchange-rate fluctuations, shortages in refining capacity, and so forth. We should put these factors aside because they do not determine the long-term trend in oil prices.

The previous discussion of lessons from the past clearly shows that the long-term oil price trends are driven by market fundamentals and underlying institutional factors. If we focus on these determinants of long-term price trends, can we identify a few key pieces to the oil-price puzzle that will cause the other pieces to fall into place? There are four key factors driving long-run oil prices:

- World GDP growth rates
- OPEC's willingness and ability to expand production capacity
- The long-run price elasticity of oil demand
- Non-OPEC supply responses from both conventional and unconventional sources

Each is taken up in turn.

### More Rapid World GDP Growth Rates?

Recall from figure 2.2 that beginning in 2003, the growth rate in world oil demand accelerated significantly as world GDP growth jumped from 2.7 percent in 2002 to 3.8 percent in 2003 and then to 4.9 percent in 2004. Interestingly, the 4.9 percent growth recorded in 2004 was sustained for the period 2005–2007, with growth averaging over 5 percent. In past decades, even though economic growth rates were faster in developing countries, world GDP was dominated by the OECD countries, which tended to grow at much slower rates. Now, faster-growing countries like China, India, other Asian countries, Russia, Middle Eastern countries, and various Latin American countries constitute a much larger share of world GDP. In addition, a number of developing countries have experienced particularly robust economic growth in recent years. Besides China and India, Russia grew at 8.1 percent and Brazil grew at 5.4 percent in 2007.[43] Since the OECD countries grew at only 2.7 percent in 2007, world GDP growth of 5.3 percent means that these other countries not only are experiencing rapid growth but are also playing a larger role in the world economy as well.

The obvious question is, How permanent is this apparent acceleration of world GDP due to growth outside the traditional OECD economies? Although some slowing is expected, there is good reason to believe that world GDP growth rates have permanently ratcheted upward by at least 1 percentage point. For example, during the 1990s, GDP growth averaged 2.8 percent per year. So far, in the first decade of the twenty-first century, the average is 3.9 percent[44]—an increase of 1.1 percentage points. Such an increase translates into about a 0.9 percent annual increase in oil consumption, or additional demand of about 750,000 barrels per day, at recent consumption rates. Faster world GDP growth rates lead to increased oil consumption. The question is whether the increased demand will be balanced with increased production from the countries most able to satisfy those demands—the OPEC producers.

### OPEC's Willingness and Ability to Expand Production Capacity

If in fact oil demand grows at a faster rate, will OPEC choose to expand capacity and oil production, or will it freeze capacity and production and simply let oil prices continue to rise? The second key to future oil prices is in OPEC's hands. The cartel's capacity to produce is an essential decision variable. Listed below are five factors that are often discussed as limitations on OPEC's ability to expand capacity:

- Physical limitations on the size of the underlying oil reserves
- The technical expertise to expand capacity
- The investment funds necessary to finance such expansions
- Geopolitical constraints
- The implications of wealth maximization

Each of these potential constraints is considered below.

PHYSICAL RESOURCE CONSTRAINTS?

As noted earlier, concerns about the adequacy of OPEC reserves are relatively new and best illustrated by Matthew Simmons's recent book, *Twilight in the Desert*. Simmons argues that the production capacity of Saudi Arabia's giant Ghawar oil field will soon decline and that Saudi reserves may well be considerably overstated.[45] Currently, the Ghawar field alone accounts for 6.2 percent of world oil production, or about 5 million barrels per day.

Simmons's assertions stand in sharp contrast to official reports that Saudi Aramco, the state-owned oil company of Saudi Arabia, has identified eighty known oil fields in Saudi Arabia and is producing from only twelve. There are apparently only about 1,000 producing wells in the kingdom, as compared with more than 300,000 in the United States.[46] Furthermore, oil reserves are like groceries on a shelf; there is not an immutably fixed supply of oil. Reserves can be replaced, *at some cost,* through additional exploration and enhanced oil recovery from existing oil fields. For this reason, we will never run out of oil; rather, producing additional quantities will at some point become cost prohibitive.

The U.S. Geological Survey (USGS) estimates that, in addition to Saudi Arabia's 264 billion barrels of known reserves, there are another 87 billion barrels that are still undiscovered. Combining these numbers gives an estimated potential reserve base of 351 billion barrels, which at current production rates could supply oil for nearly eighty-nine years. But Saudi Arabia is not the only OPEC country with enormous reserves relative to current production rates. Table 2.1 lists 2007 oil reserves for six prominent OPEC countries, as well as USGS estimates of undiscovered oil, giving an overall estimate of the potential reserve base for these countries. Dividing the estimated potential reserve base by 2006 production rates gives the number of years of supply remaining (shown in the last column of the table). Venezuela's reserves of heavy oil are not

Table 2.1  Actual reserves, undiscovered reserves, and years remaining for selected OPEC countries (billions of barrels)

| Country | Reserves[a] | Estimated undiscovered reserves[a] | Total reserves[a] | Annual production[b] | Years remaining[b] |
|---|---|---|---|---|---|
| Saudi Arabia | 264.3 | 87 | 351.3 | 3.96 | 88.7 |
| Iraq | 115.0 | 45 | 160.0 | 0.73 | 219.2 |
| Iran | 137.5 | 53 | 190.5 | 1.59 | 119.8 |
| Venezuela | 80.0 | 20 | 100.0 | 1.03 | 97.1 |
| Kuwait | 101.5 | 4 | 105.5 | 0.99 | 106.6 |
| United Arab Emirates | 97.8 | 8 | 105.8 | 1.08 | 98.0 |

*Sources:* BP (2008), and USGS (2000) for estimated undiscovered reserves.
[a]Data on reserves is as of 2007.
[b]Production data is as of 2006. The number of years remaining is based on the 2006 production rate.

even included in these figures. (If they are included, Venezuela's reserves are estimated to be 315 billion barrels.)[47] As table 2.1 indicates, at 2006 production rates, there is at least eighty-nine years' worth of oil in the total reserve bases of these six OPEC countries. In principle, these countries could double their production capacity and double production for many years before production rates would begin to decline.[48]

But even these estimates likely understate the magnitude of the resource base. When an oil field is discovered, estimates of recoverable reserves typically fall in the range of 30 to 35 percent of the original oil in place. Recent advances in enhanced oil-recovery techniques make it economic to recover up to 65 percent of the original oil in place using injections of $CO_2$ and chemical surfactants. This means that for many old fields, more oil is yet to be recovered than has been produced historically.[49] There is no *physical* constraint on the ability of these key OPEC countries to increase production capacity significantly in the foreseeable future.

TECHNICAL CONSTRAINTS ON CAPACITY EXPANSION?

A common feature of oil production in most OPEC and many non-OPEC countries is the monopoly position of their state-owned oil companies. Today, 77 percent of the world's oil reserves are in the hands of state-owned companies—including Saudi Aramco, the National Iranian Oil Company (NIOC), and Petróleos de Venezuela (PDVSA)—which represent fourteen of the twenty largest oil companies in the world in terms of production.[50] With the exception of Saudi Aramco, there is little question that these tend to be high-cost, inefficient operations compared with the international oil companies.[51] In addition, they generally lack the technical expertise of the international companies.

The more salient issue, however, is whether these state-owned companies can obtain the technological know-how necessary to exploit oil fields in their countries. In fact, a large number of privately owned oil-field service providers, such as Schlumberger, Baker Hughes, and Halliburton, and a host of international drilling companies stand ready to provide them with key technical support. Furthermore, a high level of technical expertise is not necessary for the development of most of these fields, which are predominantly onshore. Although state-owned oil companies may be high cost and inefficient, which can slow development, technical expertise is not in the end a binding constraint on the ability to expand capacity and oil production.

FINANCIAL CONSTRAINTS—LIMITED INVESTMENT FUNDS?

Rational self-interest would suggest that a government would grant favorable treatment to its major cash source, placing top priority on funding expansions in oil production capacity. Under the Socialist president Hugo Chávez, Venezuela seems to be defying this model. The conflict between PDVSA and Chavez had dire repercussions for the company and its top management. Following a widespread oil strike in December 2002, production plummeted from almost 3 million barrels per day to only 630,000 barrels per day. The top managers—along with 17,000 workers—were fired and replaced by individuals loyal to Chavez. Since then, Venezuelan production has recovered to only 2.5 million barrels per day, and the workforce loyal to Chavez has risen by 29 percent.[52] Even more inauspicious are the implications for Venezuela's ability to develop its enormous deposits of heavy oil contained in the Orinoco Belt. In the 1990s, the international oil companies were encouraged to bring their expertise to developing these reserves, which could match those of Saudi Arabia. In 2007, President Chavez proceeded to expropriate the assets of Exxon Mobil and ConocoPhillips and placed these properties under the management of PDVSA, leaving the development of the reserves in doubt.[53]

Although the paradigm of maximizing profits or wealth applies to the Exxon Mobils of the world, state-owned oil companies like PDVSA operate in an entirely different setting, with different objectives and operating constraints. Unlike private firms, which can simply go to financial markets for additional exploration or development funds, national oil companies generally face far greater impediments to obtaining funds for capacity expansions. For many, a lack of financial transparency and a history of government intervention make access to foreign capital markets prohibitively expensive. The question for these companies is whether internally generated funds can finance such expansions, or whether these funds will be diverted elsewhere.

In most OPEC countries, oil is a major source of government revenue. The national oil companies are cash cows that support diverse government expenditures, meaning that national oil companies must vie with other government agencies for development funds that they themselves provide to the government. For example, PDVSA is a major funding source for Chavez's social programs, with two-thirds of its budget dedicated to social welfare. Additionally, many national oil companies receive diminished revenues because of domestic fuel subsidies. Iran has some of the highest subsidies in the world, with gasoline selling for $0.10 per liter ($0.38 per gallon). Low prices stimulate consumption, thus reducing the crude oil available for export. Indeed, it has been estimated that by 2011, Iran will no longer be a net exporter of oil.[54]

It would be a mistake to represent all national oil companies as grossly inefficient and incapable of expanding production. Saudi Aramco stands as an example of a reasonably well-run firm whose success the government values. Even those national oil companies that are mired in government-mandated noncommercial constraints are recognized as being critical, and governments recognize that, at some point, noncommercial objectives must be subjugated to the long-run viability of oil revenues.

During periods of high oil prices, these companies are flush with cash, and the government is free to divert funds for a variety of noninvestment uses. Unlike profit-maximizing firms, national oil companies are given little incentive to expand production. Conversely, when oil prices fall, oil production must be increased to maintain oil revenues. Paradoxically, falling oil prices may provide a bigger incentive to expand capacity and output than rising prices.[55]

GEOPOLITICAL CONSTRAINTS?

Of the six OPEC countries listed in table 2.1, three appear to have been significantly constrained by geopolitical events: Iran, Iraq, and Venezuela. Before the Iranian revolution began in 1978, for instance, Iranian oil production stood at almost 6 million barrels per day. Following the revolution and the war with Iraq, production was constrained by hostilities and, with the return of peace in 1989, recovered to only 2.8 million barrels per day. In 2006, production averaged 4 million barrels per day. Meanwhile, internal consumption almost trebled during this period, leaving only 2.5 million barrels per day for export. Thus, despite Iran's impressive reserves shown in table 2.1, its role in the world oil market has diminished dramatically.

Iraqi oil production stood at 3.3 million barrels per day before Iraq invaded Kuwait in August 1990. Even with the "oil for food" program,[56] production reached only 2.5 million barrels per day in April 2003, when Iraq was itself invaded by the United States. Following the overthrow of Saddam Hussein and the ensuing civil strife, production rates fell to as low as 1.6 million barrels per day in the fourth quarter of 2005.

Geopolitical instabilities have lately emerged as particularly strong factors impeding the ability to expand production in those key countries with exceptional oil reserves. These problems, however, could abate in future years with changes in political regimes or stability. For example, Iraqi production could increase significantly with stability and the expertise of the international oil companies. By summer 2008, Iraqi production had recovered to 2.5 million barrels per day, and Iraq announced plans to allow international oil companies to rework many of the existing fields. It is estimated that Iraqi production could be ramped up to 4 million barrels per day within several years and to 6 million barrels per day sometime later.[57]

CONSTRAINTS IMPOSED BY WEALTH MAXIMIZATION?

There is yet another reason key OPEC countries might consciously decide not to expand production capacity: they might think that it is not in their economic self-interest to do so! Wealth maximization might dictate that they simply freeze production capacity at current levels, allowing prices to rise sufficiently to limit demand to available supply. Would such a strategy in fact maximize the wealth of the OPEC countries—particularly those in table 2.1 with large reserves capable of producing at current rates for eighty or more years?

The power of the time value of money is particularly instructive in answering this question. Consider the following hypothetical situation. Assume that Saudi Arabia has the choice of producing an additional barrel of oil today at a price of, say, $100 or deferring production of that barrel for, say, fifty years and selling it at some unknown future price. Suppose that Saudi Arabia could invest the $100 it gets by selling the oil today and earn a risk-free return of 5 percent on government bonds or invest in common stocks and earn a 10 percent return. Over the course of the next fifty years, the risk-free investment of $100 would grow to $1,093 and the common-stock investment would grow to $10,610. Even allowing for inflation, it seems highly unlikely that oil prices in fifty years would reach $1,093 per barrel, much less $10,610 per barrel. Indeed, even if producing more oil forced prices to half their current levels, wealth maximization would still dictate that production capacity be expanded and the oil be sold now.[58]

### The Long-Run Price Elasticity of Oil Demand

The preceding section might leave one with the impression that the future of oil prices will depend solely on the ability and willingness of OPEC countries to expand production. To be sure, that is a key consideration, but two other factors deserve particular attention—the long-run price elasticity of oil demand and the long-run price elasticity of supply of non-OPEC conventional and unconventional oil substitutes like oil sands, gas-to-liquid fuels, and biofuels.

As noted, the short-run responsiveness of energy demand to price increases is very inelastic—probably between 0.05 and 0.1. There is a good deal of evidence, however, of considerable elasticity in the long run, after consumers switch to more efficient vehicles and appliances and firms switch to more efficient equipment in response to higher prices. Using annual data for the period 1961–1999 for sixteen OECD countries, Craig Schulman and I found, as expected, a very inelastic short-run demand elasticity of 0.09. But the long-run demand elasticity for petroleum products was 0.94.[59] This means that the long-run conservation effects—the percentage decrease in demand—can be as much as ten times the short-term or one-year percentage decrease in demand in response to a price increase. The obvious question is, How rapidly do these adjustments to price increases occur? Our econometric analysis shows that even after five years, only 41 percent of the ultimate (long-run) response is realized. Even after ten years, only 65 percent of the long-run adjustment is realized.

These estimates make a lot of sense, particularly when we think about gasoline and changes in the auto fleet. In the short term, consumers respond by driving less, but the resulting decrease in gasoline consumption is only one-tenth of the ultimate decrease in consumption. The bulk of the adjustments to higher fuel prices occur through adaptations of the stock of cars and trucks on the road. For example, it takes approximately ten years to turn over the auto fleet. Higher gasoline prices will cause car buyers who are replacing old worn-out vehicles to buy more fuel-efficient models. On the other hand, a consumer who recently purchased a new SUV may find that its resale price has dropped so much that it makes no sense to trade it in for a new car. Alternatively, the SUV owner may sell it to another driver who will use it less, but it remains in the auto fleet. Ultimately, the SUV will be retired from the auto fleet, and the average fleet efficiency may increase from 20 mpg to about 35 or 40 mpg. We quickly saw ample evidence of this in the United States in response to $4.00-per-gallon gasoline: sales of hybrid cars like the Toyota Prius were phenomenal, whereas sales of SUVs and pickups were down substantially. But the full or long-term impact of the increase in gas prices will only be realized years from now.

OPEC should not take much consolation in the fact that oil demand continued to increase over the period 2004–2007 (see figure 2.2), because much the same thing happened in the period 1973–1979, as shown in figure 2.7. Initially, a rising world GDP more than offset the conservation responses to the quadrupling of oil prices. But as the medium and longer-term effects of the price increases were realized, oil consumption peaked in 1979 and declined until 1983, despite a growing world economy. Growth in oil consumption resumed after 1983, but at a slower rate. Certainly, the growth rate in consumption was considerably lower than it was during the period 1965–1973, when oil prices had been low for many years. The cumulative effects of rising oil prices in the 1970s continued to weaken demand, even into the 1990s.

The long-run conservation effects of price increases can also be seen in figure 2.10, which shows the oil input per dollar of U.S. GDP. When oil prices began to rise sharply in 1973, the ratio of oil consumption to GDP remained relatively steady until 1977 and began to fall thereafter. Between 1977 and 1985, the ratio fell from 3.9 to 2.6—a 33 percent reduction. Interestingly, even after oil prices fell sharply in the mid-1980s (see figure 2.1), the ratio of oil to GDP continued to fall until 2007. Schulman and my explanation for this continued decline is that rising oil prices in the 1970s led to the adoption of more energy-efficient technologies.[60] Rising oil prices produce incentives for technological advances that save energy. It is reasonable to believe that energy-saving innovations used in the 1990s were triggered by the price increases of the 1970s.

Rising oil prices will trigger a number of consumer behavioral responses that take time to occur. Furthermore, rising prices trigger technological advances that can save energy, just as labor shortages produce phenomenal labor-saving innovations. OPEC should not disregard the power of long-run conservation responses to higher oil prices. Precisely for these reasons, economists are critical of developing economies that choose to subsidize oil prices and politicians that propose gasoline-tax holidays in the United States.

### Non-OPEC Oil Supply

History tells us that although price-induced conservation effects can play an important role in mitigating future price increases, conservation cannot do the job by itself. Production outside of OPEC, whether it be production of natural gas liquids, conventional crude oil, oil sands, or even renewables must play a significant role in meeting future consumption. If oil prices had remained at their 2003 levels, non-OPEC supplies would likely have peaked in the period 2010–2015, but such projections are based solely on conventional crude-oil production using technologies that were economical at an oil price of $30 per barrel. These projections reflect only small contributions from nonconventional oil sources. But oil prices of more than $130 per barrel in June 2008 make such projections meaningless.

First, projections of a peak in conventional non-OPEC oil production now appear premature. Recall that after the oil price increases of the 1970s, offshore oil exploration became economic, and, as shown in figure 2.8, non-OPEC oil production increased from about 27 million barrels per day in 1973 to 46.3 million barrels per day in 2007. Interestingly, at the time of the energy crisis of the 1970s, the Workshop on Alternative Energy Strategies published a very influential study that forecast that non-OPEC oil production would peak between 1985 and 1990 and that OPEC production would peak sometime between 1990 and 1997, leaving the world starved for oil and facing economic collapse.[61] At the time, many influential policymakers bought into this premise. This pessimism is no less warranted today. Enhanced oil-recovery techniques using injections of $CO_2$ and chemical surfactants—technological developments that were not anticipated by the Workshop on Alternative Energy Strategies—means a second life for many oil fields nearing depletion. The technology has been applied on a limited basis in West Texas, and another 25 to 30 percent of the original oil in place was recovered there. Even in the United States, where current reserves are estimated at only 20.8 billion barrels, the Energy Information Administration estimates an additional 86 billion barrels of recovery using enhanced oil-recovery techniques. Obviously, at some point, production of conventional oil outside of OPEC will peak, but that time will depend critically on future prices.

Nonconventional oil production from oil sands is an economic reality. By 2005, Canadian oil-sands production[62] stood at 1.1 million barrels per day and is already ramping up to the 2015 projection of more than 4 million barrels per day. With Canadian oil-sands reserves estimated at 174 billion barrels[63] and oil prices above the estimated $40 per barrel at which production is marginally economic, Fort McMurray in northern Alberta has become a boomtown. A number of projects are proceeding with in situ (in place) methods of oil recovery, thereby avoiding the conventional open-pit mining method.

For many years, chemical engineers puzzled over how to convert natural gas into conventional petroleum products like diesel fuel. In many parts of the Middle East and the Caspian region, huge gas fields exist, yet these are "stranded" reserves. Pipelines to Europe or China are not economic.[64] Even liquefied natural gas plants are not feasible without ocean access. At last, engineers have developed gas-to-liquid technologies to convert these stranded natural-gas supplies into sulfur-free diesel fuel, which can then be transported virtually anywhere in the world by pipeline, railcar, or ship. Shell has begun construction on a 140,000-barrel-per-day liquid-to-gas plant in Qatar, which boasts almost 15 percent of the world's gas reserves and the world's largest gas field.[65] Exxon Mobil also has a 154,000-barrel-per-day plant under construction in Qatar. Virtually all the large international oil companies have plans to build gas-to-liquid plants. Although it takes twice as much energy to produce diesel fuel from natural gas than from petroleum, petroleum is very costly whereas the stranded natural gas is very cheap. It is estimated that these plants are economically viable at oil prices above $25 per barrel. Gas-to-liquid plants have huge potential not only to replace OPEC crude oil but also to produce sulfur-free diesel fuel. These plants require substantial cash outlays and construction times, so they are unlikely to play a large role over the next five years, but beyond then they could be major contributors to added supplies.

With high oil prices, there is considerable potential for biofuels such as ethanol, even without government subsidies.[66] Ethanol production is forecast to reach 570,000 barrels per day by 2010. The Energy Independence and Security Act of 2007 mandates ethanol production of 36 billion gallons (2.3 million barrels per day) by 2022. Unfortunately, corn-based ethanol places huge burdens on food supplies, so the hope is that advances in cellulosic ethanol will greatly expand supplies without this negative consequence.

Still other intriguing nonconventional oil supplies might come from the liquefaction of coal and the extraction of oil shales, both of which are abundant in the United States. Small-scale plants have demonstrated their technical feasibility, and a return to high oil prices may well make them economically viable. Investors are no doubt cautious, realizing that collapsing oil prices could render such investments unprofitable. At the same time, there are concerns about $CO_2$ emissions from coal liquefaction and oil-shale extraction and about how government policy would treat emissions from such projects. At this point, it is unclear what role, if any, such technologies will play.

## CONCLUSIONS

An underlying question of this chapter is whether markets can be trusted to provide us with cheap energy. We could have selected the U.S. coal or natural-gas markets and concluded that they have worked quite well. Instead, we chose to focus on the world oil market with all its warts and blemishes. But looking only at the period 2004–2008 to answer this question gives a distorted view of the long-term factors that drive oil prices. Thus we have gone back to 1950 in an attempt to gain a broader historical viewpoint. Both the OPEC cartel and its predecessor, the Seven Sisters, found that the ability to set prices and extract monopoly profits was undermined by a variety of market forces ranging from unexpectedly large long-run consumer responses to higher oil prices to unanticipated growth in non-OPEC oil production to the difficulties of reining in cheaters within the cartel. Despite the excesses of the 1970s, market forces exacted their revenge. On balance, it seems fair to conclude that the oil market, with all its distortions, deserves a grade of C in producing cheap energy.

Before concluding that we can do better, we should remember several empirical facts. Both short-run supply and demand are very price inelastic, which means that *price volatility is to be expected:* negative supply shocks can send prices skyrocketing, and positive supply shocks can send them plummeting. Soaring prices prompt cries to replace the free-market system with a more equitable government-managed system that avoids such volatility. Unfortunately, there is little government can do to help the oil market earn a higher grade. Indeed, well-intentioned experiments with price controls in the 1970s only made matters worse.[67] Even though polls suggest that 53 percent of Americans favor price controls on gasoline and 46 percent favor a federal gas-tax holiday, these are short-term fixes with deleterious long-term consequences. The long-run forces that work so well in oil markets are never realized in a government-managed system. Markets are the only viable alternative. The key is to expect price volatility and be patient. Market forces take time, but they are effective.

By the end of 2008, oil prices had plummeted to $40 per barrel with the onslaught of a world-wide recession. Nevertheless, the question remains, With a resumption of world economic growth, will we have seen the end of cheap oil? Four key pieces to the price puzzle are the accelerated world GDP growth rates, the ability and willingness of OPEC producers to expand capacity significantly, the responsiveness of long-run price-induced oil-conservation effects on the demand side of the market, and the responsiveness of non-OPEC supplies (both conventional and nonconventional) to higher prices. The two factors favoring higher prices are increased oil demand growth attributable to robust GDP growth rates in China and other developing countries and the difficulties faced by the national oil companies in OPEC countries in expanding production capacity. On the other side of the ledger, long-run adjustments to price increases have been quite impressive in slowing the growth of oil consumption and increasing production from outside the OPEC countries. These factors tend to limit OPEC's ability to raise prices. My opinion is that these long-term supply and demand factors will prevail, but that is not a certainty.

Whether or not we enter an era of permanently high oil prices has profound implications for achieving the goals of clean and secure energy. Since the OPEC cartel is the residual supplier, higher oil prices would reduce our dependence on Middle East oil. High oil prices would make the policy choices for secure energy much easier. They would, in themselves, lead to a more secure energy mix because they would encourage conservation and stimulate production of non-OPEC conventional and nonconventional oil substitutes. The effects of high oil prices on clean energy are not as clear-cut. If high oil prices were to stimulate widespread coal liquefaction (without carbon sequestration), the effects would be negative. However, if at high oil prices many renewables and other clean energy sources were able to compete effectively, cleaner energy could be the outcome. In effect, high oil prices would go a long way toward reducing the conflict between cheap and secure energy, and perhaps between cheap and clean energy as well. Nevertheless, the inherent conflicts between the three goals will not disappear. The political choices should be easier—a point explored later in this book.

Conversely, an era of even $50 oil prices would increase the tension between cheap and secure energy—and probably between cheap and clean energy as well. Consumers would, of course, welcome a return to an era of cheap energy. But with low prices, the supremacy of oil would reemerge. Oil consumption would grow at a faster rate because there would be less incentive to conserve. Likewise, high-cost clean fuel alternatives to oil would find it difficult to compete. Even conventional oil production from high-cost non-OPEC sources would slow, leaving the world increasingly dependent on the enormous reserves of low-cost Middle East oil. Clearly, from a security and clean-energy perspective, these would not be welcome developments. For these reasons we need a smart energy policy that is adaptable to either a high- or low-oil-price world, producing a reasonable balance between cheap, clean, and secure energy.

# Chapter 3  Oil Security in an Increasingly Insecure World

Certainly from a U.S. perspective, energy security is really about oil security, and the Middle East is the primary source of insecurity. On this most observers agree. It is when we get to the policy solutions that things go wrong. Most popular policy prescriptions include oil independence or at least bilateral oil deals with secure oil producers to insulate the U.S. economy. Also favored by many is a system of price controls designed to immunize the economy during an oil price shock. The Chinese solution has been to revert to petro-nationalism. Although these command-and-control policy prescriptions sound reasonable, they are based on a fundamental misunderstanding of the workings of the world oil market. Read on and learn the significance of the bathtub analogy.

## THE GEOPOLITICAL LANDSCAPE

There is widespread agreement that energy security is essentially an oil security problem. Whereas Europeans may have misgivings about their heavy reliance on Russian natural gas, the problem of U.S. en-

Table 3.1  Oil market disruptions, 1950–2003

| Type | Number | Average duration (months) | Average size (% of world supply) |
|---|---|---|---|
| Accidents | 5 | 5.2 | 1.1 |
| Internal political struggles | 9 | 6.5 | 2.3 |
| International embargoes and economic disputes | 4–6[a] | 11.0 (6.1[b]) | 6.2 |
| Wars in the Middle East | 4–7[a] | | |
| Total/average | 24 | 8.1 (6.0[b]) | 3.7 |

*Source:* Energy Information Administration event listing compiled in Jones, Leiby, and Paik (2004).
[a]Some events are difficult to classify.
[b]Excluding the forty-four-month Iranian oil-field nationalization.

ergy security, and for that matter world energy security, is squarely focused on oil, and particularly oil produced in the Middle East. The Middle East accounts for about 30 percent of world oil production and 62 percent of world oil reserves.[1] Historically, this region has been politically unstable, with numerous instances of oil supply disruptions. The number, duration, and significance of oil market disruptions from 1950 to 2003 are reported in table 3.1.

There were twenty-four disruptions over the fifty-three-year period, on average lasting 8.1 months and affecting 3.7 percent of world oil supply. The causes varied from accidents to internal revolutions (such as the Iranian revolution of 1978–1979) to invasions of one oil-producing country by another (such as the Iran-Iraq War of 1980–1988 and the Iraqi invasion of Kuwait in 1990) to cooperative embargoes of consuming nations (such as the Arab oil embargoes of 1957 and 1973–1974). Particularly significant is the fact that the ten nonaccidental, noninternal struggles affected 6.2 percent of world supplies and, by a conservative measure, persisted an average of 6.1 months.

Today, the Middle East is at perhaps its most volatile point in recent history. Iran, which may be pursuing the enrichment of uranium to build its own nuclear arsenal, sits on the Strait of Hormuz, through which 20 percent of world oil supplies travel. Should an embargo of Iranian oil shipments be implemented, Iran would likely sink ships passing through the strait and disrupt world oil supplies.[2] Meanwhile, Iraq, a country with immense potential oil reserves, is hopelessly embroiled in sectarian strife, with U.S. troops attempting to calm Sunni-Shia animosities while facing insurgency groups linked to al-Qaeda. Saudi Arabia, with one-fourth of world oil reserves, faces immense stresses internally and must walk a delicate line between maintaining the monarchy's control and responding to increased pressures for democratization. Compounding the country's problems is explosive growth in the population, which has increased from 7 million in 1982 to 22 million today. The fertility rate is 5.5 children per adult woman, and in 2001 more than 45 percent of the population was under the age of fifteen. The educational system has focused on Islamic law rather than providing skills for the global economy, so high unemployment and internal discontent will only intensify.[3] For a while, rising oil revenues may be able to pacify this increasingly uneasy population, but this is only a short-term solution.

Besides the developments internal to Iran, Iraq, and Saudi Arabia, the geopolitical situation has deteriorated dramatically in recent years.[4] Although Westerners tend to think of Muslims as a monolithic group, this is far from accurate. As the war in Iraq has demonstrated, animosities run strong between Sunni and Shia Muslims. The prospect of a Shia-dominated democracy in Iraq allied with Iran strikes fear into Sunni-dominated Saudi Arabia. Even within the Sunni Muslim population, the Wahhabi sect has created a schism that permeates the Saud family, which rules Saudi Arabia.[5] Finally, the terrorist organization al-Qaeda, with its avowed goal of overthrowing the Saudi monarchy, views the West as an abomination and anathema to Islam. Al-Qaeda knows the importance of oil and has called on its followers to attack energy facilities, declaring such tactics the "most powerful weapon against the United States."[6]

These geopolitical conflicts are only the beginning. As one looks further west, the emphasis shifts to Syria, Lebanon, Palestine, and Israel. Events in the summer of 2006 demonstrated the inability of the fragile democracy in Lebanon to control rocket attacks on Israel by Hezbollah, a militant party of Islamic fundamentalists. In turn, Israel's indiscriminate bombing of Lebanon only solidified support for Hezbollah and further weakened the Lebanese government. Likewise, efforts to form a Palestinian state that can coexist peacefully with Israel seem to be the pursuit of an elusive dream, and unconditional U.S. support for Israel has left Arabs bitterly distrustful of the United States and Americans in general.[7]

Another player, China, has emerged on the Middle Eastern stage. As will be discussed in more detail later, China appears to be adopting a petro-nationalist position in the Middle East, seeking to lock up "finite" oil resources to feed its rapidly expanding economy. To this end, China has tried to extend its global influence by supporting rogue nations such as Iran, Myanmar, and Sudan and making sizable investments in their oil sectors. This strategy has further thwarted U.S. efforts to neutralize Iran's nuclear developments.

## NO SIMPLE FOREIGN-POLICY FIX

Traditionally, U.S. oil security has been viewed strictly through the prism of U.S. foreign policy. Until the collapse of the Soviet Union, the U.S. strategy was to build alliances with the major oil producers in the Middle East and to support these regimes against internal as well as external threats. Concern for human rights and democracy were subjugated to "realpolitik." The premise was that U.S. military forces in the region would thwart Soviet incursions and that the West's voracious appetite for Middle East oil would provide a mutually beneficial trading arrangement. Until recently, this strategy was highly successful; consequently, oil security became viewed as the domain of the U.S. State Department, with some support from the Department of Defense.

With the military invasion of Iraq and the attempt to install democracy in the heart of the Middle East, President George W. Bush embarked on a much more aggressive strategy with high risk and high expected return. Bush's neo-conservative thesis was that voting Iraqi citizens would adopt Western consumption habits and promote liberal ideas, thereby stabilizing political institutions as well as oil supplies.[8] Instead of a smooth transition to democracy with voters settling their differences at the ballot box, however, the outcome has been a bloody civil war with American soldiers caught in the crossfire. Although history may judge Bush's efforts more favorably, the current prognosis is not good. One positive outcome is that the United States has gained a healthy respect for its own limitations of what can be done through foreign policy and military intervention to achieve oil security.

Gone is the old paradigm that oil security is essentially a foreign-policy problem with foreign-policy solutions. To be sure, as recent events confirm, U.S. foreign policy can certainly destabilize as well as stabilize a region. But even with an omniscient foreign policy, there are very real constraints on the ability of the United States or any external power to stabilize the Middle East. With the Middle East likely to remain one of the world's most volatile regions, the question is what additional measures the United States and other major oil importers should take to deal with the disruptions produced by this instability.

## ECONOMIC RAMIFICATIONS OF
## OIL SUPPLY DISRUPTIONS

A disruption in oil supplies does not always wreak economic havoc. If spare production capacity exists elsewhere, the effect of a supply disruption on oil

Table 3.2 World oil production by region, 2007

| Region | Production (millions of barrels per day) | % of world production |
|---|---|---|
| North America | 13.67 | 16.5 |
| South and Central America | 6.63 | 8.5 |
| Europe and Eurasia | 17.84 | 22.0 |
| Middle East | 25.18 | 30.8 |
| Africa | 10.32 | 12.5 |
| Asia Pacific | 7.91 | 9.7 |

*Source:* BP (2008).

prices and world GDP can be inconsequential. Such was the case during the Iranian nationalization of its oil industry in 1951–1953 and Iraq's invasion of Kuwait in 1990–1991. Conversely, in a tight oil market, characterized by little if any spare capacity elsewhere, the economic ramifications can be swift and severe. Particularly troubling is the fact that rather small disruptions can send oil prices skyrocketing and trigger a worldwide recession.[9] Such was the case during the Iranian revolution and Saudi production cutback of 1978–1979, which affected 6 percent of world oil supplies and caused oil prices to double. Table 3.2 shows that, as previously mentioned, Middle Eastern oil producers account for about 30 percent of world production. Saudi Arabia alone accounts for almost 13 percent of production, and Iran accounts for another 5 percent. The effects of losing the production of one or several of these countries in today's tight oil market could send oil prices skyrocketing and trigger a worldwide recession.

How do oil disruptions wreak economic havoc in a tight oil market? There is considerable confusion about the mechanism at work. In the absence of government intervention to control prices, a causal chain runs from an oil disruption to an oil price spike and then to a reduction in economic output. Price spikes are a predictable outcome, with the magnitude depending on the shortfall in production. Because of the short-run inelasticity of oil demand, it takes a large price spike to force consumers and businesses to reduce consumption and bring supply and demand into balance. The spike in oil prices is typically followed by an increase in inflation, resulting in rising prices for other energy supplies, transportation, labor, food, and the like. At the same time, overall economic activity, as measured by world GDP, slows or contracts as during a recession. Until fairly recently, researchers found a strong causal link between oil price shocks and decreased GDP. In 1997, Paul Leiby and colleagues surveyed available studies and found that a doubling of oil prices reduced GDP by between 2.5 percent and 6 percent.[10] However, in 2002, Stephen Brown and Mine Yucel noted that "the sensitivity of the U.S. economy to oil price shocks seems to have decreased over the past two decades."[11] This should not be surprising, since oil's share of GDP is now less than 2 percent, as contrasted with 4–6 percent during the 1970s to mid-1980s.[12] Rather surprisingly, the U.S. economy took the rising oil prices of 2004–2007 in stride, but the increases in 2007–2008 helped to push the world economy into recession. As in the 1970s, the term *stagflation* seems apropos—descriptive of a stagnant economy coupled with significant inflation.

## CONFUSED PUBLIC PERCEPTIONS AND THE
## RISE OF PETRO-NATIONALISM

Secure energy has proved to be an elusive objective because, despite widespread agreement on the nature of the situation, there are widespread misconceptions of how exactly to achieve oil security. There are four popular misconceptions:

1. *Oil independence would completely immunize the United States against the effects of an oil supply disruption.* Energy independence is a popular idea, appearing in twenty-three of the last thirty-two State of the Union addresses. Indeed, the *New York Times* columnist Thomas Friedman reports that in an August 2006 survey of the most important national-security priorities for the country, reducing dependence on foreign oil ranked highest, at 42 percent, followed by combating terrorism, with 26 percent, and the war in Iraq, with 25 percent.[13] The premise is that energy or oil independence would insulate the U.S. economy from the vagaries of the world oil market and would extricate U.S. foreign policy and troops from the Middle East.

2. *If oil independence is not possible, it is vital to import crude oil from secure countries.* The common method of evaluating a country's vulnerability to a supply disruption is to look to the sources of its oil imports. Are they secure? According to this reasoning, the United States seems relatively secure, since only 21 percent of its imports come from the Middle East, even though the Middle East accounts for about 30 percent of world oil production.

3. *Special bilateral deals with oil exporters to lock up supplies provide a secure source of supply during disruptions.* China has actively sought long-term trade agreements with various oil-producing countries, such as Iran and Sudan. China obviously thinks that such trade agreements guarantee access to key supplies.

4. *Emergency price controls can immunize the economy against the effects of a sup-ply disruption.* It is commonly believed that the above-mentioned causal chain of events, running from a supply disruption to an oil price spike to a loss in GDP, can be broken simply by instituting price controls on oil products, thereby avoiding the oil price spike. The idea is that in the absence of the oil price spike, other prices will not rise, and if consumers do not face the hardship of rising prices, they will maintain their demand for goods and services, thereby avoiding a recession. This viewpoint was quite prominent in the 1970s, when price controls on oil products were maintained before and after the Arab oil embargo of 1973–1974. A more recent example was the proposed "price-gouging" legislation following Hurricanes Katrina and Rita.

Symptomatic of misconceptions 1, 2, and 3 is the surprising growth of petro-na-tionalism,[14] which is manifesting itself in a number of ways. First, in many oil-producing countries, domestic exploration is the exclusive province of the state-owned oil company. In addition, many state-owned oil companies are now actively searching for oil outside their borders. Figure 3.1 shows the non-indigenous exploration acreage held by various state-owned oil companies in 1995 and 2005. Figure 3.2 shows the numerous countries where state-owned oil companies are actively searching for oil. Particularly active in the international arena are the four Chinese oil companies (China National Petroleum Corpora-tion, Sinopec, China National Offshore Oil Corporation, and PetroChina), the Malaysian company (Petronas), the Brazilian company (Petrobras), and the Indian company (Oil and Natural Gas Corporation). A petro-nationalist inter-pretation of this trend is that international oil companies such as Shell, BP,

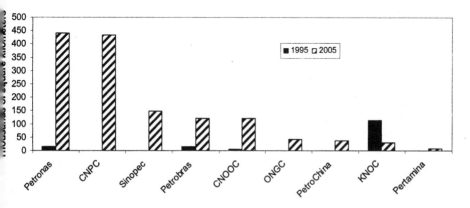

Figure 3.1
Nonindigenous acreage holdings of national oil companies
Reproduced from IHS (2006) with permission.

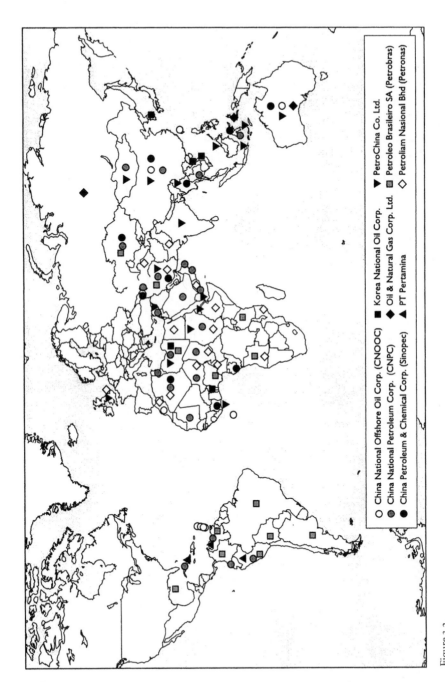

Figure 3.2

Geographic distribution of national-oil-company exploration property

Reproduced from IHS (2006) with permission

Exxon Mobil, and Chevron cannot be trusted to provide all nations with oil during a disruption. China and others probably fear that the international oil companies will become agents of their home governments—the United States, Britain, and the Netherlands.

Yet another manifestation of petro-nationalism, related to misconception 3, is for consuming nations to attempt to lock up or earmark foreign sources of oil through a set of bilateral supply agreements. China has forged such agreements with Iran and Sudan. An attempt by the China National Offshore Oil Corporation in 2006 to purchase Unocal, a mid-sized U.S.-based international oil company, set off a maelstrom of congressional denunciations calling it a matter of vital U.S. national security.

The petro-nationalist's mindset rests on two false premises. First is that the world will run out of oil, with no economically reasonable substitute. This notion equates the geological fact that the earth contains a fixed quantity of oil in its crust with the economic conclusion that the long-run supply of petroleum is fixed immutably. Some also conclude that total oil production responds neither to price increases nor to technological advances. On this basis, petro-nationalists hold that nations should seek to lock up long-term reserves of oil in order to postpone the day when they—and the world—run out of oil.

Obviously, if the premise were true, this policy would have great strategic value. But the concept of a fixed, immutable supply of oil is patently false. Just as the amount of iron ore in the earth's crust has little to do with the price and supply of steel, the amount of oil in the earth's crust is unknowable and probably irrelevant to the amount of oil that can be economically recovered.[15] The supply of oil and oil substitutes is expandable at higher prices, making previously uneconomic deposits economically viable. In addition, as will be discussed, technological advances routinely transform oil deposits that were previously uneconomical into economically recoverable reserves, as well as provide oil substitutes from such sources as oil sands, natural gas, and biomass.

The second false premise underlying petro-nationalist thinking is that oil markets are structurally fragmented so that the ramifications of disruptions are localized, rather than felt globally, and that by arranging regional supply agreements, a nation can immunize itself against a disruption elsewhere in the world. This theory harkens back to World War II, when world oil markets were bifurcated into areas held by the Axis powers and the Allies. The Allies had access to bountiful supplies from the United States and Latin America, but the Axis-controlled areas were essentially fenced off from them. Crude-oil supplies were vastly different on either side of the fence, conferring great military ad-

vantage on the Allies. In fact, Daniel Yergin argues that the abundance of petroleum supplies was a major reason the Allies won the war, citing Lord Cur-
zon's famous remark that "the Allies floated to victory on a sea of oil."[16]

Although it is certainly true that a war of the magnitude of World War II
could produce bifurcated markets, this premise is very misleading in dealing
with the more common sources of supply disruptions. Oil disruptions can occur for reasons other than world war. Eugene Gholz and Daryl Press outline
three prominent ones: natural disasters, such as Hurricanes Katrina and Rita;
instability within a major exporting industry, such as the Iranian revolution of
1978–1979 and the oil-field strikes in Venezuela in 2002–2003; and the military
conquest of one oil-producing country by another, such as the Iran-Iraq War
and Iraq's occupation of Kuwait in August 1990.[17]

Failing to comprehend the implications of a single integrated world oil market and the expandability of oil supplies and oil substitutes, policymakers continue to adopt petro-nationalist policies. Let us now examine at length the reasons such policies are both ineffective and counterproductive. Barring a world
war that might bifurcate world oil supplies, supply disruptions typically produce price shocks that are felt worldwide.

### THE BATHTUB ANALOGY

Among energy economists and students of the market, there is widespread
agreement that there is only one oil market—and it is worldwide. Daniel Yergin outlines several principles for the maintenance of energy security, one of
which is "recognizing the reality of integration. There is only one oil market . . .
For all consumers, security resides in the stability of this market. Secession is
not an option."[18]

What many think is the most appropriate analogy for this situation was devised by Morris Adelman, a professor emeritus at MIT, who compared the
world oil market to a huge bathtub with numerous faucets (the various oil-producing countries) filling it and numerous drains (oil-consuming countries)
emptying it.[19] At any single point in time, the amount of oil in the bathtub is
essentially fixed. Over time, the flow of oil into the bathtub can be turned up or
down in response to investments, which in turn are driven by oil prices and
technological advances. Consequently, over the longer term, the faucets will
not run dry, as implied by a fixed long-run supply of oil. Likewise, the rate at
which consuming nations withdraw oil from the bathtub can be adjusted in response to prices and energy-saving technologies.

But the most important implication of the bathtub analogy is that the entire world consumes oil from a common pool: the same bathtub. The consequences of this understanding are far-reaching. It means that we must think about oil security from a *worldwide* perspective rather than from an *individual country* perspective. Furthermore, oil security falls into a class of goods that economists dub "public goods." Because it is not possible to restrict the benefits of public goods to just those who pay for them, the market will generally undersupply them. By the same token, individual nations will tend to underinvest in oil security because they cannot appropriate all the benefits. Other nations will tend to free ride.

Although globalization of the oil market produces incentives for nations to free ride, it also gives rise to powerful, naturally occurring market forces that help ameliorate the macroeconomic consequences of an oil disruption. Unfortunately, these forces are not well understood, so government policies often thwart their effectiveness.

### One Big Bathtub or
### Many Separate Wash Basins?

Is the world oil market best thought of as one huge bathtub from which the whole world consumes, or is it more like a series of regional wash basins with few or no connections between them? A host of energy economists have provided empirical confirmation for Adelman's bathtub analogy.[20] To some, such confirmation may seem surprising, since crude oil can vary significantly in quality, specifically as related to gravity and sulfur content. As discussed in chapter 2, some simple refineries can process only light sweet crude oils, whereas more complex refineries have multiple processing units capable of breaking down the longer hydrocarbon chains in heavy sour crude oils. Such heterogeneity would seem to militate against the concept of a common pool of oil from which the world consumes.[21]

Also contributing to this heterogeneity is the geographic dispersion of production regions, as illustrated in table 3.2. As one would expect, oil producers and consumers tend to be linked together within regions to minimize transportation costs. For example, table 3.3 shows that the largest share of U.S. imports tends to come from oil-exporting regions located near the United States, with oil from Canada and Mexico accounting for 28 percent of U.S. imports. Again for reasons of location, sizable imports come to refineries on the East Coast and Gulf Coast from Latin America (19 percent), the western coast of Africa (27 percent), and the North Sea (2 percent). In contrast, only 21 percent

Table 3.3  Percentage of imports to the United States
and Japan by region, 2006

|  | United States | Japan |
|---|---|---|
| North America | 28 | 0 |
| Central and South America | 19 | 0 |
| Western Europe | 2 | 0 |
| Former Soviet Union | 2 | 1 |
| Middle East | 21 | 89 |
| Africa | 27 | 5 |
| Asia and Oceana | 1 | 6 |
| Total | 100 | 100 |

*Source:* United Nations (2008).

*Note:* Columns may not sum to 100 percent, because of rounding error.

of U.S. imports come from the Middle East, even though the Middle East accounts for about 30 percent of world oil production.

According to popular misconception 2, the United States should be much more secure than Japan, which derives over 89 percent of its imports from the Middle East since its nearest sources are the Middle East and East Asia (see table 3.3). But the United States is not more secure than Japan, because both consume oil from the same bathtub. Even though crude oil tends to flow to the nearest customers, these supply patterns do not indicate a series of regional wash basins or segmented markets. As we will see, the flexibility of the transportation network and the existence of complex refineries to process various crude oils make oil fungible and the market truly global.

A CHEAP, FLEXIBLE TRANSPORTATION NETWORK

Key to the world oil market are tankers that can deliver oil to almost any country at a fraction of the cost of crude oil. Over the last fifty years, tremendous efficiency gains have been made with the advent of supertankers, which can carry over 3 million barrels of oil. Today, the cost of transporting crude oil from the Persian Gulf to the U.S. Gulf Coast is normally less than $2.50 per barrel.[22] Consequently, the ability of an exporting country to charge more for its oil is quite limited because of the low costs of worldwide transportation.

REFINERY FLEXIBILITY MAKES CRUDE OILS FUNGIBLE

Although individual crude oils differ in quality, the existence of complex refineries that can process either light sweet or heavy sour crude oils means that if

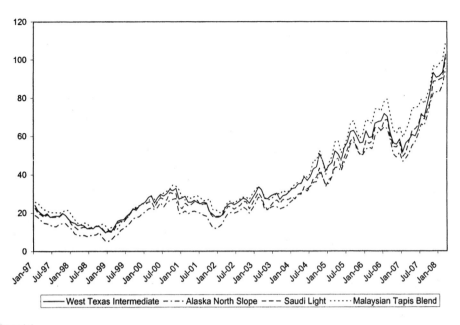

Figure 3.3
Price of crude oil by type, 1997–2008
Data from DOE (2008a).

the price of one deviates significantly from its long-term quality-based price differential, these refiners can switch between the two crude oils, forcing the prices back into their long-term relationship. This processing flexibility forces all crude-oil prices to move together with surprising rapidity.

Figure 3.3 illustrates this point by comparing the price movements of four diverse crude oils: West Texas Intermediate, Alaska North Slope, Saudi Light, and Malaysian Tapis crude oils. The quality (both gravity and sulfur content) of these crude oils differs significantly,[23] as do the geographical regions in which they are refined. For example, West Texas Intermediate crude is processed in Midwest and Gulf Coast refineries. By contrast, Alaska North Slope crude is processed in West Coast refineries. Saudi Light crude is exported primarily to Europe and Asia. Malaysian crude oil is sold primarily in Asia; only token amounts come to the U.S. West Coast. If these geographically and molecularly distinct crude oils were sold in separate markets, one would not expect their prices to move together, because local supply and demand conditions would determine their prices. But as shown in figure 3.3, the prices move together, clearly indicating a common worldwide market. If the price of an individual crude were to fall outside this band, oil traders would profit by selling oil in the high-price area (causing its price to decrease) and reducing supplies to the low-price region (thus causing its prices to increase).

In a recent study, Lance Bachmeier and I used daily crude-oil prices to estimate the speed with which prices of different crude oils adjust back into parity with one another.[24] We found that a $1 increase per barrel in Dubai crude oil, for example, resulted in a $0.98 increase in the price of West Texas Intermediate crude oil *on the same day.* Interestingly, only a small amount of Dubai crude finds its way to U.S. Gulf Coast refineries, which process West Texas Intermediate crude. Furthermore, Dubai crude is a sour crude with a sulfur content of over 2 percent, whereas West Texas Intermediate crude is a sweet crude with sulfur content of 0.5 percent.

As shown in figure 3.3, after 2004, all crude-oil prices increased, but light sweet crudes like West Texas Intermediate and Malaysian Tapis Blend increased in value relative to the heavier sour crude oils. In the vernacular of the oil patch, the sweet-sour price differential widened because of the tight refining capacity of complex refineries discussed in chapter 2. In contrast, with ample spare capacity in simple refineries (designed to process only light sweet crude oils), prices of light sweet crude oils were bid up proportionally more. Does the shortage of complex refining capacity to process heavy crudes disprove the bathtub analogy? No; even heavy sour crude oils became more valuable after 2004. Furthermore, as noted earlier, future additions to refining capacity will focus on complex refineries capable of converting heavy sour crude oils, because of their attractive prices vis-à-vis light sweet crude oils. Refinery flexibility makes molecularly heterogeneous crude oils fungible, allowing them to be used to produce generic petroleum products like gasoline, diesel fuel, and jet fuel.

### Faucets in the Bathtub

Another important element of the bathtub analogy is how faucets (which represent the various oil-producing countries) regulate the *rate* at which oil flows into the bathtub. In the short term, a country's installed capacity to produce oil effectively caps the flow rate from its faucet. With most countries' faucets turned wide open, there is little flexibility in the short run, which explains why supply disruptions under "tight" market conditions can produce price shocks with dire economic consequences.

But over time, the flow rates are adjustable. Economic forces and technological advances combine in several ways to affect the long-run supply from any faucet:

- Oil deposits in the earth's crust are arrayed in a wide spectrum of reservoir sizes. As oil prices rise, it becomes economically attractive to develop smaller reservoirs that were previously uneconomical to develop.
- Primary recovery techniques recover only about 15 to 20 percent of the original oil in place. Secondary recovery techniques, including waterflood and the injection of natural gas, have boosted recovery to around 30 to 35 percent. With higher oil prices, it becomes economical to invest in tertiary techniques called "enhanced oil-recovery" projects, which can boost recovery to between 50 and 65 percent depending on the reservoir.
- As noted in chapter 2, vast reserves of oil sands in Canada and Venezuela have become economical to exploit at today's prices.[25] Consequently, as Morris Adelman points out, there is no such thing as a fixed stock of oil that must be divided between the current and future generations.[26]

In sum, technological advances in seismic techniques, horizontal drilling, and tertiary recovery methods mean that previously uneconomical oil deposits can now be developed. Examples from Texas, a mature oil-producing region, illustrate the potential to wring more and more oil out of existing reservoirs—many of which have been producing for seventy years. Additions to reserves can be made through new discoveries, extensions of known fields, and "revisions" of previous estimates of reserves. Interestingly, of all the oil reserve additions made in the continental United States since 1980, discoveries accounted for only 22.5 percent, whereas revisions due to improved recovery techniques accounted for the lion's share, 50 percent.[27] If there were a fixed, immutable supply of oil, there would be no role for price and technology—the primary drivers of reserve revisions.

## THE BATHTUB'S IMPLICATIONS
## FOR OIL SECURITY

In this section I develop a simple stylized model that I will use to make predictions of how the world oil market behaves during a supply disruption. Readers not accustomed to economic theorizing may need to be patient with this analysis. To obtain clear-cut predictions, economists like to postulate a simplistic world that abstracts from many real-world complexities. In this case, a very simple construct is all that is needed.

### Seven Assumptions

Imagine a simplified world oil market with the following seven characteristics:

1. There are two oil-producing countries, Country 1 and Country 2, each producing 50 barrels per day of identical-quality crude.
2. There are two oil-consuming countries, Country A and Country B, each consuming 50 barrels per day.[28]
3. Producer 1 is secure. Producer 2 is insecure, and is subject to natural disasters, internal political instability, and possible invasion by a neighbor.
4. An independent, competitive oil-tanker transportation market makes it possible to move crude between countries at low cost.
5. Producer 1 is located near oil-consuming Country A. Producer 2 is located near oil-consuming Country B.
6. In both consuming countries, the short-run price elasticity of oil demand is 0.1; the long-run elasticity is 0.5.[29]
7. At any instant, both producing countries have a maximum capacity to produce 50 barrels per day.

Several of these assumptions require elaboration. The first two are designed to simplify the world to two producing and two consuming countries. Differences in crude-oil quality are assumed to be inconsequential, so the issue of refining complexity can be ignored. Making each producing country and each consuming country equal in size further simplifies the model so that each country has either 50 percent of world oil production or 50 percent of world oil consumption.[30]

The third assumption allows us to distinguish between oil production from relatively secure countries and that from insecure countries. The fourth assumption is the critical one; it is necessary for a world oil market in which competitive tanker operators will move crude oil to the highest-priced market. Thus, arbitrage coupled with low-cost, flexible tankers ensures a single world price for crude oil.[31]

The sixth assumption, regarding the short-run and long-run price elasticities of demand, tells us that for the consuming countries to achieve a 10 percent reduction in consumption in the short run, the price of oil must rise by 100 percent.[32] The long-run price elasticity of 0.5 indicates much greater price responsiveness. As a result of adjustments to the stock of oil-consuming equipment, a 100 percent price increases produces a 50 percent reduction in consumption in the long run.

The magnitude of the price shock is the relevant statistic in determining the macroeconomic impacts of a supply disruption, because it signals the extent of the disruption. As noted in chapter 1, the reason that short-run demand is so inelastic is that no short-run substitutes exist for gasoline, diesel, or jet fuel in the transportation sector. Long-run demand is much more elastic because cars, trucks, and airplanes can be redesigned to be more fuel efficient. Fully realizing the efficiency gains from such new designs typically requires the turnover of the whole fleet, which can take many years.

Finally, the seventh assumption is designed for convenience—a supply disruption in Country 2 means that Country 1 cannot offset the disruption by making up the lost production. Given the current tight oil market, this assumption is justified, and it simplifies the analysis.

### Impacts of a Supply Disruption

The stylized model described above focuses on the *short-run* ability of oil exporters to produce, not on the long-run availability and price of oil or oil substitutes. The focus is on the existing production capacity of each oil-producing country, not on current oil reserves or estimated undiscovered reserves. From the perspective of oil security, it is the *short-run* ability of consumers and producers to react to a supply disruption, given the current infrastructure to produce oil, and not the long-run availability of oil or oil substitutes, that is important.

Figure 3.4 describes a market in which, during a normal period, oil flows to the nearest buyer without disruptions. Because, under the fifth assumption, oil-producing Country 1 is located near oil-consuming Country A and Country 2 is located near Country B, transportation costs dictate that Country A will purchase all 50 barrels per day of Country 1's oil and Country B will buy all 50 barrels per day of Country 2's oil. There will be a common world oil price in both countries because, under the fourth assumption, if prices in one consuming country rose relative to prices in the other, crude traders would quickly arbitrage away any price differences between the two countries by increasing shipments to the high-price country and reducing shipments to the low-price country, thus driving the prices in the two countries back into parity.

Consider the effect of a complete supply disruption in Country 2, as illustrated in the bottom half of figure 3.4. Since both oil-producing countries are producing at their capacity of 50 barrels per day, the loss of Country 2's production will reduce world oil supply from 100 to 50 barrels per day. With a price elasticity of demand of 0.1, a 50 percent drop in production implies a 500 per-

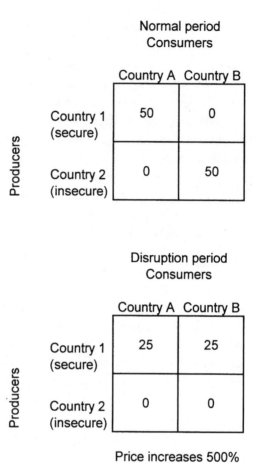

Figure 3.4
Free market: Oil flows to nearest buyer

cent price increase.[33] Both consuming countries will experience the same 500 percent price increase, as production from Country 1 will now flow equally to Countries A and B, even though in the pre-disruption situation, all of Country 1's production was shipped to country A—Country B will simply bid away oil supplies originally destined for Country A.

The key conclusion is that Country A suffers the same price shock as Country B. Neither Country A nor Country B is immune to the price shock resulting from a supply disruption, *irrespective* of who bought the insecure oil from Country 2 during the normal period. This simple example explains why popular misconception 2, which suggests that oil security can be obtained by im-

porting crude oil from secure countries, is fallacious. In a world where both secure and insecure oil is fungible, the origin of a country's imports is irrelevant.

## BILATERAL TRADE DEALS

Now turn to popular misconception 3, that special bilateral oil deals can provide a secure source of supply during disruptions. Consider various bilateral
policies Country B might pursue, and ask whether these policies would actually result in improved security. Suppose, for instance, that Country B, which is
dependent entirely on insecure oil from Country 2, decides to lock up secure oil
from Country 1 and signs a supply agreement to pay Country 1 a premium for
its oil sufficient to overcome the differential in transportation costs. Under such
an agreement, all 50 barrels per day of secure oil would flow from Country 1 to
Country B, instead of to Country A.

But would such a bilateral agreement protect Country B against a supply
disruption in Country 2? Certainly not. If Country A lost supplies from insecure Country 2, it would simply bid away supplies from Country 1 that were
previously destined for Country B. Just as before, a 50 percent reduction in
world supply would cause a 500 percent worldwide price spike, and Countries
A and B would equally share the 50 barrels per day of available secure oil. Country B's special bilateral agreement comes at the cost of higher oil prices during
the normal period. Yet during the disruption period, competitive bidding between A and B ensures that B receives the same 25 barrels as in figure 3.4, not the
50 barrels it received prior to the disruption.

Now consider a special bilateral agreement with an added feature: a long-
term contract between Country B and Country 1 to sell oil to Country B *at a
predetermined price,* regardless of market disruptions elsewhere. In principle,
Country B might sign a long-term purchase contract with Country 1 specifying
*a fixed price and volume commitment.* Country 1, knowing the probability of
disruption in Country 2 and the likely magnitude of a price spike, would, of
course, extract a premium designed to compensate it for the windfall profits it
would otherwise earn during a disruption. Thus, such an insurance policy
would not be free to Country B. Nevertheless, assume that Country B chose to
pay such a premium. Now assume a supply disruption in Country 2. Three
different outcomes are possible.

One possibility is that Country 1 honors its contract and Country B hoards
its oil. In this case, the price level in Country A would rise by 1,000 percent instead of 500 percent because the entire shortfall would be concentrated in

Country A. But would such a hoarding strategy be economically rational? Clearly not, because the oil would be worth far more in Country A than in Country B. Country B could profit handsomely by reselling oil to Country A, to say nothing of the benefits it would receive indirectly for helping reduce the economic calamity in Country A. Obviously, noneconomic considerations could dominate the hoarding decision. Unless the two countries were belligerents, it seems more plausible that Country B would choose a second option—reselling oil to Country A.

There is, however, a third option. It centers on the incentives for Country 1 to renege on its supply obligations and sell its oil to the highest bidder. The incentives to renege would be enormous during a disruption, and Country 1 might well sell directly to Country A, keeping for itself the windfall profits of a 500 percent price spike. Country B would have little recourse, as there would be significant legal problems with enforcing a contract between sovereign nations. Military action might be possible, but it would be risky and costly as well.

Long-term supply contracts are thus unlikely to confer any special advantages on Country B, either because it would choose to resell its oil to Country A or because Country 1 would renege on the contract and sell to Country A. The likelihood of these problems occurring probably explains why crude-oil sale contracts do not involve fixed long-term prices; rather, prices are based on the world price on the date of delivery.

### OIL INDEPENDENCE

If bilateral policies are ineffective in achieving oil security, would oil independence work? The idea that oil independence could immunize a country against the effects of a supply disruption is popular misconception 1.

In principle, oil independence can be achieved by price-induced conservation or increased supply of domestic oil and non-oil substitutes. Going back to the original example, assume that Country B, finding itself an importer of insecure oil, embarks on a massive program designed to reduce its oil consumption from 50 to 25 barrels per day. At the same time, it will stimulate its own production of costly but technologically feasible domestic oil and non-oil substitutes from 0 to 25 barrels per day. Of course, to cause consumers to reduce consumption substantially, the effective price of oil and oil products must be increased.[34] In turn, a higher domestic price would stimulate the production of high-cost domestic oil and non-oil substitutes.

For simplicity, assume that policymakers in Country B use the most transparent device to induce conservation and increase production of domestic oil (or oil substitutes)—a tariff on all imported crude oil. The tariff should be set high enough to reduce consumption and increase domestic production by 25 barrels. For simplicity, we will assume that a 100 percent oil tariff would reduce consumption from 50 to 25 barrels per day and that doubling the domestic price for oil would raise long-run domestic production to 25 barrels per day.

Figure 3.5 shows the long-run effect of a 100 percent oil tariff in Country B under these assumptions. Worldwide consumption would fall from 100 to 75 barrels per day as consuming Country B cut its consumption from 50 to 25 barrels per day. Note that Country B has also become an oil producer, selling 25 barrels per day to itself. But in this case, country B has removed itself from the world oil market; its domestic price is set by supply and demand conditions within its borders.

Assume that, as Country B withdraws from the world market and world demand (excluding Country B) shrinks to 50 barrels per day, the productive capacity of Countries 1 and 2 shrinks proportionally.[35] Thus, as figure 3.5 indicates, after Country B has become oil-independent, Country A will buy 25 barrels from each of Country 1 and Country 2, and both will be producing at capacity.

What happens during an oil disruption in Country 2? The bottom portion of figure 3.5 describes two situations. On the bottom left, it is assumed that Country B does not trade oil with Country A during the disruption. On the bottom right, it is assumed that A and B trade oil to mitigate the worldwide effects on GDP. In considering the case involving no trade between the two countries, we must remember that the world oil market now consists of only 50 barrels per day. With a loss of 25 barrels per day from Country 2, world oil consumption has fallen by 50 percent, triggering the same 500 percent price spike as in figure 3.4. The only difference is that Country A alone is experiencing the price shock. In this case, oil-independent Country B would keep its oil for domestic consumption and suffer no price shock.

But what if Countries A and B are linked together with strong trade ties in other goods, as in the second case? Because of the feedback effects on B, it would not be in B's interest to see A's economy crippled. Therefore, with a globalized economy, a more likely scenario is that Country B would sell oil on the world market, allowing Country A to access its oil. In the bottom right of figure 3.5, we see Country B selling 4 barrels of oil to Country A during the disruption and reducing its own consumption from 25 to 21 barrels per day. Clearly, prices in both countries will rise. As a consequence of B sharing its oil

Normal period

Consumers

| Producers | Country A | Country B |
|---|---|---|
| Country 1 (secure) | 25 | 0 |
| Country 2 (insecure) | 25 | 0 |
| B | 0 | 25 |

Disruption period:
No trade between A and B

Consumers

| Producers | Country A | Country B |
|---|---|---|
| Country 1 (secure) | 25 | 0 |
| Country 2 (insecure) | 0 | 0 |
| B | 0 | 25 |

Disruption period:
Trade between A and B

Consumers

| Producers | Country A | Country B |
|---|---|---|
| Country 1 (secure) | 25 | 0 |
| Country 2 (insecure) | 0 | 0 |
| B | 4 | 21 |

Figure 3.5
Country B becomes energy independent

with A, the magnitude of the world oil price shock would be diminished from a 500 percent increase to a 420 percent increase.[36] But in selling its oil to A, B experienced the same high price levels as in A.

What can be learned from this example? Clearly, Country B's oil-independence policy improved world security, as evidenced by the diminished magnitude of the world price shock. But did Country B really immunize itself against price shocks? It would be immunized only if it chose not to trade with A, and this seems improbable.

This example illustrates several additional important points. First, because of globalization, oil security is a world problem, not an individual-country problem. Because oil security is a world problem, it is another example of a public good. Country B's actions to alleviate its own security problem provided security benefits for all in the form of a smaller price shock. Yet the costs fell entirely on B. Consumers in Country B paid 100 percent higher oil prices during normal conditions, reducing its competitiveness in world markets. In contrast, with lower oil prices, Country A enjoyed a substantial trade advantage as a lower-cost producer in world markets.

The implications of oil security being a public good are quite predictable: individual countries are unlikely to impose substantial costs on themselves when a large portion of the benefits accrue to all.[37]

Returning to popular misconception 1, would a policy of energy independence immunize the United States against the effects of oil disruptions? As shown in the above example, Country B became self-sufficient at the cost of doubling its oil costs. Assuming oil trade with Country A, Country B still felt the impact of the oil disruption because its domestic oil and oil substitutes were bid up during the disruption and diverted to Country A.

A policy of oil independence would enhance worldwide security, but the cost burden would fall entirely on the United States—and even then the United States would not be immune to oil disruptions. Energy independence is not the panacea its advocates would have us believe. Arguments that it would create numerous jobs at home fail to recognize that these jobs and resources would otherwise be employed elsewhere, producing other products. Nor do its proponents consider the trade implications of making the United States an even higher-cost producer in world markets.

## THE THREE KEYS TO THINKING
## ABOUT OIL SECURITY

The previous discussions point to some generally pessimistic conclusions. Bilateral supply agreements between producing and consuming countries are ineffective and unenforceable as well as politically counterproductive because they feed the petro-nationalist phobia. Unilateral actions by countries to reduce dramatically their own domestic oil consumption—like oil independence—are very costly to the countries initiating such programs. Does it follow, then, that there is little policymakers can do to reduce the vulnerability of the world economy to oil supply disruptions? Fortunately, the bathtub analogy suggests three general principles for enhancing security.

### 1. Adding More Faucets
### to the Bathtub Increases Security

In the example above, there were only two oil-producing countries: Country 1, the secure producer, and Country 2, the insecure producer. Both had faucets filling the bathtub at equal rates. Clearly, adding more faucets in the form of different producing countries means that the disruption of any one faucet is likely to cause a much smaller percentage disruption of world supplies and thus a smaller price shock. It also matters greatly whether the probability of disruption of any one faucet is correlated with a disruption of other faucets. For example, a supply disruption in one country is likely to trigger a supply disruption in another country if the two countries share a similar geopolitical background, as in the Middle East.

The solution lies in diversifying world supplies: adding more faucets—and preferably more secure ones. Obviously, there are a number of producers in the Middle East, and supply disruptions by any one country have a nontrivial probability of spreading to other countries in the region. Nevertheless, disruptions rarely encompass a whole region and typically involve only one or two producing countries.[38] During the Iranian revolution, for instance, Iranian production fell from 6 million barrels per day in September 1978 to 0.7 million barrels per day in January 1979 amid widespread instability. In September 1980, the Iran-Iraq War erupted; combined production in November of that year was less than 1 million barrels per day, compared with 6.5 million barrels per day a year earlier. In 1990, Iraq's occupation of Kuwait led to a combined loss of about 5 million barrels per day from Iraq and Kuwait, but other key Middle Eastern countries were unaffected.

Outside the Middle East, supply disruptions have been limited to individual countries. Even though production in Africa and Venezuela may be subject to political upheavals, it provides useful diversification because these disruptions tend to be unrelated to those in the Middle East. For example, Nigerian oil production has historically been quite volatile; in many instances, it has fallen by more than 1 million barrels per day for reasons unrelated to the Middle East. In a world oil market of more than 85 million barrels per day, these disruptions have not resulted in large price shocks. Venezuela historically has been a much larger producer than Nigeria and has been more politically stable, but the oil strikes following the election of President Hugo Chávez led to a production decline of 2.3 million barrels per day between November 2002 and January 2003.

Let us look at the math of supply disruptions to see how adding more faucets, especially independent faucets, enhances security. For example, relax the second assumption in our model (that there are two oil producers) and instead assume that there are five equal-size producers. Also relax the third assumption (that one producer is secure and the other insecure) and assume that all five producers are subject to random oil disruptions 5 percent of the time and that disruptions in any one country are *independent* of disruptions else-where. What is the probability in any one period of a supply disruption affect-ing 20 percent of the world's oil supply? A disruption in any one country would cut supply by 20 percent, and the binomial distribution suggests that the prob-ability of that happening is 0.204[39]—in other words, even though the proba-bility of a disruption in any one of the five producers is only 5 percent, the prob-ability that any one country will experience a supply disruption in a given period is 20 percent.

Now change the example to ten equal-sized producers, each with the same 5 percent probability of a disruption. To create a 20 percent supply disruption, two countries must experience disruptions simultaneously. The probability of observing a 20 percent disruption to world supplies thus drops to 0.075[40]—that is, it falls by almost a factor of three as a consequence of doubling the number of producers from five to ten. An even more dramatic reduction in the probability of a 20 percent disruption occurs when twenty oil producers are considered; the probability drops to only 0.013.[41] In that case, four producers would have to experience a simultaneous disruption to cause a 20 percent world supply disruption.

Hence, the sharp decline in the probability of a severe disruption to world oil supplies depends critically on the *number* of producers and the *independence* of disruptions across countries. If the independence assumption is relaxed and it is assumed that disruptions are perfectly correlated between adjoining coun-tries, then adding more faucets does not necessarily increase security.

Yet another mechanism for adding faucets to the bathtub is maintaining emergency oil supplies that can be used during disruptions. In Europe, refiners are required to maintain supplies of crude oil and petroleum products to be used during emergencies. The United States has the Strategic Petroleum Re-serve (SPR), in which about 750 million barrels of crude oil are stored in salt domes along the Gulf Coast. In the event of a supply disruption, this oil can be quickly tapped and transported to the large number of refineries located in the area.

Countries that incur the costs of maintaining such reserves can recoup these costs when they sell oil during disruptions at much higher prices. Thus, unlike oil independence, a strategic petroleum reserve has some attractive features for the country investing in the facilities. Although adding these supplies to the bathtub benefits the whole world, a country investing in a reserve can recoup part of its costs by selling oil at high disruption prices.

To put the 750-million-barrel SPR into perspective, consider the following hypothetical example. Suppose an oil supply disruption resulted in a 10 percent shortfall in crude supplies, or a shortfall of 8.5 million barrels per day. If half of that shortfall, 4.25 million barrels per day, were offset by a drawdown from the SPR, the SPR would last for 176 days or almost half a year. Certainly, the SPR is an important source of oil security. At issue is its optimal size, which depends on the probability of disruption and the anticipated duration of a disruption. Work is underway to enlarge the SPR to 1 billion barrels.

### 2. Reducing Withdrawals from the Bathtub Enhances Security

If diversifying the supply of oil into the bathtub enhances security, so too would reducing the rate of withdrawal from the bathtub. Reduced worldwide consumption has two security-enhancing effects. First, reducing the oil dependency of an economy likely reduces the effects of a given price spike on GDP. Second, when worldwide consumption is decreased, the mix of secure oil available in the bathtub likely increases, which means that the magnitude of the price spike is likely to be smaller. Recall from chapter 2 that when oil consumption fell in the 1980s, it was the OPEC producers that suffered the loss of sales.

In principle, reduced dependence on the bathtub is very attractive. Achieving international cooperation for an oil consumption tax would address the public-good aspect of the problem, but such cooperation may be difficult to achieve. Nonetheless, in the absence of such an agreement, the oil price increases since 2004 should have some beneficial, though unintended, consequences. With a return to high prices, individual countries will choose to conserve oil, and oil substitutes will enter the market on a large scale, reducing the share of OPEC oil from the Middle East. In effect, high oil prices are the friend of oil security.

### 3. The Globalization of the Bathtub Facilitates Security

Admittedly, oil prices remain highly volatile, but is the global market the cause of this volatility? Most economists and political scientists disagree with the more common view that the globalization of the world oil market exacerbates insecurity, and they persuasively argue just the opposite.[42] Eugene Gholz and Daryl Press's argument rests on what they dub a "strategic adaptation theory," according to which markets, firms, and consumers worldwide have much more ability to respond to disruptions than is commonly thought.

Today, worldwide oil futures markets enable supplies of oil to be substituted both intertemporally and internationally to the time period and country where the disruption is most acute.[43] Firms in industries particularly vulnerable to price spikes, such as airlines, can purchase an insurance policy in the form of options to purchase oil futures at a predetermined price, effectively insulating themselves from the price spikes. On the other side of such transactions are firms that find these risks more tolerable, such as domestic oil producers or re-finers, which would actually benefit from a price shock. Likewise, the advent of heating-oil futures markets enable heating-oil suppliers to guarantee their cus-tomers a predetermined price for an impending heating season. Risk-averse consumers with little ability to reduce consumption will pay a premium for such a price guarantee, whereas more adaptable consumers will opt to self-insure.

To be sure, futures markets can exist within a country whether or not that country is linked to the world oil market. Being a part of the bathtub means that a supply disruption is spread over the whole world. Consequently, the risk sharing occurs on a worldwide basis rather than on an individual-country basis. Those firms and consumers worldwide who can reduce consumption most eas-ily will do so. In effect, the globalization of the world oil market facilitates risk sharing and therefore attenuates the magnitude of a price spike.[44] Even though globalization probably tends to reduce price volatility, it is nevertheless a grim reality that oil markets have been and will continue to be volatile. Price volatil-ity is the result of highly inelastic short-run demand and supply, not a global-ized market.

For those who remain confused or unconvinced, consider the case of crude oil and gasoline before and after hurricanes Katrina and Rita in 2005. As shown in figure 3.6, gasoline markets and prices behaved exactly as basic economics textbooks would have anticipated—increased gasoline imports from abroad, coupled with the normal workings of supply and demand here at home, helped minimize the effects of these disruptions.

On August 1, 2005, four weeks before Katrina struck, the price of West Texas Intermediate crude oil stood at $61.55 per barrel, and wholesale gasoline prices stood at $73.38 per barrel, which translates into $1.75 per gallon. After the addition of taxes and local distribution costs, the national average retail gasoline price at the time was $2.29 per gallon. Under normal conditions, the price of crude oil is the primary determinant of gasoline prices, constituting about 85 percent of the wholesale price and about 65 percent of the retail price. As shown in figure 3.6, on August 26, three days prior to Hurricane Katrina's landfall, wholesale gasoline prices rose from $73.38 to $80.93 per barrel, pri-

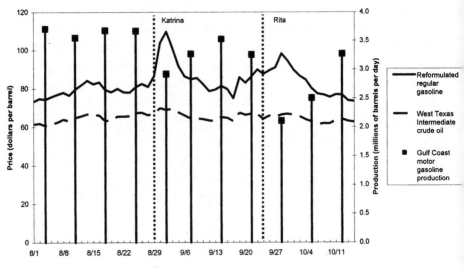

Figure 3.6
Crude-oil prices, wholesale gasoline prices, and Gulf Coast gasoline production
Data from DOE (2008a).

marily because of rising world oil prices in anticipation of crude-oil production shutdowns in the Gulf.

As the evidence of Katrina's destruction to refineries in the area mounted, gasoline prices decoupled from crude-oil prices and continued to rise sharply, reaching $109.81 per barrel on August 31, 2005—an increase of $28.88 per barrel. Over the same period, crude-oil prices increased by less than $3 per barrel because lost oil production from the Gulf of Mexico accounted for less than 1.5 percent of world supplies. Furthermore, all but 0.5 percent was offset by increased production from the SPR and elsewhere.[45] The reason for the sharp increase in gasoline prices vis-à-vis crude oil was that at this point the bottleneck was U.S. refining capacity—not crude oil supplies. Corresponding to the Katrina-induced peak in gasoline prices was a trough in Gulf Coast gasoline production at 2.9 million barrels per day because a number of refineries closed.

As the refining industry began to recover from Katrina, Gulf Coast gasoline production rebounded to 3.5 million barrels per day during the week of September 12–16, which was almost back to pre-Katrina levels.[46] Over the same period, wholesale gasoline prices fell sharply to $74.97 per barrel, near the initial price in early August.

But then as reports of Rita's ferocity and anticipated landfall along the upper

Texas coast began to circulate, wholesale gasoline markets rose steadily in *anticipation* of the potential destruction, reaching $98.25 per barrel on September 28—four days after Rita's landfall. As shown in figure 3.6, by September 26–30, Gulf Coast gasoline production had fallen to only 2.1 million barrels per day from weekly production of 3.5 million barrels per day in September 12–16. An important contribution to the recovery process was the surge of gasoline imports, from 938,000 barrels per day during the week of September 12–16 to 1,431,000 barrels per day during the week of October 3–7. The Bush administration moved quickly to suspend EPA mandates regarding boutique gasoline blends so that imported gasoline could enter without any geographic restrictions.[47] Not surprisingly, over this period wholesale gasoline prices fell by almost $25 per barrel compared with their peak during Rita.

The story of Katrina and Rita brings us back to popular misconception 4 regarding oil security—the belief that price controls during disruptions can prevent the macroeconomic dislocations that accompany sharply rising oil prices. The idea is that oil prices are like a thermometer that measures an economy's health. Preventing price shocks during a disruption masks the effects of the shortage, and the macroeconomy continues performing well. As noted in chapter 1, this logic was very popular in the United States during the energy crisis of the 1970s, when elaborate price controls were instituted. Unfortunately, these well-intentioned policies had the opposite effect of actually inviting further OPEC price hikes.[48]

Especially during price shocks, higher prices serve to move oil to its highest-value uses, ensuring that scarce supplies are not wasted on low-value uses. Higher prices lead to a surge in gasoline imports that help ameliorate the crisis. Furthermore, in anticipation of being able to earn huge profits during an emergency, gasoline stations will invest in holding higher-than-normal inventories, and these higher inventories make future emergencies less severe.

Regrettably, the lesson Congress learned from Katrina and Rita was that it felt compelled to pass legislation that would empower the government to ban price gouging during emergencies. Lost was the lesson that markets had actually functioned well and had prevented a bad situation from becoming much worse.

## POLICIES TO ENHANCE OIL SECURITY

The worldwide problem of oil security has to be addressed on a worldwide level. Solutions must involve either augmenting the sources of oil and the flow rate *into* the global bathtub or reducing the world's consumption rate *from* the bathtub, while preserving markets as the facilitators. Unfortunately, the leading policy prescriptions do not serve these ends. The petro-nationalist mentality of seeking bilateral oil deals does nothing to achieve these goals, so such deals are doomed to failure. Likewise, well-intentioned but misguided legislation that prohibits price gouging during oil price shocks only thwarts the market's ability to allocate scarce supplies and minimize the economic impacts of emergencies.

So what approaches would be effective? One example of a policy that individual countries find in their interests is investment in strategic petroleum reserves. As noted previously, individual countries may well choose to invest in reserves that can be released during an emergency. They can recoup their investment when they sell emergency supplies into the world market at inflated prices; yet, by providing additional supplies, they lessen the magnitude of the price spike. In effect, strategic petroleum reserves are analogous to additional faucets that can be turned on during an emergency.

But the question remains whether the price of a barrel of insecure oil in world markets reflects its true social cost if we must buy an insurance policy in the form of adding a barrel of oil to a strategic petroleum reserve. Isn't the true social cost of the insecure oil in this case its purchase price *plus* the cost of the insurance policy? In principle, we should impose an oil security tax on the insecure oil equal to the cost of the insurance policy, thereby internalizing the full social cost of the oil.

In a perfect world, all the consuming nations would agree on which oil sources were "secure" and which were "insecure," and all importing countries would impose a common tariff on the "insecure" oil equal to the externality it imposes. Unfortunately, this elegant policy prescription is not likely to work in practice. Given the fungibility of oil, any attempt to differentiate secure from insecure oil would be subject to abuses such as the repackaging of insecure oil as secure oil, the effect of which would be to thwart the desired security effects.

Since the theoretically optimal policy prescription is not practical, probably the next best alternative is to opt for some type of international security tax aimed at reducing worldwide oil consumption. Although increased prices due to an oil consumption or security tax will *not* increase the flow of oil from conventional production into the bathtub, the higher oil prices will promote conservation, accelerate the development of substitutes for conventional oil, and reduce dependence on Middle East oil.

The most straightforward method of reducing worldwide oil consumption would be a cooperative multicountry security tax. Given the incentives to free ride, the tax should not be set so high as to pose a major obstacle to international cooperation. Fortunately, Leiby and others estimate that the externally borne costs of an oil price shock lie somewhere between $0.21 and $9.91 per barrel, depending on disruption probabilities.[49] Ian Parry and Joel Darmstadter conclude that most analysts believe that the premium is nontrivial and go on to recommend an oil security tax of $5 per barrel.[50] Given that these estimates were developed when oil prices were in the $20 to $30 range, the question arises whether the proposed tax should be increased in a world of $130-plus oil prices. Since at higher oil prices world dependence on Middle East oil will fall, it can be argued that such a tax rate should, if anything, decrease.[51] The bathtub analogy forces us to recognize that a unilateral U.S. oil security tax without some international cooperation would place all the burden on the United States. Rather, the United States should seek the cooperation of other industrialized countries to adopt a similar tax. An agreement among developing countries not to subsidize petroleum products would be a good quid pro quo.

But what role should markets play in providing security? Although maintaining and increasing the SPR, encouraging R&D on oil substitutes, and imposing an oil security tax are eminently sensible policy prescriptions, markets provide the most powerful forces for energy security in at least three ways. First, all things equal, international oil companies prefer to base their exploration efforts in relatively secure countries because revolutions, wars, and nationalization mean financial ruin. In effect, the market rewards secure countries that protect property rights and offer stable political and economic institutions, and punishes insecure countries, which must offer potential bonanzas before oil companies will accept such risks.

Second, emergency supplies can contribute to energy security. All along the supply chain—from the oil field to the refinery to the local gasoline station—inventories must be held to handle fluctuations in supply and demand and maintain a continuous flow of product to consumers. Additional inventories can be held for speculative motives. If firms anticipate that oil prices will rise sharply, they will accumulate inventory. Likewise, if prices are expected to fall, firms will reduce their holdings to the minimum level necessary to maintain production. Although it is the expectation of windfall profits during a supply shortage that animates the decision to maintain emergency supplies, such supplies mitigate the magnitude of price shocks as they are released into the market.

Third, the existence of a world market as opposed to regional markets means that a supply disruption spreads the price shock over the whole world, inducing adaptations worldwide. With localized markets, a disruption is concentrated in one trading area, and a much greater price adjustment is necessary to reduce consumption to available supply. Consumers in the affected region bear the full brunt of making all the required adaptations.

As Daniel Yergin has noted, "Secession [from the world market] is not an option."[52] For most consuming countries, energy or oil independence would be prohibitively expensive. Instead, policymakers should think of ways to increase the number of faucets in the bathtub and reduce the drainage from it. Furthermore, it is imperative that policymakers come to view markets and globalization as allies, rather than as enemies, in the struggle for energy security. Shedding the petro-nationalist mind-set is a necessary first step.

# Chapter 4 Climate Change and the Search for Clean Energy

In chapter 1 I emphasized that one of the three goals of energy policy should be clean energy. In industrialized economies, clean energy becomes increasingly important as a policy goal as incomes rise and standards become more exacting, and it will probably always be so as those standards remain perpetually out of reach. Indeed, today there is no perfectly clean technology free of some negative attribute. Even solar panels and wind farms have aesthetic characteristics that are bothersome to some. The choice is among imperfect alternatives.

Because substantial progress has already been made in reducing other air pollutants, as discussed in chapter 1, analysis of the clean-energy challenge is limited to the problem of carbon emissions from fossil fuels and their effects on climate change. Carbon dioxide poses a different problem than other pollutants because it remains suspended in the atmosphere for very long periods of time and its effects are not limited to the emitting country's borders. The bathtub analogy that was so useful in thinking about oil security can also apply to $CO_2$ if we are willing to use a little imagination. Imagine a huge glass bathtub suspended upside down above the earth. In effect, the bathtub is catching the world's $CO_2$ emissions. The more it catches, the greater the temperature increase. Most importantly, since all countries emit $CO_2$ into the bathtub, we have a worldwide problem.

The Intergovernmental Panel on Climate Change states in its 2007 report that "warming of the climate system is unequivocal."[1] Eleven of the twelve years from 1995 to 2006 rank among the warmest since the instrumental recording of surface temperatures began in 1850.[2]

Global climate change poses a whole set of scientific, economic, political, and ethical problems. Indeed, it has been described as the "mother of all problems." This rhetoric suggests that apocalyptic events will unfold as humanity marches blindly forward, demanding more and more automobiles, jet travel, and air-conditioned homes. Once we cross over the precipice, there will be no returning to the earlier world. The earth's atmosphere will have been irreversibly violated, and humans will be forced to reap forever the consequences of their profligate lifestyle.

Whether this alarmist view is correct is open to debate. But as an *intellectual* exercise, climate change appears to be the mother of all problems because of its complexity. Anyone who has attempted to understand the carbon cycle, the climatological interactions of $CO_2$ with the atmosphere, the effects of climate change on market and nonmarket activities, the technological options to abate carbon emissions, the functioning of a market-based trading system for $CO_2$ permits, or the international organizations needed to deal with global warming usually comes away frustrated and hopelessly bewildered. Climate change brings together the disciplines of botany, biology, climatology, atmospheric and oceanic chemistry, glaciology, systems modeling, cloud physics, statistics, economics, and political science. For any one person to achieve proficiency in all these areas seems impossible.

Despite this complexity, a layperson can come to understand in a general way the various issues from which reasonable policy prescriptions follow. For those of us with a healthy respect for what we do not know, the reward may be a clear view of the choices before us and the uncertainties on which they hinge.

A good starting point is to acquire a basic knowledge of the issues. This chapter draws extensively on a conference volume from the Bush School of Government and Public Service at Texas A&M University, in which eminent scholars summarized the prevailing wisdom in their fields.[3] They offered their opinions regarding the following eight "big picture" questions:

- What is the link between fossil-fuel consumption and $CO_2$ concentrations in the atmosphere?

- What is the relationship between $CO_2$ concentrations and global warming?
- Is the principal tool of economic analysis, benefit-cost analysis, adequate for recommending policies to address global climate change?
- In a business-as-usual world, what are the market effects of global warming?
- In a business-as-usual world, what are the most significant nonmarket effects of climate change?
- What are the mitigation costs of various policies, and what technologies are available to reduce $CO_2$ emissions significantly?
- How vigorously should we be working to reduce $CO_2$ emissions?
- Are existing institutions and agreements, like the Kyoto Protocol, up to the task, and if not, what other policy options are likely to lead to cooperative efforts to reduce carbon emissions?

Answers to these complex questions are not always clear-cut, and opinions differ considerably. But by focusing on the prevailing wisdom of experts in their fields, we can gain a general understanding. The remainder of this chapter and the next is devoted to answering these questions on the basis of the prevailing wisdom.

### WHY THE EMPHASIS ON $CO_2$?

Before jumping headfirst into discussions of the carbon cycle, it is important to acquire some background facts. Why focus on $CO_2$ as the primary determinant of global warming?

Carbon dioxide is a greenhouse gas that regulates the rate at which the earth can radiate heat energy back into space. Greenhouse gases are transparent to incoming solar radiation but largely opaque to the passage of outgoing infrared radiation. In effect, these gases form a type of greenhouse that traps solar heat near the earth's surface, preventing extremely frigid nighttime temperatures from occurring. Besides $CO_2$, other greenhouse gases include halocarbons, nitrous oxide, methane, tropospheric ozone, and water vapor. Most of them, along with $CO_2$, occur naturally and are essential for providing the temperate conditions under which life on earth is possible. Greenhouse gases clearly do not belong on the list of toxic air pollutants, but, as we shall see, there can be too much of a good thing.

Since 1950, human-induced (anthropogenic) factors have eclipsed natural factors as the dominant cause of climate change. Disentangling natural from anthropogenic causes is an inexact science, but several statistics stand out. In a study for the Pew Center on Global Climate Change, Tom Wigley reports that from 1950 to 2000, the global mean temperature increased by approximately 0.5 degrees Celsius (°C) or 0.9 degrees Fahrenheit (°F), and about 75 percent of radiative forcing[4] was attributable to anthropogenic sources.[5] $CO_2$ has historically accounted for about 53 percent of the anthropogenic forcing associated with greenhouse gases.[6] Other contributors include methane gas (17 percent), tropospheric ozone (13 percent), halocarbons (12 percent), and nitrous oxides (5 percent).

One might ask why $CO_2$ receives so much attention if it accounts for less than half of only a 0.9°F temperature change over the last fifty-plus years. The explanation is complicated, but, in a nutshell, $CO_2$ emissions and temperature changes in the next half century are not likely to be as benign as in the previous half century. There are at least five reasons $CO_2$ will become an increasingly serious problem.

First, $CO_2$ is a very long-lived gas. Carbon that is emitted today will persist in the atmosphere for several centuries before atmospheric removal mechanisms purge it. In contrast, methane is estimated to have a lifetime of just twelve years. The effects of $CO_2$ emissions, therefore, are cumulative.

Second, $CO_2$, fossil fuels, and energy consumption are linked. Fossil fuels, which account for 87 percent of world energy consumption, are responsible for almost all current $CO_2$ emissions. For example, in the United States, 98 percent of $CO_2$ emissions come from fossil fuels. Table 4.1 ranks the world's twenty largest energy consumers and shows the mix of fossil fuels and hydroelectric, nuclear, and other energy forms that each nation uses. In France, which relies heavily on nuclear power for electricity generation, fossil fuels account for only 56 percent of total energy requirements. Solar, biomass, and other miscellaneous energy sources account for less than 4 percent in all the countries surveyed. This last statistic is striking in light of all the public efforts to jumpstart alternative energy sources following the energy crisis of the 1970s. For the foreseeable future, fossil fuels will continue to be the backbone of world energy supplies.

The third reason the $CO_2$ problem will become increasingly serious is that economic output requires energy inputs. GDP and energy use are highly correlated, as shown in figure 4.1. As worldwide economic development spreads to China, India, and other rapidly developing countries, worldwide energy use will reach levels never dreamed of fifty years ago. Since fossil fuels will provide most of these supplies, $CO_2$ emissions are expected to grow rapidly and to account for the bulk of greenhouse-gas forcing.[7]

A fourth reason to be particularly concerned about $CO_2$ is that fossil fuels

Table 4.1  Fuel mix of the twenty largest energy-consuming
nations, 2007

| | Total energy[a] | Fossil fuels (%) | Nuclear energy (%) | Hydroelectric (%) |
|---|---|---|---|---|
| United States | 2361.4 | 89.5 | 8.1 | 2.4 |
| China | 1863.4 | 93.4 | 0.8 | 5.9 |
| Russia | 692.0 | 88.9 | 5.2 | 5.9 |
| Japan | 517.5 | 84.1 | 12.2 | 3.7 |
| India | 404.4 | 92.2 | 1.0 | 6.8 |
| Canada | 321.7 | 67.5 | 6.6 | 25.9 |
| Germany | 311.0 | 87.8 | 10.2 | 2.0 |
| France | 255.1 | 55.3 | 39.1 | 5.6 |
| South Korea | 234.0 | 85.7 | 13.8 | 0.5 |
| Brazil | 216.8 | 59.9 | 1.3 | 38.8 |
| United Kingdom | 215.9 | 92.5 | 6.5 | 1.0 |
| Iran | 182.9 | 97.8 | 0.0 | 2.2 |
| Italy | 179.6 | 95.1 | 0.0 | 4.9 |
| Saudi Arabia | 167.6 | 100.0 | 0.0 | 0.0 |
| Mexico | 155.5 | 94.5 | 1.5 | 3.9 |
| Spain | 150.3 | 86.8 | 8.3 | 4.9 |
| Ukraine | 136.0 | 82.9 | 15.4 | 1.7 |
| South Africa | 127.8 | 96.7 | 2.3 | 1.0 |
| Australia | 121.8 | 96.9 | 0.0 | 3.1 |
| Taiwan | 115.1 | 90.5 | 8.0 | 1.5 |

*Source:* BP (2008).

*Note:* Excludes biofuels as well as wind, geothermal, and solar power. Rows may not sum to 100, because of rounding error.

[a]Million tonnes of oil equivalent.

will remain abundant and the fuels of choice. As discussed in chapter 2, even if conventional oil production peaks over the next forty years, waiting in the wings are plentiful supplies of oil sands, heavy oils, oil shale, and natural gas for gas-to-liquid fuels, along with enormous coal reserves. In the absence of major cost-reducing advances in alternative fuel technologies, fossil fuels are and will continue to be the incumbent fuels.

Finally, the earth's natural carbon absorption mechanisms are maxed out. The ability of the earth to absorb $CO_2$, which depends on a variety of factors, including the weathering of rocks, ocean uptake of $CO_2$, and photosynthesis by plants and trees, has in the last decades been exceeded by the levels of $CO_2$

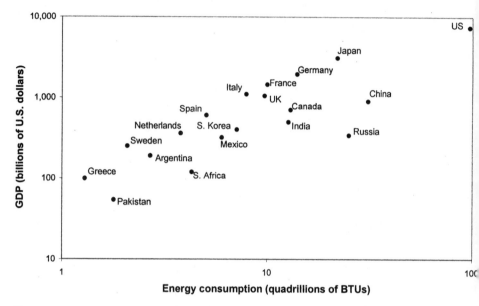

Figure 4.1
Energy use and GDP for selected countries, 2000
Reproduced from Griffin (2003b, fig. 1.1).

emissions—in other words, the planet's carbon absorption mechanism is maxed out.[8]

A simple inventory equation describes the level of $CO_2$ concentrations in period $t$ as follows:

$$CO_2 \text{ concentrations}_t = CO_2 \text{ concentrations}_{t-1} + CO_2 \text{ emissions}_t - CO_2 \text{ absorption}_t$$

The idea is that the current inventory of $CO_2$ concentrations depends on last year's inventory of $CO_2$ concentrations plus $CO_2$ emissions in the current year less what is absorbed by natural forces. Currently, $CO_2$ emissions exceed absorption by about 2 parts per million (ppm) annually, so $CO_2$ concentrations are growing at a rate of 2 ppm. But this is likely to increase sharply in the years ahead as $CO_2$ emissions continue to grow and the absorption mechanism is unable to offset it.

Having zeroed in on $CO_2$ as the primary future greenhouse gas, scientists typically focus on the following two questions: How long will it take before $CO_2$ concentrations in the atmosphere double? What climate changes will result from this doubling of $CO_2$ concentrations? Note that these two questions center on $CO_2$ *concentrations*, not $CO_2$ *emissions*.

Climate change depends on $CO_2$ concentrations, not emissions in any one year, so even if we could quickly adjust our annual emissions, it would not quickly translate into temperature adjustments. And a one-time reduction in annual emissions will have no meaningful impact on total $CO_2$ concentrations. It is *cumulative* emissions that matter. But the exact timing of emissions reductions does not matter as long as cumulative reductions are sufficient to enable $CO_2$ concentration to stabilize at some reasonable level. Accordingly, if future technological advances provide low-cost abatement techniques, it may be prudent to concentrate the major reductions in the future.

Furthermore, atmospheric $CO_2$ concentrations have already risen from 280 ppm during the Industrial Revolution to approximately 380 ppm today—an average annual increase of about 0.4 ppm per year. But today the annual increase in $CO_2$ concentrations is on the order of 2.0 ppm and could rise to 4.0 ppm per year by 2030.[9] The Intergovernmental Panel on Climate Change has forecast that, under a business-as-usual scenario, $CO_2$ concentrations could reach 550 ppm by 2050 and 750 ppm by 2100.[10] The world is consuming fossil fuels on a scale never before realized.[11] Even if emissions were stabilized at current rates, $CO_2$ concentrations would continue to rise for a number of years. Increased economic development will only accelerate the rate of increase in $CO_2$ concentrations. Robert Socolow has calculated that worldwide consumption of fossil fuels by electric power plants alone from 2003 to 2030 will equal 69 percent of all fossil fuels consumed over the previous 252 years.[12] And remember, fossil-fuel-fired power plants account for only about one-fourth of current $CO_2$ emissions!

## THE EFFECT OF $CO_2$ CONCENTRATIONS
## ON GLOBAL WARMING

In forecasting future global warming patterns, climatologists face two general types of uncertainty. First is the difficulty in estimating future $CO_2$ concentrations because, as noted above, a number of factors influence the increase in these concentrations over time. Second is the uncertainty in the process of translating a given level of $CO_2$ concentrations into temperature change. For example, as temperatures rise, so will the rate of water evaporation, creating additional greenhouse gases and further warming the planet. Climatologists have devised elaborate models to predict differential patterns of global warming, but the science is still highly inexact.

Even though there are substantial differences in the predictions of the various models of climate change, certain broad conclusions appear inescapable. As noted, under a business-as-usual scenario, $CO_2$ concentrations will rise sharply over the next fifty to one hundred years.[13] Although the various models show a wide array of predicted temperature changes, all point to significant increases over current levels. The Intergovernmental Panel on Climate Change's best estimate of the global average surface warming due to a doubling of $CO_2$ concentrations from preindustrial levels is 3°C (5.4°F).[14] Using today's temperatures as a benchmark, $CO_2$ concentrations of 550 ppm imply a temperature increase of 2.3°C (4.1°F). If $CO_2$ concentrations reached 750 ppm by 2100, the estimated temperature increase would be 3.8°C (6.8°F).

Not only is the mean temperature likely to rise significantly, but its effects will be spread quite unevenly across the globe. The models predict an amplification of the warming toward both poles, with the equatorial areas experiencing more moderate temperature increases. For example, the warming in Siberia and northern Canada could be as much as 5.5°C to 6.1°C (10°F to 11°F).[15]

### PROSPECTS FOR DEFERRING THE DATE AT WHICH CO$_2$ CONCENTRATIONS DOUBLE

Are the dates 2050 and 2100, when $CO_2$ concentrations are projected to reach 550 ppm and 750 ppm, respectively, cast in stone? No. Fortunately, the world community can push back these dates through the price mechanism and technological advances.

Given time to work, the price mechanism has the power to alter long-term $CO_2$ emissions by three means, the first of which is the substitution of low-carbon for high-carbon fossil fuels. An important and often forgotten point is that all fossil fuels are not created equal. On a per-Btu basis, coal emits 77 percent more $CO_2$ than natural gas; petroleum emits 39 percent more $CO_2$ than natural gas, but 22 percent less than coal.[16] Table 4.2 shows that the mix of fossil fuels differs considerably across countries, demonstrating the ability to substitute fossil fuels with lower emissions for fuels with higher emissions. Although these differences may not seem large, consider, for example, that if China employed the same mix of fossil fuels as the Netherlands, it would reduce its $CO_2$ emissions by 30 percent. The Netherlands relies extensively on natural gas to produce electricity and for home heating, whereas China relies extensively on coal.

The possibility also exists of substituting nonfossil fuels for fossil fuels. As

Table 4.2  Fossil-fuel mix of the twenty largest energy-consuming nations, 2007

|                | Coal (%) | Oil (%) | Natural gas (%) |
| -------------- | -------- | ------- | --------------- |
| South Africa   | 76.5     | 20.2    | 0.0             |
| China          | 70.4     | 19.7    | 3.3             |
| India          | 51.4     | 31.8    | 8.9             |
| Australia      | 43.6     | 34.7    | 18.6            |
| Taiwan         | 35.7     | 45.6    | 9.2             |
| Ukraine        | 28.9     | 11.3    | 42.8            |
| Germany        | 27.7     | 36.2    | 23.9            |
| South Korea    | 25.5     | 46.0    | 14.2            |
| United States  | 24.3     | 39.9    | 25.2            |
| Japan          | 24.2     | 44.2    | 15.7            |
| United Kingdom | 18.1     | 36.2    | 38.1            |
| Russia         | 13.7     | 18.2    | 57.1            |
| Spain          | 13.4     | 52.4    | 21.0            |
| Italy          | 9.7      | 46.4    | 39.0            |
| Canada         | 9.5      | 31.8    | 26.3            |
| Brazil         | 6.3      | 44.5    | 9.1             |
| Mexico         | 5.9      | 57.4    | 31.3            |
| France         | 4.7      | 35.8    | 14.8            |
| Iran           | 0.6      | 42.1    | 55.0            |
| Saudi Arabia   | 0.0      | 59.2    | 40.8            |

*Source:* BP (2008).

table 4.1 shows, the mix of nonfossil fuels can be varied even with existing energy technologies. France is the prime example of this type of substitution.

Finally, there is the substitution of non-energy-intensive for energy-intensive goods. The energy crisis of the 1970s taught us that the energy input of a dollar's worth of GDP can be reduced dramatically as firms substitute capital and labor for energy and consumers choose less energy-intensive products.

All these substitution responses—lower-emissions fossil fuels for higher-emissions fossil fuels, nonfossil fuels for fossil fuels, and non-energy-intensive for energy-intensive goods—are the direct result of the price mechanism. Higher prices for fossil fuels will bring all three of them into action.

Besides the price mechanism, the second major factor altering our date with destiny is technological change, which can manifest itself in a variety of ways, including cheap methods of $CO_2$ sequestration,[17] greater fuel efficiency, and clean alternative energy sources. Over longer periods of time, breakthroughs in

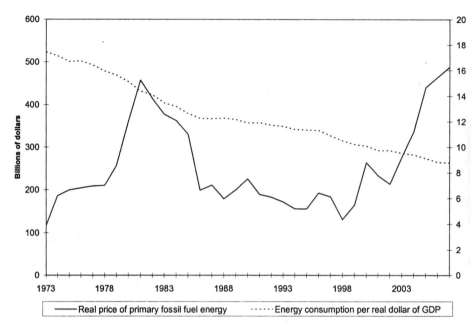

Fig. 4.2
Energy intensity of real GDP versus real price of energy, 1973–2007
Data from DOE (2008c) and DOC (2008).

basic R&D may be commercialized, allowing for the diffusion of new technologies and the possibility of profoundly reshaping the energy landscape.
These advances will not be without cost—nor will they occur quickly—but
they can occur if we make the effort. Anyone doubting the ability of technological change to fundamentally alter the energy landscape should visit the Smith-
sonian National Air and Space Museum or the Disney theme park Epcot.

Figure 4.2 shows the combined effects of price-induced substitution responses and energy-saving technological change on the energy input per dollar
of U.S. GDP since the energy crisis of the 1970s, providing additional evidence
for our ability to change the future. It also shows the real price of energy, with
its meteoric rise in the 1970s and early 1980s, followed by a long period of declining real prices. Notice that the sharply rising real prices in this early period
triggered the substitution and technological responses, which persisted well
into the 1990s and led to a substantially lower energy content of GDP.

The price mechanism coupled with technological advances have tremendous potential to alter the future, but harnessing them to achieve these outcomes is a tricky policy issue about which much more is said later.

## CHOOSING AMONG CO$_2$-ABATEMENT STRATEGIES

The fact that the doubling date for CO$_2$ concentrations can be altered tells us that we have choices. Putting aside for the moment the serious issue of obtaining international cooperation to control CO$_2$ emissions, it is useful to consider what benefit-cost analysis, the economist's stock in trade, has to say about the speed at which carbon emissions should be reduced and the magnitude of such reductions. Admittedly, the world seldom operates according to the principles of economic efficiency, but it is at least beneficial to ask what economic efficiency has to say about the timing and intensity of efforts to reduce CO$_2$ emissions.

### A Conceptual Framework for Choice

We must begin by asking, Does an effective approach to the problem of global warming require a massive investment in carbon abatement right away, or a more moderate strategy that spreads the costs many years into the future? How can we go about determining this?

Traditionally, economics has held forth benefit-cost analysis as the preferred framework for answering these questions. The idea is straightforward: find a strategy that yields the greatest benefits relative to costs over time. In calculating benefits and costs, one applies a social discount rate—that is, a percentage used to convert future costs and benefits to their "present value." This makes it possible to determine whether the cost of an investment today is worth the benefits it will yield in the future.[18]

Mathematically, the idea is to choose an abatement strategy that maximizes the present value (PV) of benefits ($B$) less costs ($C$) as follows:

$$PV = B_0 - C_0 + \frac{B_1 - C_1}{1+r} + \ldots + \frac{B_{50} - C_{50}}{(1+r)^{50}} + \ldots + \frac{B_{100} - C_{100}}{(1+r)^{100}} + \ldots$$

For each time period starting in the current period ($i = 0$), one computes the benefits ($B_i$) and the costs ($C_i$) of a particular abatement strategy and discounts the difference back to the current period using the social discount rate $r$. The benefits of a particular abatement strategy in period $i$ are computed so as to include both the market and nonmarket valuation of benefits from lower concentrations of CO$_2$ in each period $i$. Costs are the costs associated with the abatement strategy society chooses in each period $i$. For each abatement strategy and the resulting CO$_2$ emissions and concentrations over time, one can compute the present value of benefits less costs, as shown above. Economic efficiency says to select the strategy with the highest present value.

This framework treats the whole world as a single entity, aggregating benefits and costs across all regions. An objection to benefit-cost analysis is that there may be large distributional effects—some areas may be big winners and others big losers. Benefit-cost analysis puts these distributional issues aside, leaving it to the policymakers to compensate the losers, if necessary, from the benefits accruing to the winners.

There is also a great deal of contention as to what social discount rate should be applied, since the results of the analysis depend critically on this measure.[19] Programs that would significantly reduce today's $CO_2$ emissions will cost a lot now, with very little offsetting benefit accruing to the generation making the investment. Instead, the benefits will be realized primarily in the distant future, when temperatures will be lower than they would have been if the investment had not been made. When the future benefits are divided by $(1 + r)^n$, where $n$ is, say, fifty years from now, the present value is much smaller depending on the social discount rate chosen. For example, $1 in benefits fifty years from now is worth only 8.7¢ today if $r$ equals 0.05, implying a 5 percent discount rate. Alternatively, if we use a 2 percent social discount rate ($r = 0.02$), the present value of the same dollar is worth 37.2¢—about four times as much as at a 5 percent rate.

In most benefit-cost analyses, the social discount rates applied is in the range of 3 to 5 percent ($r = 0.03–0.05$), reflecting current real rates of return on invested capital.[20] Applied to the issue of global warming, however, such rates would make abatement strategies focused on massive investments to achieve immediate large emissions reductions prohibitively expensive; they would flunk the benefit-cost test and yield a negative present value. The reason is that the costs are immediate whereas the benefits are likely to accrue many years in the future, and after we discount these future benefits back to the present, the present value of these investments is negative.

To those calling for such immediate large-scale actions, benefit-cost analysis is anathema—something to be thrown out or altered dramatically. For example, to justify massive immediate initiatives to halt the growth of greenhouse gases, Sir Nicholas Stern in the *Economics of Climate Change: The Stern Review* argues that a lower social discount rate of near zero should be applied, stressing that future generations, who will be the primary beneficiaries of current emissions reductions, should be treated on an equal footing with present generations.[21] As shown by William Nordhaus, a near-zero discount rate assumption allows Stern to justify a carbon tax of \$85 per ton of $CO_2$.[22]

To see just how important this one parameter is to the policy debate, consider that a tax this high would raise the current price of coal, natural gas, and crude oil by 870 percent, 66 percent, and 75 percent, respectively. Consider further that, following the logic of a zero discount rate, the abatement of a ton of $CO_2$ emissions has the same value now as in 2100. But this makes no sense. Surely, the value to society of a ton of abatements would be much greater in 2100, when concentrations might be approaching 750 ppm, than it would today.

Furthermore, investing in programs to address global warming is only one way to benefit mankind. Particularly in the developing world, funds invested in carbon abatement must compete with investments in human health, education, and rural infrastructure. If current generations can make capital investments that will yield real returns around 4 percent, why should we choose to bequeath to future generations investments yielding a zero return? As Thomas Schelling notes in a work on intergenerational discounting, singling out global warming for preferential treatment by using an artificially low discount rate makes no sense to most economists.[23]

Opponents of adopting conventional discount rates fail to recognize that the standard benefit-cost equation provides greater incentives for carbon abatement in the distant future—that is, the net benefit of carbon abatement rises over time at the rate of social discount. For example, a \$5 per ton tax on $CO_2$— one-seventeenth the level proposed in the *Stern Review*—rising at 4 percent in real terms would, by 2080, equal the \$85-per-ton tax proposed in the *Stern Review*. The conclusion is clear: applying conventional discount rates in the range of 3 to 5 percent can greatly alter the timing of carbon-abatement investments, leading us to spread them over time and begin them slowly now. Now that we have figured out the appropriate social discount rate, we need to decide what benefits and costs to factor into the benefit-cost equation.

### Benefits of Carbon Abatement

Researchers attempting to measure the benefits from carbon abatement (which here refer to damages avoided from global warming by investing in abatement strategies) typically divide their analyses into two types of effects of climate change: market and nonmarket effects. Market effects are reflected in GDP— the benefits of an abatement strategy for agricultural output, forest output, household energy consumption, water consumption, and coastal economies.

Nonmarket effects refer to things not traded in markets but nevertheless valuable, such as natural ecosystems, human lifestyles, health, amenity values, and the avoidance of catastrophic risk. Although much more is known about the market effects of global warming than about nonmarket effects, considerable uncertainty surrounds both. Unfortunately, this uncertainty is not likely to be eliminated over the next few decades.

MARKET DAMAGE FROM CLIMATE CHANGE

There has been substantial research about the effects of climate change on the U.S. economy, but much less about the effects on the world economy. Studies conducted in the early and mid-1990s, based on an increase in $CO_2$ concentrations to 550 ppm and an increase in temperatures of 2.3°C (4.1°F) over current temperatures, produced estimates of annual damages ranging from a low of 0.1 percent to a high of 0.9 percent of U.S. GDP.[24] The next generation of studies by Robert Mendelsohn and James Neumann suggested that the earlier studies grossly overestimated the benefits of carbon abatement to the U.S. economy.[25] Indeed, they found that small increases in temperature could actually be beneficial to the United States. Why the difference?

A key advancement of Mendelsohn's work over earlier estimates is that he incorporates *adaptation* into his analysis.[26] For example, global warming in agriculture might make a particular geographic region unsuitable for growing some traditional crops; however, farmers can typically adapt by selecting some other crop that is more suitable for warmer weather. According to Mendelsohn, society will adapt to climate change not only in agriculture but in a multitude of other dimensions as well.

This more refined body of work highlights another extremely important consideration: differences across regions and sectors. Mendelsohn shows that looking only at aggregate U.S. effects masks big differences between regions and between the various sectors of the economy.[27] Warming benefits the agricultural sector and the timber industry generally via $CO_2$ fertilization;[28] the energy sector, water sector, and coastal areas, however, are negatively affected. Consumers pay more in summer air-conditioning bills than they save in lower winter heating bills. Also, different regions of the United States are affected unequally. The Northeast, Midwest, and Northern Plains would benefit from a 2.5°C (4.5°F) warming, whereas the Southeast, the Southern Plains, and Southwest would generally be worse off.

Mendelsohn applies a similar methodology to estimate the global consequences of warming. Again, he finds that in the aggregate, moderate warming (less than 2.5°C) would result in a small net gain to world GDP of about 0.1 percent. The biggest beneficiaries would be Asia, western Europe, and North America, whereas Africa and India would be losers.

Perhaps the most scientifically convincing aspect of Mendelsohn's work is the finding that, beyond some level of warming, further temperature increases would result in significant damages. In climates that are already warm, any further warming would result unambiguously in increased damages. With a 5°C temperature increase, Mendelsohn finds, all regions would be unambiguously worse off.

What are the policy implications of these estimates? Although his is the best work available, Mendelsohn is careful to emphasize the large uncertainty that surrounds it and earlier work in the area. Nevertheless, the finding that adaptation is likely to hold down damages for modest warming resonates with intuition. Similarly, the finding that the damages are unambiguously negative for large temperature increases seems plausible. Even if Mendelsohn's estimates are off by a factor of ten, they counsel policymakers that, on average, the market benefits of carbon abatement appear to be small for a warming of 2.5°C or less. For greater levels of warming associated with $CO_2$ concentrations of 550 ppm or greater, however, damages become potentially quite serious. As $CO_2$ concentrations rise to 550 ppm or beyond, the marginal benefits of carbon abatement are likely to rise steadily over time. This has important implications for carbon policy because it suggests that abatement efforts should be concentrated when the benefits are highest.

Yet another implication of Mendelsohn's work is that, even for small temperature changes, some areas will be significant losers—even here in the United States, issues of equity will only intensify. The industrialized nations must find ways to compensate the losers—particularly in the poorest regions—through investments in health, education, and the like.

NONMARKET DAMAGES FROM CLIMATE CHANGE

The measurement of damages associated with market-traded goods is fraught with uncertainty; determining the value of nonmarket goods is even more conjectural. There is a whole host of environmental and quality-of-life effects that have no observable market prices, are not traded, and do not constitute part of GDP, yet they routinely affect individuals' sense of well-being. For example, climate change may lead to the destruction of an entire ecosystem and its replacement by some other ecosystem with less biological diversity. Valuing such losses is a daunting task; yet to assume they are negligible is not acceptable to most students of the subject.

Indeed, Joel Smith, Jeffrey Lazo, and Brian Hurd conclude that nonmarket damages from warming are potentially much greater than the market-related damages estimated by Mendelsohn.[29] Their survey of potential losses suggests that with respect to recreation, tourism, and amenities, some regions will be winners and others will be losers. To find substantial worldwide negative effects of global warming, they argue, we must look beyond these areas—to the natural ecosystem, human health, and potential catastrophic outcomes.

In terms of the ecosystem, earlier work by William Nordhaus and Joseph Boyer provides estimates of "willingness to pay" to avoid further damages. They estimate that the United States is willing to pay 0.1 percent of GDP;[30] Richard Tol estimates that the world is willing to pay 0.2 percent of global GDP.[31] These estimates, although the best available, should be interpreted with considerable caution. Whether based on the judgment of experts or on contingent valuation studies (in which respondents are asked hypothetically what they would be willing to pay to avoid a particular outcome), these estimates are flawed for two reasons. First, we simply do not know what the ecosystem loss is likely to be. Second, respondents to hypothetical questions regarding what they would be willing to pay to avoid some climate outcome have little ability to assess the significance of the hypothetical damage conjectured; nor must they back up their valuations with actual cash contributions.

Although the effects will not be universal, damages to human health appear to be another potentially important nonmarket effect of global warming. Given the large populations in tropical countries and their relatively poor health-care systems, higher mortality rates are likely to result.

More important even than health is the issue of avoiding a catastrophic climate event, such as the breakup of the West Antarctic ice sheet or a slowdown of the North Atlantic current's thermohaline circulation. And although climate scientists have not been able to identify a temperature change that would produce such catastrophic events, one cannot rule out the possibility, and prudence suggests that we should be willing to pay some amount to insure the world against such events.

Nordhaus and Boyer investigate such an outcome of climate change, postulating a catastrophe that could result in a 30 percent drop in income.[32] Associated with a warming of 2.5°C, they find a "willingness to pay" of 0.45 percent of GDP; for a 5°C warming, 2.5 percent. In other words, the warmer the postulated temperature change, the more expensive an insurance policy the public is willing to buy. In focusing on catastrophic outcomes, Nordhaus and Boyer have put their finger on the issue most important to countries' willingness to pay to ameliorate global warming.

Avoiding a catastrophic outcome can generate significant benefits that should be factored into the benefit-cost equation. Prudence dictates risk aversion. Accordingly, insurance against such outcomes becomes more and more valuable at greater levels of $CO_2$ concentrations. This means that the benefits from carbon abatement, although small today, are likely to increase significantly in the future as $CO_2$ concentrations reach much higher levels.

### Costs of Carbon Abatement

Much more is known about the costs of carbon abatement than about the damages associated with global warming. Although fossil fuels remain the dominant fuel source, society has a number of choices, including nonfossil fuels such as renewables. Renewable fuels in the form of biofuels or grain-sourced ethanol, do, it is true, emit $CO_2$ when consumed. However, the crops or grains used in the production of these fuels absorbed $CO_2$ while they were growing, so the net $CO_2$ emissions of these fuels are, in principle, zero.[33]

Another option is continued reliance on fossil fuels coupled with carbon sequestration. A number of sequestration alternatives are available, including geologic storage of $CO_2$ (in depleted oil and gas fields, deep saline reservoirs, coal seams that cannot be mined, and basalt formations), ocean storage (mid-depth dispersion in deep lakes and as hydrates), and storage as a solid (in carbon form, as solid $CO_2$, and as a mineral carbonate), as well as terrestrial sequestration by soils and trees.[34] James Edmonds and Ronald Sands emphasize that there does not appear to be one dominant technology.

When it comes to carbon abatement, there is no silver bullet. Rather, these various options are likely to compete with one another; some will be preferred in some situations but not in others.

Such trade-offs are captured in a projected cost comparison, published by the Electric Power Research Institute (EPRI), of electric power generated by various existing technologies in 2010 and potential future technologies in 2020.[35] Table 4.3 summarizes the analysis for 2010. The first column presents a cost comparison based on existing technologies for the year 2010. Pulverized coal is the lowest-cost fuel, at 4.1¢ per kilowatt hour (kwh). However, $CO_2$ emissions from this fuel, shown in the second column, are 722 grams per kwh. The other technologies are ranked in order of their costs. The third column

Table 4.3 Comparative costs of electricity generation in 2010
with existing technologies

| Generation technology | Cost (¢/kwh) | Carbon emissions (g/kwh) | Carbon tax parity ($/ton of $CO_2$) |
|---|---|---|---|
| Pulverized coal | 4.1 | 722 | 0 |
| Nuclear power | 4.7 | 0 | 7 |
| IGCC coal | 6.3 | 710 | 18 |
| Biomass | 6.4 | 0 | 30 |
| Natural gas combined cycle[a] | 6.9 | 370 | 35 |
| Wind power[b] | 7.6 | 0 | 42 |

*Source:* Electric Power Research Institute (2006). Estimates of $CO_2$ emissions from Edmonds and Sands (2003).

[a]Assumes natural gas cost of $6 per million Btu.

[b]Assumes 29 percent capacity factor, implying widespread adoption in lower wind-speed areas.

provides EPRI's estimate of the necessary carbon tax to cause a power company to choose a given technology over a pulverized coal plant. For nuclear power to compete with coal, a carbon tax of $7 per ton would be required, whereas a tax of $42 per ton would be required to make wind power competitive with coal.

Even though nuclear power would appear, given existing technology, to be the most cost-effective energy source to displace pulverized coal, EPRI believes that the technology landscape could change dramatically by 2020. Integrated gasification combined-cycle (IGCC) coal technology[36] is projected to cost less than pulverized coal and become the lowest-cost technology. Furthermore, a carbon tax of $20 per ton of $CO_2$ would make it economical to include carbon sequestration in these IGCC plants, with a total cost of 5.5¢ per kwh. EPRI projects that improvements in wind-power technology will reduce costs from 7.6¢ to 5.2¢ per kwh. By 2020, biomass could be the biggest winner, with costs falling to 4.4¢ per kwh.

EPRI's forecasts give us hope that we will be able to choose from a menu of alternative technologies at reasonable costs. Rather than one fuel or technology dominating the landscape, we are likely to see a variety, including IGCC with carbon sequestration, nuclear power, biomass (from areas with abundant supplies), and wind power (in areas offering adequate wind speed).

Evidence of the rising costs of more stringent emissions abatement has been reported by Stanford University's Energy Modeling Forum and is shown in figure 4.3.[37] Various models, whose symbols are shown on the right-hand side, were used to compute the discounted costs of limiting $CO_2$ concentrations in

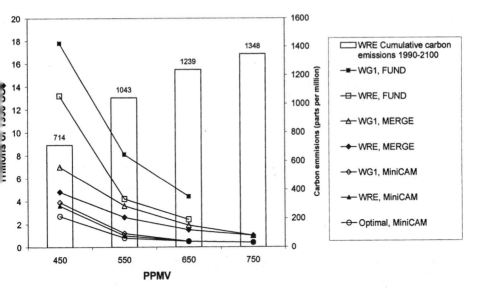

Figure 4.3
Costs (discounted present value) of stabilizing $CO_2$ concentrations at 450–750 ppm
Data from Energy Modeling Forum (1995).

2100 to the following levels: 450 ppm, 550 ppm, 650 ppm, and 750 ppm. The left vertical axis shows the discounted present value of the costs of stabilizing $CO_2$ at these levels, and the right vertical axis shows cumulative emissions over the period 1990–2100. The additional costs of achieving ever more stringent levels of abatement rise sharply as $CO_2$ concentrations are reduced from 750 ppm to 650 ppm to 550 ppm. Going from $CO_2$ concentrations of 550 ppm to 450 ppm results in a particularly sharp increase, with most models showing a doubling of costs.

The forum concludes that whatever the targeted level of $CO_2$ concentrations, the lowest-cost strategy involves a gradual transition, with a small initial departure from current trends and a gradual move toward a lower path of $CO_2$ emissions. This follows for several reasons. First, as discussed, a carbon tax should rise over time at the rate of social discount, causing abatement efforts to be much more intensive at higher tax rates in the future than in the present.

Second, it would be exorbitantly expensive to scrap the existing capital infrastructure to achieve massive immediate reductions in $CO_2$ emissions. Waiting until the stock of power plants is replaced would be the least costly strategy.

Third, as the EPRI study shows, future technological advances appear likely to reduce dramatically the costs of carbon sequestration, as well as the costs of nonfossil fuels. As the emphasis on carbon abatement intensifies over time, technological advances are sure to reduce its costs.

### SOLVING THE BENEFIT-COST EQUATION

Even though the benefit-cost paradigm gives us a clear conceptual framework for finding the optimal combination of strategies, solving the problem mathematically is fraught with practical difficulties.

Alan Manne and William Nordhaus use highly aggregated mathematical models to answer the key question of what benefit-cost analysis tells us.[38] The chief conclusion from Manne's model is that an optimal policy would call for a moderate tax of approximately $3 per ton of $CO_2$ emitted, rising at 4 percent annually (in real dollars) over time to $16 per ton by 2050. A tax of $3 per ton of $CO_2$ would boost the price of gasoline by about $0.03 per gallon initially. Most significantly, it would raise the current cost of coal by about 25 percent, from an average of $24 per ton to $30.50 per ton.

Nordhaus's recalibrated DICE model of 2007 concludes that the optimal tax should be set at $7.35 per ton of $CO_2$ and rise at an average rate of 2.8 percent over time, reaching about $26 per ton (in 2005 dollars) by 2050—a quadrupling of the initial amount in forty-three years.[39]

Richard Tol surveys twenty-eight studies attempting to estimate the marginal costs of $CO_2$ and finds wide variations.[40] The combined mean estimate is $4.35 per ton of $CO_2$, based on conventional assumptions about the social discount rate (4–5 percent). Thus, Manne's and Nordhaus's estimates reflect the prevailing wisdom.

To some, imposing Manne's carbon tax of $3 per ton (or even Nordhaus's tax of $7.35 per ton) may seem like a do-nothing strategy, but Manne carefully explains that this is not the case. The quintupling of his carbon tax by 2050 would affect long-lived investments and point the economy toward a low-carbon future over time. Since the incremental benefits of emissions abatement will be rising while the costs of abatement will be falling, it makes sense to defer the bulk of the transition to a low-carbon economy. Nevertheless, actions taken now send both the price and the technology signals necessary to initiate the transition, particularly for power plants that will remain operational for fifty years. Such an approach recognizes that the stock of energy-using equipment must be replaced over time, and if investors are aware that future carbon taxes will be increasing substantially, these adaptations can proceed in an orderly and efficient manner.

## Chapter 5 Climate Change and the Difficult Search for Institutions and Policies

Chapter 4 provided a general understanding of the science, economics, and engineering issues involved in climate change. In this chapter I consider the politics of climate change, the adequacy of existing institutions to effect change, and the specific policy options available. Let us begin by reviewing the political problems involved in getting numerous nation-states with diverse interests committed to policies to abate greenhouse gases and to cooperate on oil security.

### IMPEDIMENTS TO COOPERATION ON GLOBAL WARMING

As discussed in the previous chapter, Alan Manne's calculation of the optimal carbon tax is an interesting intellectual exercise; but convincing more than two hundred nations to adopt such a tax or an equivalent policy throws us squarely into the world of international politics, with its own set of constraints. Suddenly, the question shifts from what is economically optimal to what is politically achievable. What are the obstacles to international cooperation on global warming?

Reaching an international consensus on how to confront climate change is complicated by a number of inescapable impediments resting on the differences between nations in their motivations and abilities to deal with global warming:

- In this political climate, reaching a consensus on a problem that will not become serious until the distant future is extremely difficult. Increases in $CO_2$ concentrations since the Industrial Revolution have been small compared with the likely increases over the next forty or fifty years. Likewise, temperature increases to date appear insignificant, especially compared with likely future increases as the world economy grows and consumes fossil fuels on a scale not dreamed of a few years ago.

- A long lead time exists between making expenditures to abate $CO_2$ emissions and ultimately lowering $CO_2$ concentrations and temperatures. Large expenditures are required up front to improve conditions in the distant future. Consequently, the current generation cannot readily observe the benefits it is conferring on future generations, but it can observe the costs. There is a great temptation to defer action altogether—to wait until the scientific uncertainties are reduced.

- Not all countries will be affected equally by global warming. Temperate climates might actually benefit from a modest amount of warming, whereas already warm climates will suffer the largest and most immediate consequences. In effect, for temperature increases of 2.5°C (4.5°F) or less, there may be winners as well as losers. For larger increases, the effects appear uniformly negative, but these effects may not occur for seventy-five or a hundred years.

- Even if global warming affected all equally, nations would tend to act as free riders. Individual nations would likely reason that their participation in a carbon-abatement program would not affect whether other nations chose to participate. Following this logic, the best course of action would be to free ride, deriving the same benefits as those who participate without incurring any costs.

- Carbon-free energy forms are likely to be considerably more expensive than even the high-cost fossil fuels prevalent today. The fact that fossil fuels currently supply 87 percent of the world's energy is no accident. One should not be sanguine about asking consumers worldwide to pay substantially higher prices for energy. Of course, as noted in chapter 2, if oil prices return to summer 2008 levels, alternative fuels will emerge, but many of these will be fossil fuels such as those derived from oil sands and gas-to-liquid technology.

Table 5.1  Ten largest emitters of carbon from fossil fuels, and their
per capita incomes

| Rank | Country | Carbon emissions[a] | % of total | Per capita GDP[b] ($) |
|------|---------|---------------------|------------|------------------------|
| 1 | United States | 6.0 | 21.1 | 46,000 |
| 2 | China | 5.3 | 18.9 | 5,300 |
| 3 | EU-27 | 4.3 | 15.1 | 32,900 |
| 4 | Russia | 1.7 | 6.0 | 14,600 |
| 5 | Japan | 1.2 | 4.4 | 33,800 |
| 6 | India | 1.2 | 4.1 | 2,700 |
| 7 | Canada | 0.6 | 2.2 | 38,200 |
| 8 | South Korea | 0.5 | 1.8 | 24,600 |
| 9 | Iran | 0.5 | 1.6 | 12,300 |
| 10 | South Africa | 0.4 | 1.5 | 10,600 |
| Total | | | 76.7 | |

*Sources:* DOE (2007b, table h.1co2) and CIA (2008).
[a]Billions of metric tons of carbon dioxide from fossil fuels in 2005.
[b]Estimated per capita GDP in 2007, adjusted for purchasing power parity.

- It is unrealistic to expect many countries in the developing world to participate voluntarily in policy actions that will significantly increase energy costs and thus reduce their competitiveness in world markets. As noted in chapter 1, developing countries simply do not value clean energy very much.

To illustrate this last point, table 5.1 ranks the ten largest $CO_2$-emitting countries according to their estimated $CO_2$ emissions in 2005. If the twenty-seven countries of the European Union are treated as a single entity, the top ten emitters account for about 77 percent of global emissions. The table also reports the 2007 estimated per capita income of each country in U.S. dollars, adjusted for the purchasing power of the country's currency.

Two important points emerge from the ranking. Two lower-income countries—China and India—rank second and sixth in total carbon emissions. As noted in chapter 1, clean energy becomes a priority only in higher-income countries. But more affluent countries may find it galling that poorer ones with high emissions might be exempted from any international agreement.

As table 5.1 makes clear, not only will the benefits from reduced $CO_2$ concentrations be spread quite unevenly across the globe, but the costs of abatement will be spread quite unevenly across space and time as well. *High-benefit regions rarely match high-abatement-cost regions.* Ideally, each country would find it individually advantageous to reduce $CO_2$ emissions and would voluntarily comply with abatement programs. Unfortunately, the reality is quite different. The primary beneficiaries of lower $CO_2$ concentrations are the poorer countries located in already warm regions, such as Africa and India—the countries with the least capacity to pay to avoid the consequences of global warming. By contrast, the industrialized countries, located in more temperate zones, can afford to pay but derive fewer benefits.

Even if all countries' economic interests were mutually aligned, game theory suggests a disturbing outcome. Each country's best response is to choose *not* to enter into a worldwide agreement to reduce $CO_2$ emissions. There is a further advantage to becoming a free rider by opting out of any agreement: the individual country avoids higher energy prices and thus becomes a low-cost producer vis-à-vis other participating nations. This has been referred to as the "leakage" problem, as carbon-intensive industries could, in principle, migrate to nonparticipant countries, leaving global emissions unchanged and nonparticipants richer. Furthermore, small nonparticipating countries could reason that their nonparticipation would not significantly affect worldwide $CO_2$ concentrations. And if that argument cannot be plausibly made by larger newly industrializing countries like India and China, they can always point out that they are small contributors to existing $CO_2$ *concentration* levels, even though they are significant contributors to current emissions.

Pursuing one's own economic self-interest suggests strong incentives for nonparticipation. Can these be overcome? Let us begin by reviewing progress under the Kyoto Protocol.

## THE ELUSIVE SEARCH FOR THE BEST
## INTERNATIONAL INSTITUTIONAL STRUCTURE

### The Kyoto Protocol in Theory

According to the conventional wisdom, the Kyoto Protocol will solve the knotty problem of bringing the world's nation-states together to curb greenhouse-gas emissions effectively and efficiently. The agreement rests on four pillars: universal participation, binding emissions targets and timetables for compliance, integrated emissions trading, and compensation of developing countries to ensure their participation.[1]

The architects of the agreement based the first pillar—universal participation—on the premise that sovereign nation-states would find it in their self-in-terest (or could be coerced) to cooperate and participate in the agreement. The second pillar—quantitative targets for individual nations for reducing emissions from greenhouse gases, which must be met by certain dates—was designed to ensure compliance. To minimize the global costs of meeting these targets, the agreement called for the third pillar, the trading of emissions allowances within and between countries. Low-cost-abatement countries would be able to sell their allowances to high-cost emitters, ensuring that emissions targets would be met at the lowest cost. Finally, even developing countries' participation could be achieved by the fourth pillar—compensation—through the clean development mechanism, whereby emitters in developed countries would compensate developing countries for instituting low-cost abatement projects, which could be counted as offsets to emissions allowances in the developed countries.

In principle, the Kyoto Protocol would function like the highly successful sulfur oxide ($SO_x$) permit market in the United States, in which a specific number of emissions permits or allowances are issued.[2] In the $SO_x$ system, low-cost abaters sell their allowances to high-cost abatement sources. Monitoring technology—sensors installed in smokestacks of stationary-source emitters—provides the EPA with a low-cost method of policing $SO_x$ emissions. Limits on total $SO_x$ emissions are set for each air-quality region in the United States to satisfy local air-quality standards imposed by legislation. Of course, the price of $SO_x$ emissions allowances fluctuates over time, depending on electricity output, the availability of low-sulfur coal, and the installed capacity of stack-gas scrubbers.[3] Prices have fluctuated from as low as $70 per ton in 1996 to as high as $1,500 per ton in 2005.[4] Fluctuating prices of $SO_x$ allowances, however, are not a large component of the overall cost of fuels, so their volatility has not been disruptive.

Drafters of the Kyoto Protocol saw in the $SO_x$ "cap-and-trade system"[5] the basis for an analogous method to reduce carbon emissions worldwide. It was envisioned that under the agreement, each member country would be assigned a number of tradable $CO_2$ emissions allowances proportional to its benchmark emissions in 1990. Each country would then take its total allowances and divide them between tradable and nontradable sources. In general, stationary sources of $CO_2$ emissions would be subject to tradable allowances. Although tradable allowances could, in principle, be auctioned to the highest bidders, they would typically be given away or grandfathered to the sources of carbon emissions. Since some countries would be able to reach their targets at lower cost than others, overall costs of abatement could be reduced by encouraging the trading of emissions permits between countries, and certainly among $CO_2$ emitters within countries.

With respect to cap-and-trade arrangements, ardent environmentalists and industries with high levels of carbon emissions find themselves strange bedfellows, each supporting tradable emissions rights for very different reasons. Environmentalists like the idea that the number of emissions permits is frozen at a fixed, immutable level, such as the 1990 benchmark levels. Carbon-intensive industries generally prefer tradable emissions rights over the alternatives because in the initial distribution such allowances are usually assigned to the firms that have historically been high $CO_2$ emitters. If these firms reduce their emissions below their allotted amounts, they can sell their unneeded allowances to new entrants at a profit; and even if they are not able to do so, at least the allowances are free.

Another attractive feature of the Kyoto Protocol is that the system is readily expandable to enlist new participants, furthering the prospects of universal participation. New participants can simply be assigned allowances equal to some agreed-upon amount of emissions. For example, Russia and Ukraine had incentives to join because allowances were set at 1990 emissions levels, which far exceeded their emissions when they signed the protocol. These countries could profit by selling unneeded allowances to other participants. In this same vein, one could envision securing the future participation of China and India by granting allowances equal to projected emissions at some future date. In the interim, China and India could sell their unneeded allowances and profit handsomely. Even the very poor countries are allowed by the clean development mechanism to effectively sell carbon allowances by making carbon-reducing investments at home, thereby achieving "offsets" for buyers in the participating countries. To the extent that carbon emissions can be reduced at lower costs in these countries, such efficiency-enhancing investments are laudable.

Although the international trading of carbon allowances has not been fully implemented under the Kyoto Protocol, the European Union initiated an emissions trading system in January 2005. This market within the European Union offers valuable insights as to how a decentralized system involving all of the Kyoto signatories might work. Basically, the European Union specifies trading sectors (iron and steel, certain mineral industries, pulp and paper, and energy) and nontrading sectors and assigns total emissions targets based on Kyoto levels to the member states. Individual member states, in turn, are free to allocate their national quotas of allowances as they deem appropriate to the

12,000 stationary factories and power plants in the European Union that fall in the trading sectors. (Targets in the nontrading sector must be met by direct controls on fuel uses.) Interestingly, allowances are typically given to the carbon-emitting plants instead of being auctioned. Indeed, the European Union explicitly limits the fraction that can be auctioned to 5 percent, although in practice this limit has never been reached.

Giving the allowances to large $CO_2$ emitters rather than forcing them to purchase allowances via an auction reveals an interesting perspective. It seems to suggest that these carbon-intensive sectors are entitled to a property right to emit $CO_2$ and that it would be unfair to force them now to buy that right. Like the Kyoto Protocol, the E.U. emissions trading system also allows firms to buy foreign offsets from the clean development mechanism. Of particular note are the consistency and accuracy of monitoring, reporting, and verification of emissions from these 12,000 plants. Member states retain considerable autonomy in regulating monitoring techniques and approving the use of third-party verification services. An unresolved issue is whether punishment for fraud will result in equal civil and criminal penalties across the member states.[6]

### Problems with the Kyoto Protocol in Practice

Increasingly, it is becoming evident that all four pillars of the Kyoto Protocol, which seem so desirable in theory, have serious defects in practice.[7] The first pillar—universal participation—flies in the face of the differing interests of the nation-states. Indeed, the United States failed to ratify the treaty, and Canada chose to withdraw after initially committing. The Russians followed suit when it appeared they might have to change their energy consumption habits. In Japan and the European Union, efforts have focused on an accounting shell game that will probably yield formal legal compliance but little actual reduction in emissions.[8] Unlike $SO_x$ trading in the United States, the Kyoto Protocol lacks an institution to monitor and enforce compliance. Participating countries and emitting firms do not have the same incentives to monitor, report, and verify carbon emissions as under the EPA's $SO_x$ trading mechanism. And without the ability to punish lax enforcement by participating countries, the second pillar—binding emissions targets and timetables—represents an ideal goal but lacks teeth.

Even the third pillar—integrated emissions trading—has become subject to growing skepticism. Setting a cap on sulfur emissions made a lot of sense in the United States, since each region must adhere to specified limits on sulfur emissions under the Clean Air Act. As discussed in chapter 4, however, the idea of

freezing carbon emissions at some fixed level has no scientific or economic basis, and the exact timing of carbon emissions abatement is immaterial. What
matters is that we choose a cost-effective emissions path that prevents $CO_2$
concentrations from reaching levels that produce significant damages.

The current trading prices of allowances under the E.U. emissions trading
system signal costs far in excess of their benefits, as reported by Alan Manne
and William Nordhaus.[9] In April 2006, allowances sold for more than $42 per
ton of $CO_2$, and, in early 2007, 2008 allowances were trading in the range of
$23 per ton. Again, as discussed in chapter 4, an economically optimal strategy
would call for making only those emissions abatements that could be justified
today at a cost of at most $7 per ton. With annual escalations in the carbon tax,
emissions reductions will be concentrated in the future, when the existing energy infrastructure is due for replacement and future technologies are available
to reduce the cost of carbon abatement.

The E.U. trading experiment has revealed yet another problem with the
third pillar: extreme price volatility. Between April 2006 and February 2007,
the price of $CO_2$ allowances fell from about $42 to $0.65 per ton. Why? Because by February 2007, it was clear that emissions were well below the target
and that the value of the allowances for the remainder of the year was negligible. Since 2007 allowances were set to expire in December 2007, however, the
2008 emissions rights were, as we have said, selling for about $23 per ton of
$CO_2$.

Price volatility of this magnitude is terribly destabilizing. Investors contemplating building new plants in sectors subject to tradable emissions allowances
face extreme uncertainty. At prices of $0.65 per ton of $CO_2$, they might choose
a highly carbon-intensive technology, whereas at $42 per ton they will either
proceed with a low-carbon design or simply choose not to expand capacity. Potential entrants recognize that output prices might not adjust sufficiently to justify the $42-per-ton cost of $CO_2$ allowances. Such price volatility of an item so
fundamental to economic activity could have serious macroeconomic repercussions as well. With carbon allowances at $42 per ton of $CO_2$, the cost of
burning coal in the United States could potentially rise from $24 to about $127
per ton. Such increases could lead to a doubling of electricity prices, which
would be highly disruptive to the economy.

If extreme price volatility is so tough on investors contemplating new plants
and so potentially destabilizing to the macroeconomy, why do carbon-intensive industries ally themselves with ardent environmentalists to support and
lobby for a cap-and-trade system? Curiously, the price volatility confers poten-

tially huge profits on the incumbent carbon emitters. Furthermore, emissions allowances in the E.U. system are given away rather than auctioned, so incumbent firms receive an extremely valuable property right that becomes even more valuable with spikes in allowance prices. Although some allowances are set aside for new entrants, for the most part, new entrants receive few allowances and are thus forced to buy allowances at the market price.[10]

Since, under conventional economic theory, the costs of the marginal supplier set the output price of the carbon-intensive good, incumbent carbon-intensive firms with free allowances stand to profit both from the sale of allowances and from the sale of their outputs at higher prices. For example, the price of electricity generated from coal could skyrocket to compensate the new entrant for the allowances it had to purchase. But the cost of coal for the incumbent electricity suppliers, who received free allowances, would remain at $24 per ton. Electricity prices would rise to cover the costs of the new entrant's allowances, and the incumbents' profits would skyrocket. Free allowances confer a huge economic benefit on incumbent coal-burning power companies and deter the entry of new firms, who must buy allowances from the incumbents. It is no wonder that the incumbent carbon emitters lobby so intensely in favor of a cap-and-trade system.

Finally, even the fourth pillar of the Kyoto Protocol—compensation to encourage participation by developing countries—is ill conceived and, as Michael Wara argues, has not worked as anticipated. As previously mentioned, Kyoto's attempt to achieve emissions reduction in developing countries centered on the clean development mechanism, under which carbon emitters in participating countries can receive "offsets," or credits, for carrying on certified abatement projects in developing countries. Under the Kyoto Protocol, projects to reduce emissions of any of the six greenhouse gases, not just $CO_2$, can generate credits. Today, only about a third of the projects involve the actual reduction of $CO_2$. Instead, the bulk of credits come from reducing trifluoromethane (HFC-23) and nitrogen oxides ($NO_x$). HFC-23 is a by-product of the manufacture of refrigerant gases and can be captured at low cost. Indeed, Wara estimates that the actual cost of capturing the volumes of HFC-23 sold through the clean development mechanism was less than 100 million euros. Yet their value in terms of allowances in the E.U. emissions trading system was 4.6 billion euros.[11] Instead of encouraging power plants to convert from coal-fired plants to natural gas or nuclear plants, the clean development mechanism has proved to have little effect on the energy infrastructure in the developing world. Offsets such as those under the Kyoto Protocol's clean development mechanism undermine the effectiveness of the original emissions targets because they create a loophole for carbon emitters in the participating countries.

### An Alternative to the Kyoto Protocol:
### The Club Approach

Given the institutional flaws of Kyoto, are there alternatives worth considering? David Victor sets forth an alternative system that differs from the Kyoto Protocol in the following important dimensions:

- Participation would be limited to a small club of countries that are major contributors to $CO_2$ emissions.
- The system would allow for a variety of efforts that are tailored to each member's capabilities and interests.
- The system would offer a framework with sufficient accountability so that commitments would become connected to action.[12]

Organizations such as the G8 and the World Trade Organization have proved very effective at dealing with specific problems related to the world economy and world trade. Likewise, Victor argues, an organization limited to the major $CO_2$ emitters offers prospects of achieving similar cohesion and coordinated effort. Stopping short of suggesting which countries should be in the club, he notes that it must be small enough to be functional. As shown in table 5.1, the top ten emitting countries (with the twenty-seven members of the European Union treated as one) in terms of their percentage share of 2005 emissions account for 77 percent of the world's emissions. Consequently, under the club approach, it would be critical to get the cooperation of these countries. Recall that the United States accounts for 21.1 percent of $CO_2$ emissions, followed closely by China with 18.9 percent, and the European Union with 15.1 percent. Then comes Russia with 6 percent, Japan with 4.4 percent, India with 4.1 percent, Canada with 2.2 percent, and South Korea with 2 percent. Other contributors, such as Iran and South Africa, seem unlikely participants. So even with a club membership of eight, almost 75 percent of emissions would be covered.

Under this club system, a variety of policy approaches to dealing with greenhouse-gas emissions might emerge. Since different club members face different incentives to participate, it may not be realistic to expect all to participate in, say, a cap-and-trade system. Rather, different club members may choose different policies to abate $CO_2$ emissions. The per capita income differences shown in table 5.1 are a sobering reminder of the heterogeneity of the eight potential club members and their willingness to participate at the same level of intensity.

For example, under this more flexible club approach, not all members would necessarily commit to the same proportionate reductions in carbon emissions. It is unrealistic to expect China and India, with their rapidly growing economies, to commit to freezing emissions at current levels. They may, nevertheless, be willing to commit to policies that would substantially slow the growth rate of their $CO_2$ emissions.

Whatever institutional form future international cooperative efforts take, it is important to recognize that prospects for cooperation among key carbon emitters is reasonably good. Let us assess prospects for cooperation.

## PROSPECTS FOR OVERCOMING THE OBSTACLES TO INTERNATIONAL COOPERATION

Despite all the obstacles, there are two persuasive reasons to be optimistic about prospects for international cooperation on climate change. First, the United States would not have to proceed unilaterally, since there are widespread concerns in the developed world that global warming and oil security pose serious problems. U.S. leadership in this area is likely to be warmly received and to engender substantial international cooperation—cooperation among countries accounting for more than half of worldwide fossil-fuel consumption. Second, there are mechanisms that offer promise for including rapidly growing developing economies like China and India in a cooperative effort. If these efforts are successful, participation by contributors of about three-fourths of $CO_2$ emissions appears possible.

### Prospects Are Good for International Cooperation in the Developed World

As emphasized in chapter 1, the goals of clean and secure energy gain increasing importance as per capita incomes rise. Accordingly, the United States should look to other industrialized nations as partners. The thirty members of the OECD are likely partners, since they include the countries of the European Union, plus Japan and other developed nations. As a group, they account for 51.4 percent of world fossil-fuel consumption and 59 percent of world oil consumption. If Russia is added to this group, the percentages rise to 58 percent and 62.5 percent, respectively.[13] Clearly, cooperation among countries accounting for so much consumption would significantly increase the incentives to adopt more aggressive policies.

Table 5.2 Taxes as a percentage of retail energy prices for selected OECD countries, second quarter 2006

| Country | Gasoline | Household natural gas | Heating oil | Household electricity |
|---------|----------|----------------------|-------------|------------------------|
| France | 62 | 5 | 25 | 25 |
| Germany | 62 | 24 | 25 | 25 |
| Italy | 59 | n.a. | 53 | 29 |
| Japan | 45 | 5 | 5 | 7 |
| Spain | 51 | 4 | 28 | 18 |
| Sweden | 61 | n.a. | 54 | n.a. |
| United Kingdom | 64 | 5 | 24 | 5 |
| United States | 13 | 0 | <1 | 0 |

*Source:* OECD (2006).

To varying degrees, members of the European Union have demonstrated a resolve to strive for clean and secure energy. All signed the Kyoto Protocol, and although the European Union as a whole appears unlikely to achieve the 8 percent reduction from 1990 emissions levels required under the agreement, emissions levels will be significantly lower than they would have been absent the agreement.[14] Coal consumption in the European Union fell by 31 percent from 1990 to 2004, and consumption of petroleum products increased by only 15 percent during that period.[15]

European countries have long used stiff taxes to discourage the use of petroleum products and thereby slow the growth in consumption of such products. As shown in table 5.2, taxes on various petroleum products and other energy sources account for a much larger fraction of the retail price in selected OECD countries than in the United States. For example, taxes on gasoline as a proportion of the retail price vary from a low of 13 percent in the United States to more than 60 percent in France, Germany, Sweden, and the United Kingdom. The percentage of taxes on natural gas for household uses varies from a low of 0 percent in the United States to a high of 24 percent in Germany. Home-heating-oil taxes are less onerous than gasoline taxes but tend to be higher than those on natural gas, ranging from 24 percent to 54 percent for the European countries. A similar pattern holds for household electricity. Taxes range from 0 percent in the United States to 29 percent in Italy. Besides taxes on individual fuels, Sweden, Norway, Finland, and the Netherlands have implemented carbon taxes on fossil fuels.

Significant fuel taxes are an accepted fact of life in Europe and Japan. In the

OECD countries the United States has a group of potential partners who have demonstrated their willingness to tax energy to promote conservation and reduce greenhouse-gas emissions. Far from the United States finding itself alone in the search for clean and secure energy, we have an economically powerful group of nations looking to the United States for leadership in this area.

### Mechanisms Exist to Bring along China and India

Looking beyond the developed countries, we see in table 5.1 that China and India are major $CO_2$ emitters, despite their relatively low per capita incomes. With their rapid rates of economic growth, China will soon displace the United States as the world's largest $CO_2$ emitter and India's rank on the list will surely rise. Consequently, some ways must be found to at least slow the growth of $CO_2$ emissions from China and India. Remember that China and India face far more pressing social problems than climate change, so it is unrealistic to expect the same level of urgency from China and India as from the developed nations.

Consequently, we must look for good solutions, not perfect solutions. Perfection cannot be allowed to become the enemy of the good; nor can its nonattainment become a justification for inaction by the United States. Recognizing that the geopolitics of obtaining China's and India's cooperation could easily fill a book, let us briefly review some possible mechanisms for ensuring their partial cooperation.

The most powerful, but most dangerous, lever to induce China and India to cooperate is trade policy. Both countries benefit greatly from access to markets in the European Union, the United States, and Japan. Compared with the United States or the European Union, China and India are heavily dependent on trade. For example, the combined ratio of exports plus imports to GDP is 68.3 percent in China and 46.8 percent in India. In contrast, the ratios are only 22 percent in the United States and 20.4 percent in the European Union.[16] Clearly, access to markets in the OECD countries has been a major contributor to China's and India's phenomenal rates of economic growth.

A popular policy suggestion in both the European Union and the United States is to impose an environmental fee on imported goods from China and India proportional to the carbon emissions associated with that particular good's production. Tying the environmental fee *to the specific $CO_2$ emissions associated with the good in question* would make it clear that the fee has a reasonable basis and is not intended to punish Chinese or Indian goods generally. The justification for such a fee would be that domestic firms are subject to costly carbon-emissions regulations. Domestic carbon-intensive industries facing competition from India and China ask why imported goods not subject to costly carbon-abatement policies should be able to come into the United States and undermine their ability to compete. On the face of it, such carbon-based tariffs would seem imminently sensible. We can at the same time force China and India to cooperate on carbon and protect domestic industries from unfair competition.

Opponents, such as researchers at the Peter G. Peterson Institute for International Economics and the World Resources Institute,[17] counter that besides being a nightmare to administer, such a tariff is unlikely to force cooperation by India and China; nor is it likely to significantly improve the competitiveness of American industry in general. Furthermore, they contend that it would set back efforts at trade liberalization and sour the prospects for international cooperation. Administratively, measuring the carbon emissions associated with a toy or dress is no simple matter since it is virtually impossible to trace the carbon emissions at various stages of production of the intermediate inputs (for example, cloth, zippers, buttons, thread). Carbon emissions intensity is likely to vary greatly between countries and within firms in a given country. In addition, China's exports of carbon-intensive goods to the United States are relatively small. Apparel and electronics, the two largest import items, have very low direct energy intensity, so a tariff on these items would not materially affect the ability of U.S. firms to compete. Opponents of a carbon tariff argue that for the trade-exposed domestic industries (such as ferrous and nonferrous metals and chemicals), which account for less than 6 percent of U.S. emissions, separate domestic policies can be structured without the need for unilateral carbon tariffs at the U.S. border.

These groups argue that climate policy should not be tied to trade policy and vice versa. The most salient argument against tying climate change to trade policy is probably that it could prove to be a slippery slope with potentially disastrous outcomes for both. Opening markets to free trade has been an arduous process, and these gains could evaporate if cooperation in taming carbon were to become a precondition for trade. We cannot forget that international relations and world economic prosperity have benefited immensely from globalization, and we would not want to jeopardize these gains. Although separating trade policy from carbon-emissions policies makes much sense, in today's political environment, separating the two will be a dicey exercise.

An entirely different approach that avoids using trade policy is to focus on ways of directly reducing China's and India's voracious consumption of coal in power plants.[18] China is already experiencing a severe air-pollution problem from its coal-powered electricity plants. Structuring a deal with Russia for natural gas would reduce both conventional air pollutants and $CO_2$ emissions. With the rapid growth of electricity demand in China, replacing coal-fired electricity plants with natural-gas-fired combined-cycle generating plants could cut carbon emissions by two-thirds.[19] Furthermore, China might find it in its own interest to make such a substitution, particularly if international assurances on price and deliverability could be structured. Not only are these coal-fired plants large $CO_2$ emitters, but they are heavy contributors of other air pollutants—$SO_x$, particulates, and hydrocarbons—as well. China faces strong internal pressures to reduce these emissions and, as a by-product, to reduce carbon emissions. Surely, as per capita income rises, the Chinese people will demand clean energy.

For India, the effects of global warming could be particularly severe, so that country should be sympathetic toward efforts to avoid global warming. The problems are that coal is relatively cheap in India, the country's appetite for electricity is increasing rapidly, and per capita income is still low. Access to either natural gas from the Caspian region or reactor-grade nuclear fuel could significantly reduce India's dependence on coal for power generation. Even though there are huge reserves of natural gas in the Caspian region, transporting natural gas from Turkmenistan across Afghanistan and Pakistan pose major security issues. Victor believes that the most promising alternative is nuclear power.[20] Already, U.S. support for supplying reactor fuel for India's nuclear plants has triggered construction.

In addition to the built-in incentives that India and China have for reducing carbon emissions, international diplomacy could help significantly. Particularly if the other major carbon emitters (especially the United States) can agree to take meaningful actions, India and China seem likely to cooperate at some level. The great merit of the club approach is that its members can pursue a variety of measures to reduce emissions. It is not necessary that all members participate at the same level. If the United States and the European Union commit to major initiatives, it is reasonable to expect that China and India will make some commitments as well. Creative diplomatic solutions promoting cooperation are needed since there are clear benefits to all sides from cooperation. In the end, surely both China and India know that they benefit greatly by participating in the world economy and that the current situation of unrestrained emissions growth is not sustainable.

## POLICY OPTIONS IN A POST-KYOTO ERA

If club members were free to pursue alternative emissions-abatement strategies under Victor's alternative architecture, what specific strategies might the United States and other club members choose? Five options have been proposed, ranging from a purely technological approach to a carbon tax. In fact, policymakers can choose a mixture of these alternatives.

### A Purely Technological Approach

The easiest approach to gaining cooperation among club members would be jointly funded energy R&D efforts. Substantial technological advances will be required to tame carbon, and on this all club members can surely agree. Indeed, this has been the approach followed by the George W. Bush administration.[21] Recognizing that substantial progress in reducing greenhouse-gas emissions will require major technological advances, the primary U.S. focus has been on science and technology. As part of this strategy, the U.S. government created the Climate Change Science Program, which has an annual budget of $2 billion and whose mission is to narrow the scientific uncertainties regarding the magnitude and effects of climate change. The second key piece of this strategy was the formation of the Climate Change Technology Program (CCTP) to promote R&D in technologies that can reduce greenhouse gases. The CCTP has an annual budget of $3 billion and is administered by the U.S. Department of Energy.

In principle, there are three alternative types of technologies that can be pursued: technologies to reduce the cost of greenhouse-gas abatement, geoengineering technologies that would cancel out the warming effects of $CO_2$ while allowing continued use of fossil fuels, and technologies that facilitate adaptation to climate change. The CCTP focuses almost entirely on the first—reducing greenhouse-gas emissions. The question remains whether expenditures on the remaining two technologies are justified. Several distinguished scientists argue for some R&D expenditures on geoengineering, such as placing reflective sulfate aerosols in the upper atmosphere to counteract greenhouse warming. If we were to discover that the world was facing a point of no return in climate change with dire consequences, the scientists maintain, the ability to utilize geoengineering technologies to halt or even reverse the effects of greenhouse gases in the atmosphere would have considerable value.[22]

Another suggestion for modifying the Bush program is to spend more on technology. Indeed, there have been calls for raising the budget of CCTP from $3 billion to $5 billion or more.[23]

Quite independent of the question of the magnitude of funding of federal R&D is the question of the types of R&D projects targeted for funding. After all, the private sector has been a prolific source of technological advances. If federal money simply duplicates projects that would otherwise be funded by the private sector, it is wasteful to expend federal funds. A primary conclusion of research on the economics of R&D is that the social rate of return resulting from new innovations often greatly exceeds the private rate of return earned by the successful innovator. This result tells us that there is a tendency for the private sector to underinvest in R&D because it cannot appropriate all the benefits flowing from its innovation. Even with patent laws to protect intellectual property, the inventor is unable to collect all the benefits. This provides a clear justification for government's role in supplementing R&D expenditures. But does this mean that federal R&D funds should be expended across the full gamut of both basic and applied R&D?

Consider a continuum of R&D projects ranging from basic research, in which the scientist has no idea of the potential application of the technology, to applied research, which has a clearly defined application. The appropriation problem facing private innovators is greatest in the case of basic research.[24] Often, the potential applications of a breakthrough in basic research cannot be known at the time, so the inventor is unlikely to capture the benefits of the invention. Consequently, private R&D tends to focus almost exclusively on applied R&D. In effect, the closer a technology is to commercialization, the better able the innovator is to appropriate the benefits of the innovation. As a consequence, private R&D investments typically focus on projects that are on the cusp of development. The optimal focus for publicly funded R&D, therefore, is on basic research, where the benefits can be huge but the inventor is unlikely to capture those benefits. Also, for particularly high-cost projects involving applied research, government R&D funding can be critical because the high costs can deter private expenditures. In contrast, perfecting a commercial version of a new technology can typically be done by private R&D labs. In essence, government R&D can play an extremely valuable role in providing new energy technologies, but these funds should be concentrated in those areas where private investors are unlikely to invest. Specifically, basic research and high-cost applied research projects should be the target of federal funds.

Publicly funded R&D targeted at basic research and high-cost applied projects is a necessary condition for a sound energy policy, but is it a sufficient condition? Proponents of the Bush strategy would argue that new technology is both necessary and sufficient to obtain clean energy at a reasonable cost. For R&D to do the job by itself, however, it must lead to the development of new carbon-free technologies that are technically feasible *and cheaper* than the existing fossil fuels. For example, new technologies for a hydrogen-powered automobile not only must provide hydrogen at a cheaper price than gasoline but also must include a low-cost, convenient distribution infrastructure. Many feel that even with dramatic technological breakthroughs, low-carbon or zero-carbon fuels are likely to be more expensive than the incumbent fossil fuels. Consequently, the prevailing wisdom is that a purely technological approach is a necessary component of a successful energy policy but that it is not sufficient in itself. We need other policies that complement the pure technology approach because of the incumbent advantages that fossil fuels enjoy.

To level the playing field on which the new fuels must compete, club members would have four additional complementary options to go along with the purely technological approach: use command-and-control approaches to reduce carbon emissions, subsidize the use of alternative fuels, implement tradable allowances on $CO_2$ emissions, or adopt a carbon tax. Let us consider each of these as a complement to the purely technological strategy.

### The Command-and-Control Approach

One way to ensure that the products of R&D are both technically and economically feasible is to force their adoption through such means as mandated standards for automobile efficiency, for the ethanol content of motor fuels, for appliance efficiency, and for the fraction of electric power coming from renewables. As explained in chapter 1, these policies are called *command-and-control* mandates. Energy producers must comply with the command, and consumers must pay the higher prices that result. Indeed, the Energy Independence and Security Act of 2007 is full of commands and controls, ranging from corporate average fuel economy (CAFE) standards to the types of lightbulbs we can purchase. The act raised the mandated CAFE standard to 35 miles per gallon (mpg) on all passenger automobiles and light trucks by 2020. Mandates also call for the biofuel content of gasoline to increase from 6.5 billion gallons in 2007 to 36 billion gallons by 2022, with 21 billion gallons to come from non-cornstarch products[25] Even the incandescent lightbulb will be banned from sale after 2014, although there are exceptions for certain specialty uses.

Depending on the particular command-and-control mechanisms chosen, many segments of society find them quite acceptable, whereas others find them totally unreasonable. For example, residents of large inner cities might enthusiastically support a combined CAFE standard of 35 mpg. Yet ranchers in western states who rely extensively on light pickups would be unhappy to find that to comply with the corporate average of 35 mpg, auto manufacturers would sharply increase the price of light trucks to reduce the share of light trucks sold and thereby meet the fleetwide average efficiency.

The biggest difficulty with command-and-control solutions is that Congress has little ability to balance the trade-offs between various commands and controls. The result is typically a mishmash of controls. Some, like the CAFE standards, may be cost-effective, and might even be adopted voluntarily, even without regulation. For example because of $4 per gallon gasoline, it is reasonable that consumers would choose far more fuel-efficient autos and light trucks. Others, such as mandating the use of biofuels, are not likely to be cost-effective given the potential of importing Brazilian ethanol made from sugarcane. Worse, these controls are not fashioned in a political vacuum. To appease certain interest groups, the government often adopts conflicting policies that only complicate the trade-offs between cheap, clean, and secure energy.

### Subsidies for Alternative Fuels
### (a.k.a. Congressional Beauty Contests)

As noted in chapter 1, hosting beauty pageants for alternative fuels is a popular congressional mode of operation that uses a grab bag of subsidies and tax credits to alter the mix of fuels produced. Unlike command-and-control policies, which are simply policy directives, subsidies use incentives to encourage the adoption of particular fuels or technologies.

There are many problems with using subsidies as a means of facilitating the adoption of new or existing technologies. First, the exact amount of the subsidy necessary to level the playing field with fossil fuels is rarely known with great precision, and it changes over time with advances in technology. Second, as the fiasco with corn-based ethanol illustrates,[26] there is no assurance that Congress will select the most promising technology; worse, once subsidies have been created for a particular technology, a political lobby will grow to protect its favored place vis-à-vis rival technologies, thus potentially thwarting the development of superior technologies. Utilities with wind farms, for example, will lobby, hard to protect their subsidies, even though they are economically viable without subsidies. Third, subsidies—particularly for vast quantities of low- or zero-carbon fuels—are likely to be very expensive, necessitating either increases in income taxes or further deficit spending. Finally, subsidies do not encourage conservation; rather, they promote overconsumption and waste.

With all these poor attributes, why are subsidies so popular? The answer is that once subsidies are enacted, the costs of those subsidies are spread out and disguised in various ways, whereas the benefits are concentrated to the advantage of well-connected lobbies. Subsidies are hidden on a line in a company's tax return for investment tax credits. Or in the case of ethanol, the subsidized price is simply blended with that of regular gasoline and gets hidden in the price at the gasoline pump. In neither case does Congress write a check. Rather, the U.S. Treasury simply collects less revenue. No one knows how much more would have been collected in the absence of the subsidy. Of course, because of the subsidies, Americans all pay more taxes (either immediately in the form of higher income taxes or in the future through increased deficits), but the linkage is not visible.

### Tradable Emissions Allowances without Kyoto's Flaws

Academic economists have become increasingly skeptical of carbon-emissions trading as currently implemented, but Congress, many environmental groups, and carbon-intensive industries remain solidly behind it. Indeed, in 2007, seven major carbon-trading bills came before Congress. The sponsors include some household names such as Joseph Lieberman, John McCain, John Kerry, Olympia Snowe, Dianne Feinstein, Bernie Sanders, Barbara Boxer, Jeff Bingaman, Arlen Specter, Tom Udall, Tom Petri, and Henry Waxman.

An interesting question is the extent to which these bills correct for the defects of the E.U. emissions trading system. Three major proposals have been made to fix the defects. First, many observers would recommend auctioning rather than freely granting the emissions allowances, which would allow the government to capture the value of the property right. Also, new entrants would not be competitively disadvantaged vis-à-vis the incumbent producers in $CO_2$-intensive industries. Since this would not solve the problem of extreme price volatility, many recent cap-and-trade proposals incorporate, second, a "safety valve" to prevent extremely high allowance prices and, third, the concept of "banking" to prevent extremely low allowance prices.[27]

The ideas are straightforward. Firms would be allowed to purchase additional allowances from the government at a set safety-valve price, say, $20 per ton of $CO_2$, which would prevent allowance prices from becoming too high. Firms would also be allowed to "bank" unused allowances for use in future years, which would place a floor on the price of allowances, further reducing volatility and correcting the anomalies witnessed in the E.U. emissions trading system—namely, 2007 allowances selling for $0.65 per ton and 2008 allowances selling for $23 per ton. Indeed, if the safety-valve price were set in the range of the carbon tax proposed by Manne and Nordhaus, price volatility would disappear altogether and the system would function essentially as a carbon tax. The existing allowance allocation would be given away in the form of tax credits to carbon-intensive firms, and additional allowances would be sold at the safety-valve price.

A survey of the seven 2007 carbon-trading bills by the MIT Joint Program on the Science and Policy of Global Change revealed that the defects of the E.U. emissions trading system are apparently being recognized only gradually.[28] Four of the seven bills allow emitters to bank allowances for future use.[29] Only two include the important feature of a safety-valve price to avoid skyrocketing allowance prices.[30] As for auctioning the allowances, five bills do not specify any percentage to be auctioned, and the other two call for 55 percent and 20 percent, respectively, of the allowances to be granted for free.

Estimating the price of $CO_2$ allowances under these bills is a highly inexact endeavor, but the MIT Joint Program study provides the best estimates available. According to the study, the bills that include a safety valve would lead to much lower allowance prices: $7 per ton in 2015, rising to $39 per ton in 2050. In contrast, the five bills without safety valves would result in dramatically higher allowance prices—ranging from $31 per ton in 2015 to $121 per ton in 2050, at the low end, and from $53 per ton in 2015 to $210 per ton in 2050, at the high end—depending on the mandated reductions that must be achieved by 2050.[31]

To get some idea of the magnitude of the likely increase in fossil-fuel prices, consider that an allowance price of $40 per ton of $CO_2$ would increase the effective cost of coal by almost 400 percent, the cost of natural gas by 37 percent, and the cost of crude oil by about 28 percent.[32] With an allowance price of $200 per ton, those percentages would be five times as great. Clearly, it matters greatly whether there is a safety-valve price and how fast that price increases over time.

Politically, it should not be surprising that five of the seven proposals explicitly exclude a safety valve and fail to specify how the allowances will be distributed. Carbon-intensive industries receiving free allowances know that their free property right will become even more valuable with more stringent mandated reductions in emissions. Potential new entrants, without the advantage of free allowances, will face much higher costs, ensuring higher prices for electricity and other carbon-intensive goods and thus higher profits to the incumbents. At the same time, environmental groups intent on capping carbon emissions will likely prefer greater emissions reductions without the prospect of firms being able to buy additional rights. Consumers preferring cheap energy and cheap energy-intensive goods are, of course, the losers if the safety-valve price is set much above the levels advocated by Manne and Nordhaus.[33]

Interestingly, the Bingaman-Specter and Udall-Petri bills—calling for a safety-valve price that starts at $7 per ton in 2015 and rises to $39 per ton in 2050—proposed something more akin to a carbon tax than to a cap-and-trade system. At the safety-valve prices they have stipulated, there is likely to be demand for additional allowances, so the safety valve price will likely apply and the system will function much as a carbon tax would.

### A Carbon Tax

Economists generally favor a carbon tax for a number of reasons. First, a carbon tax fixes the price that society is willing to pay for $CO_2$ abatement and creates a more level playing field for new technologies. Second, a carbon tax avoids the potential problem of uncertain and highly fluctuating prices of emission rights. Investors in new plants know with certainty the current carbon tax and the rate at which it will escalate in the future and thus can develop sensible plans. Third, a carbon tax offers flexibility so that emissions reductions occur optimally over time. As new technologies are gradually developed and the existing stock of energy-consuming capital is gradually replaced, a carbon tax gives carbon emitters the option to pay the tax if indeed it becomes too costly to abate the $CO_2$. With steadily rising carbon taxes and future technological advances, it becomes more advantageous to make large emission reductions in the future. This flexibility is especially important as we make the transition to lower carbon emissions.

In principle, tradable emissions allowances with banking and an appropriately low safety-valve price could achieve these same three advantages, but there are two additional properties that distinguish a carbon tax.

A carbon tax is clearly much more transparent than tradable emissions allowances and potentially less subject to manipulation. There would be no offsets or "allowance credits" for farmers or foresters that could be sold; nor would there be the clean development mechanisms that have resulted in abuses under the Kyoto Protocol. It is hoped that, as with the gasoline tax in the

United States, there would be no special exemptions. The tax would be assessed on the carbon content of the fuel, which is readily measurable. For firms installing carbon-sequestration technologies in coal plants, credits would be allowed only on the basis of measured quantities of $CO_2$ sequestered.

In addition, to the extent that revenues from carbon taxes are used to reduce other distorting taxes elsewhere in the economy, the economy gets a double dividend.[34] It has long been recognized that income and payroll taxes create a welfare loss by creating a disincentive to work. Yet these taxes have been needed to raise the revenues necessary to fund government expenditures. By replacing revenues from income and payroll taxes with environmental-tax revenues, policymakers can correct two distortions. Economists are enamored with the potential to correct a source of welfare loss in the environment while reducing disincentives to work.[35]

Even for those who view every federal tax dollar as an invitation for increased federal expenditures, it would be a simple matter to couple carbon-tax revenues with offsetting income- or payroll-tax reductions, producing a revenue neutral effect.[36] Consequently, economists generally prefer carbon taxes not only because they are the best way to deal with the carbon problem but also because of their double dividend.

Finally, a carbon tax is likely to have two advantages in the international arena. First, because carbon taxes start low and increase over time, they are likely to be much more palatable to developing countries like China and India, who would face major coal price increases under a cap-and-trade system. As discussed later, the likely initial price of a ton of $CO_2$ emissions under a cap-and-trade system could easily be five or six times the price that would result from a carbon tax, making a cap-and-trade system a political nonstarter for China and India. Second, as the carbon tax ratchets up over time, club members can assess whether other countries are meeting their commitments. Escalations could be postponed as a bargaining chip in obtaining the compliance of others. In effect, the incrementalism of a carbon tax has some very desirable characteristics in bringing along other nation-states.

## IMPLICATIONS FOR U.S. POLICY

Just as the scientists are groping to better understand the magnitude and implications of climate change, nation-states are busily weighing their own interests against those of the world community. Institutions to deal with climate change are in a state of flux. For a variety of reasons, the Kyoto Protocol has not achieved its lofty ambitions. Whether a club-type organization of large carbon emitters will evolve in its place is unclear.

In such a vacuum, the United States has a unique opportunity both to set its own course and to lead by example. Doing nothing is not an option. Although others may choose such a course, the right thing to do is to treat climate change as a potentially serious problem. At the same time, we must recognize that the bathtub analogy applies as well to $CO_2$ as it does to oil security. Achieving international cooperation is vital.

The question then becomes which combination of the five policy options discussed above are to be preferred. There is no question that federal R&D expenditures are necessary, but they must be targeted at basic research and high-cost applied research projects that the private sector is unlikely to invest in. But beyond federal R&D, which of the remaining policy options should be embraced? All policy approaches are not equal. Moreover, existing command-and-control policies and congressional beauty contests are off course and designed to fail. Both the cap-and-trade system and the carbon tax use the price mechanism to steer us to a low-carbon world. But even here, there are important differences.

# Chapter 6  A Smart
# Energy Policy

Balancing cheap, clean, and secure energy will require major techno-logical breakthroughs. The critical question is, How best can society facilitate these technological advances? As discussed in chapter 5, Congress has neither the expertise nor the objectivity to select promis-ing technologies as winners of its beauty pageants for alternative fuels or to mandate the use of certain fuels through command-and-control regulations. There is also the widespread—but unrealistic—view that government-funded R&D will by itself solve the problem. To be clear, as discussed in chapter 5, government-funded R&D has an important role to play in supporting basic research and high-cost, risky applied research projects that the private sector is unlikely to undertake. Our universities and federal R&D labs have enormous potential to make breakthroughs in basic research that will in turn feed applied research efforts. When it comes to applied R&D, the bulk of the technological breakthroughs and their diffusion must originate in the private sector. But these advances will not occur automatically. Newly emerging technologies and future technologies on the horizon, likewise, hold great promise, but markets must bring them to fruition.

If harnessing the private sector to produce these technological advances is the key, how can policymakers facilitate these advances? The answer to this question leads us to the major theme of the book—getting the prices right is critical for developing these new technologies and promoting their diffusion. Some very simple policy recommendations follow from this.

## HOW TO HARNESS TECHNOLOGY

Major technological advances do not fall from the sky; nor do they frequently emanate from federal R&D labs. Rather, history is replete with examples pointing to the genius of the inventor, visionary entrepreneurial companies, and an economic system that rewards innovation. The fact that the market has played a vital role in providing these technologies in the past should give us considerable comfort that it can in the future. Let us review just a few of the phenomenal advances in technology since the Arab oil embargo of 1973–1974. Then let us look at new technologies that are already emerging and still others on the horizon. When we consider the problems that new technologies will face in becoming economically viable, we realize how important it is to "get the prices right."

### Past Achievements Suggest Hope for the Future

One should not forget that the market has been an amazing provider of new technologies since the Arab oil embargo of 1973–1974. Virtually all these advances have been the result of the genius of the inventors, the entrepreneurial skill of the companies commercializing these technologies, and economic incentives. Let us consider just a few examples.

In the oil and natural-gas industry, significant advances have been recorded in seismic technology, horizontal drilling technology, fracturing technologies, enhanced oil-recovery techniques, and offshore drilling technology. With three-dimensional seismic technology, the incidence of dry holes has been dramatically reduced. Horizontal drilling techniques with sensors on the drill bit allow for the penetration of the most prolific source rock, greatly enhancing the fraction of oil recovered. Advances in hydraulic fracturing techniques now allow huge quantities of natural gas trapped in very tight shale formations to be economically recovered.

Enhanced oil-recovery techniques have given many old oil fields not only a second life but also a third life. In the 1950s, secondary recovery techniques—

waterflood and gas repressurization—came along to give oil fields a second life. Then in the 1970s and 1980s, tertiary recovery techniques, frequently using $CO_2$ and chemical injectants, gave these fields a third life. The Department of Energy estimates that tertiary recovery techniques such as $CO_2$ injection can double the oil recovery of many oil fields, potentially adding 89 billion barrels of additional reserves—four times current U.S. reserves.[1] Finally, advances in offshore drilling technology have been phenomenal, opening up vast areas of the world's surface heretofore inaccessible. Today, almost one-fourth of U.S. oil production comes from offshore production in the Gulf of Mexico.

One should not forget conservation technologies. Higher energy prices following the energy crisis of the 1970s forced us to conserve by using less energy, but it also stimulated energy-saving technological advances—combined-cycle electric generation plants, more fuel-efficient cars, and high-efficiency central air-conditioning units, to name just a few. The traditional steam-powered electric generation plant requires 3 Btu of fuel input (coal, natural gas, or oil) to produce 1 Btu of electricity, whereas the newer natural-gas-fired combined-cycle power plants require only 1.5 Btu to produce 1 Btu of electricity. Advances in autos and appliances have been equally impressive. Compare one of the most maligned SUVs, the Chevy Suburban, with its gas-guzzling counterpart of 1972, the Chevy Impala. The Impala got only about 12 to 14 mpg on the highway, compared with the 2007 Suburban's 21 mpg. And it was only in the late 1970s that the government required manufacturers to display the efficiency, as measured by the Seasonal Energy Efficiency Ratio (SEER), of air-conditioning units. At the time, the most popular units typically had a SEER rating of 6 or 7. Today, SEERs of 13 are commonplace and units with SEERs as high as 18 are on the market. It could be argued that government-mandated fuel-efficiency standards for autos and appliances account for these advances, but this overlooks the fact that rising gasoline prices and electricity prices would by themselves have achieved these outcomes.

### Newly Emerging Technologies

The future portends even more spectacular advances in energy technology. Let us review just a few that are already in the marketplace. It seems clear that over the next several decades, natural gas will become the preferred fossil fuel for reasons of both cleanliness and security. There are enormous reserves of stranded natural gas all over the world, much of which is inaccessible by pipeline to the world's major consuming markets. Two developments are at work to solve this problem. The first is liquefied-natural-gas technology—natural gas is liquefied at a port and then transferred in refrigerated tankers to destinations in Japan, Europe, and the United States. At its destination, the liquefied natural gas is re-gasified and injected into the local pipeline network. Another potentially huge technological breakthrough is the gas-to-liquid technology that allows natural gas to be converted directly into sulfur-free diesel fuel. Shell is currently build-ing a 140,000-barrel-per-day facility in Qatar. Since diesel and heating oil ac-count for roughly 28 percent of petroleum products worldwide, a huge poten-tial exists to substitute natural gas for oil and thereby diversify our sources of petroleum products.[2]

As discussed earlier, ethanol produced from corn and sugarcane has already emerged as a "green" renewable gasoline substitute. In Brazil, ethanol produced from sugarcane enables motorists with flex-fuel cars to switch between con-ventional gasoline and pure ethanol. In the United States, ethanol initially emerged as an oxygenate supplement to gasoline to boost octane, but with tariffs on cheaper Brazilian ethanol and a 51¢-per-gallon tax credit, it is now in-creasingly used as much more than a gasoline supplement. Ethanol pumps for E85 fuels are already in operation.

Advances in economically viable energy-conservation technologies have been equally impressive. Most impressive is the hybrid gasoline-electric vehicle. Hybrid cars with efficiencies of up to 60 mpg have enormous potential to halve the demand for gasoline. There are waiting lists for new hybrids, whereas sales of conventional gasoline-powered SUVs have fallen sharply. Even the simple incandescent lightbulb faces technological obsolescence as a result of new light-emitting diodes that use one-eighth the power.[3] Likewise, wind power has emerged as a rapidly growing source of electric power, expanding tenfold over the period 2001–2006.[4] Advances in design have led to spectacular cost reduc-tions—from 25¢ per kwh in 1985 to about 5¢ per kwh in 2006.[5] Today, even though government subsidies persist, wind power is economically viable on its own and further substantial cost reductions are on the horizon.[6]

Finally, one should not write off nuclear power, despite its history of being a high-cost fuel source even with an abundance of government subsidies. The key will be to reduce capital and operating costs, particularly the costs associ-ated with construction and the approval process. The last nuclear plant built in the United States took twenty-four years to complete. Recent regulatory changes have streamlined the process, allowing a single combined construction and operating license and a preapproved design certification for the reactors. In addition, public attitudes toward nuclear power are softening, and once the issue of nuclear waste disposal is resolved, nuclear power may yet emerge as a viable part of the energy equation.

### New Technologies on the Horizon

History often makes a mockery of technology forecasts; today's most promising technologies become flops, and obscure, seldom-considered technologies emerge as tomorrow's successes. Imagine a huge smorgasbord of potential technologies. A very few will emerge as major innovations along the lines of electricity and the internal combustion engine. Another larger set of technologies will play niche roles, and most will forever remain on the shelf of the smorgasbord because they could not pass the market test. Let us review just a few to convince ourselves that the smorgasbord has many interesting possibilities awaiting commercialization.

Perhaps the most intriguing alternative energy source is hydrogen because it is potentially both clean and secure. It is hoped that technology advances will make it cheap. Hydrogen-powered vehicles that emit only water offer great appeal. The keys to the successful commercialization of hydrogen-powered vehicles center on providing hydrogen at multiple locations, reducing the size and cost of the hydrogen fuel cells used to power the vehicles, providing less cumbersome hydrogen storage tanks in the vehicles, and, of course, providing a low-cost hydrogen source. On the face of it, these seem like overwhelming hurdles, but as Vijay Vaitheeswaran points out, significant progress is being made on all these fronts.[7] Because the potential rewards for a commercially viable hydrogen-powered vehicle are so high, considerable privately funded R&D efforts are ongoing. At the same time, government-funded R&D can still pay huge dividends because these projects are very risky and it is difficult for private investors to appropriate the benefits of their inventions.

In automobile construction and design there are exciting possibilities. In *Winning the Oil Endgame,* Amory Lovins and others emphasize that the primary determinant of gasoline consumption is the weight of the vehicle.[8] Advances in plastics and steel alloys have already resulted in lighter, more fuel-efficient cars, but they believe that the next wave will be cars made of strong ultralight carbon fibers. Carbon composites, which are already used extensively in aerospace, could cut the weight of cars in half—effectively doubling the mileage.

Another intriguing technology is the development of fuels from biomass. Particularly promising is the potential to make cellulosic ethanol from wheat and rice straw, cornstalks, switchgrass, or even fast-growing saplings and small trees. The idea is to use enzymes to turn various forms of biomass into sugars, which can then be fermented into ethanol. Many proponents believe that switchgrass, a prairie grass that grows naturally in the South and the Midwest, might serve as a sufficiently large source of cellulosic ethanol. At the same time, it would avoid the huge release of $CO_2$ that results from converting pastureland to cropland to grow corn used for corn-based ethanol. However, relatively little is known about the economics and feasibility of large-scale ethanol plants fueled by switchgrass.

According to the *Economist,* photovoltaic or solar cells are the fastest-growing type of alternative energy, with an annual growth rate of 50 percent. The cost of electricity generated by solar cells fell from 50¢ per kwh in 1995 to 20¢ per kwh in 2005. Recent advances hold promise for further cost reductions.

Today's talk of "clean coal" technologies with carbon sequestration calls for dramatically reduced $CO_2$ emissions. Proponents of clean coal point out that we do not necessarily have to abandon our use of this abundant fuel if we can find ways to reduce the associated carbon emissions. One possibility is to adapt existing pulverized coal combustion units, sequester the $CO_2$ from the flue gases, and inject the $CO_2$ either into an underground formation or into deep ocean water. Another possibility is integrated gasification combined-cycle (IGCC) coal technology that would gasify the coal, recover hydrogen and $CO_2$ for sequestration as by-products, and use the gas to produce electricity in a combined-cycle power plant. Given the enormous coal reserves in the United States, the ability to make either of these technologies economically viable would have enormous security and environmental benefits.

### Reality: Alternative Technologies at a Disadvantage

As promising as these new technologies sound, it is necessary to interject a strong dose of realism. New technologies will face a tough uphill battle against the incumbent fossil fuels for two reasons. First, fossil fuels enjoy a significant cost advantage because their consumption is tied to the existing stock of energy-consuming equipment and the existing fuel delivery system. For many new technologies, overcoming these advantages will be quite difficult. Coal-fired electricity-generation plants, for example, have an economic life of thirty to fifty years. New technologies intended to displace them will take long periods to reach a substantial market penetration. Likewise, gasoline enjoys a significant incumbent's advantage over rival automotive fuels that require an alternative fuel-distribution infrastructure. The existing stock of pipelines and terminals used to transport gasoline, coupled with existing service stations, makes very difficult the proliferation of certain new technologies, such as hydrogen-powered cars or compressed natural gas, that would require significant modifications to this network.

Second, traditional fuels are artificially cheap. This is why "getting the prices right" is essential. The market prices of fossil fuels do not reflect their true social costs—they do not reflect the external security and environmental costs. Take, for example, a new-generation clean-coal-technology plant featuring carbon sequestration competing against a conventional coal-fired plant. The conventional coal-fired plant wins hands down. Why? Because it faces no penalties for its carbon emissions.

Similarly, conservation technologies face a tough time in gaining acceptance because the prices of incumbent fuels do not include the externalities associated with carbon emissions and security issues. At lower prices, consumers have less incentive to conserve. If, instead, the externalities associated with carbon emissions were internalized in, say, the cost of electricity, consumers would face higher electricity prices, which would prompt a whole host of electricity-conserving actions, including the adoption of new cleaner, more fuel-efficient technologies. The problem is leveling the playing field for these new technologies so that they can gain a foothold in the energy market.

### Existing Policies Fail to Level the Playing Field

The current policy approach to leveling the playing field is, of course, the congressional beauty pageant, coupled with some command-and-control regulations. Instead of raising the prices of fossil fuels by putting taxes on them, Congress identifies those alternative technologies that it considers the most promising and steps in with special tax credits, subsidies, or R&D grants targeted specifically for them. The result is that these finalists in the beauty pageant are made artificially cheap, which presumably enables them to compete with the incumbent fossil fuels.

For example, in the 2005 energy bill, Congress chose to offer tax credits of up to $3,400 for the purchase of hybrid gasoline-electric cars and of up to $500 for the purchase of energy-efficiency home improvements, such as metal roofs and energy-efficient air conditioners. The bill also provided generous tax credits for wind farms, new nuclear plants, and even offshore drilling in the Gulf of Mexico. On the other hand, Congress decided not to subsidize vehicles constructed of carbon fibers, hydrogen-powered vehicles, and a host of R&D projects focused on more fundamental technological breakthroughs. The bulk of the subsidies went to mature technologies—such as corn-based ethanol—many of which hold little promise for additional breakthroughs.

In light of this experience, we have to wonder whether Congress has the ability to select the winners among the new energy technologies of the future. Do politicians have the expertise to decide that some technologies are so promising that they should receive tax credits or subsidies whereas others are not? Are the judges of the beauty pageant likely to select technologies according to the likelihood of a successful innovation, or are the choices more likely to depend on which states stand to obtain the greatest benefits or which lobbyists have been most effective? And in the absence of the advantages conferred on Congress's pageant finalists, would other, perhaps more promising, technologies have been introduced instead?

Congress does not have a good track record on these questions. Given the ethanol legislation discussed in chapter 1, Congress cannot be considered an impartial judge. Even if all congressmen were impartial and had the expertise to pick the most promising technologies, the process would still be flawed. Not knowing the future costs of these new technologies, Congress would likely provide the wrong level of subsidy. If tax credits and subsidies are set too low, for instance, the technology will fail to compete. If subsidies are set too high, the technology may be quite successful, but society ends up subsidizing wasteful, high-cost technologies.

Meanwhile, by failing to tax fossil fuels and thereby raise their prices, Congress's strategy does not promote conservation. As emphasized in chapter 2, consumers, when given time to adjust to higher energy prices, have shown a remarkable ability to conserve. By artificially *lowering* overall energy prices via subsidies, the congressional beauty pageant fails to motivate people to conserve and thus fails to use a major tool in the battle to reduce carbon emissions.

**THE SMART ALTERNATIVE: TAXES**

If congressional subsidies and tax breaks for alternative energy technologies are not the way to attain the correct balance between cheap, clean, and secure energy sources, the critical question becomes, How, then, should energy policy be used to level the playing field with the incumbent fossil fuels?

Instead of targeting specific alternative fuels with subsidies and tax credits, why not level the playing field by getting the prices right for incumbent fossil fuels? Specifically, Congress should enact a carbon tax per ton of emissions and a security tax per barrel of oil, raising the prices of these fuels to reflect their true social cost.

This strategy has several advantages over the congressional beauty pageant:

- *All* new technologies would enjoy a more level playing field, not just those selected as pageant finalists.
- The market, not government, would determine which of the new technologies will succeed.
- This approach would be more transparent. With the current patchwork of subsidies and tax credits, it is extremely difficult to assess their costs (in terms of lost tax revenues) or their effectiveness in achieving their intended goals. In contrast, the carbon and security taxes would force us to ask how much we are willing to pay for cleaner air and added oil security.
- A focus on getting the prices right for incumbent fossil fuels would limit the scope of Congress to pass legislation designed to enrich particular private-interest groups.
- Getting the prices right would greatly simplify the existing approach. Congress would have to struggle with only two parameters—the amounts of the carbon and security taxes. By so limiting the focus, public attention and oversight could be much more easily concentrated. New technologies would then compete against the incumbent fossil fuels, and the market would winnow out the successful from the unsuccessful technologies. If a fuel could not pass the market test, there would be no justification for special tax breaks.

### The Oil Security Tax

As discussed in chapter 3, the analogy of the world oil market as one huge bathtub provides useful insights. Oil security is a worldwide problem, and there is a built-in incentive for countries to underinvest in security since any one country cannot capture all the benefits. Oil security is achieved either by reducing world oil consumption or by increasing the amount of secure oil in the mix. Investment in the storage of emergency oil supplies, such as the United States' Strategic Petroleum Reserve, is an example of a means to accomplish the latter.

But the question remains whether the price of a barrel of oil in the world market reflects its true social cost if associated with its consumption we must buy an insurance policy in the form of a adding a barrel of oil to a strategic petroleum reserve. Isn't the true social cost of oil in this case its purchase price *plus* the cost of the insurance policy? In principle, then, the oil security tax should be set equal to the cost of the insurance policy, thereby internalizing into the price the full social cost of the oil.

In a perfect world, all the consuming nations would agree on which oil sources were "secure" and which were "insecure," and all importing countries would impose a common tariff on the "insecure" oil equal to the externality it imposes. Unfortunately, this elegant policy prescription does not hold up if only part of the world adopts such a tax. Given the fungibility of oil, any attempt to differentiate secure from insecure oil would be subject to abuses such as the repackaging of insecure oil as secure oil, the effect of which would be to thwart the desired security effects.

Since the theoretically optimal policy prescription is not practical, the best alternative is a security tax on all oil consumed *domestically*, the purpose of which would be to raise the price to the consumer and thereby reduce consumption. Although increased prices due to an oil security tax will *not* increase the flow of oil from conventional production into the bathtub, the higher oil prices will promote conservation and accelerate the development of substitutes for conventional oil, such as fuel from oil sands, gas-to-liquid fuels, and renewable fuels. As noted in chapter 3, the appropriate amount for an oil security tax has proved elusive to economic modelers. The consensus is roughly $5 per barrel. Over time, the tax should be adjusted for inflation.

The effect on retail petroleum products of a $5-per-barrel security tax is on the order of $0.12 per gallon, which at today's gasoline prices is not likely to unleash a sizable conservation effect on worldwide gasoline consumption or petroleum demand in general. Remember the lessons from the bathtub analogy. The key is to induce cooperative efforts to reduce worldwide oil consumption. As a starter, in return for adopting such a security tax, the United States should seek commitments from developing countries to discontinue harmful oil subsidies. In effect, we should use such a tax as a bargaining chip to obtain the cooperation of others.

### The Carbon Tax

Economists generally favor a carbon tax for a number of reasons. First, a carbon tax establishes an observable price that society is willing to pay for $CO_2$ abatement and creates a more level playing field for new technologies. Second, a carbon tax avoids the potential problem of uncertain and highly fluctuating prices of emissions rights. Investors in new plants know with certainty the current carbon tax and the rate at which it will escalate in the future and thus can formulate sensible investment plans. Third, a carbon tax offers flexibility so that emissions reductions occur optimally over time. As new technologies are gradually developed and the existing stock of energy-consuming capital is gradually replaced, carbon emitters have the option to pay the tax if, indeed, it becomes too costly to abate the $CO_2$. With steadily rising carbon taxes and future technological advances, making large emissions reductions in the future becomes more advantageous. This flexibility is especially important as we make the transition to lower carbon emissions.

In principle, tradable emissions allowances, combined with banking and an appropriately low safety-valve price, could have these same advantages; but there are two additional properties that distinguish a carbon tax. One is that a carbon tax would be much more transparent than tradable emissions allowances and potentially less subject to manipulation. There would be no offsets, for example, for farmers or foresters that could be sold; nor would there be the clean development mechanisms that have resulted in abuses under the Kyoto Protocol. It is hoped that, as with the gasoline tax in the United States, there would be no special exemptions. The tax would be assessed on the carbon content of the fuel, which is readily measurable. For firms installing carbon-sequestration technologies in coal plants, credits would be allowed only on the basis of measured quantities of $CO_2$ sequestered.

The other is that revenues from a carbon tax can be used to reduce other taxes.[9] It has long been recognized that income and payroll taxes cause a welfare loss by creating a disincentive to work, but these taxes have been needed to fund government expenditures. Environmental-tax revenues could be used to reduce income and payroll taxes, correcting two economic distortions at once and giving society a double dividend.[10] It would be a simple matter to couple carbon-tax revenues with offsetting income- or payroll-tax reductions, producing a revenue-neutral carbon tax.[11]

Getting the prices of energy right essentially involves two numbers—the appropriate carbon tax and the appropriate oil security tax. Economic theory offers a straightforward policy prescription for setting optimal tax rates: set the rate where the marginal cost of controlling the externality equals the marginal benefit received from its abatement. In effect, to set the carbon-tax rate, create a supply and demand curve for $CO_2$ abatement; the price at which the two curves intersect reflects society's willingness to pay for carbon abatement and thus the optimal tax. The carbon and oil security taxes will raise the prices of fossil fuels to reflect the true social costs of such fuels. The higher prices will make alternative fuels more economically attractive and induce more energy conservation.

In chapter 4 I discussed the analyses of Alan Manne and William Nordhaus, who concluded that the optimal carbon tax should be set initially somewhere between \$3 and \$7.35 per ton of $CO_2$. Over time, Manne's carbon tax would be increased in inflation-adjusted dollars by about 4 percent per year, reaching \$16 per ton by 2050, and Nordhaus's tax would rise at a slower rate, reaching \$26 per ton by 2050.[12] Prudence suggests a tax rate initially closer to the Nordhaus estimate. I prefer an initial tax of \$5 per ton of $CO_2$ in 2009 that would increase annually at 4 percent plus inflation, resulting in a tax rate of \$25 per ton by 2050. *Providing for automatic increases in the carbon tax is essential to provide stability and predictability to the market and to prevent Congress from revisiting the issue yearly.* Building in these future increases sharpens the incentives to begin finding substitutions for fossil fuels now, placing the economy on a path toward substantially lower emissions.

We can put an initial \$5-per-ton $CO_2$ tax into perspective by considering how such a tax would have affected the prices of the primary fossil fuels—coal, oil, and natural gas—if it had been implemented in 2007 (even though at earliest such a tax would not be implemented before 2009). To simplify the analysis, let us assume that the full amount of the tax is passed on in higher prices to consumers. Figure 6.1 shows the effect of the oil security tax and the carbon tax on the 2007 price of the three fuels. To compare the prices of crude oil, natural gas, and coal, we index the prices, setting the 2007 price to 100, and then add the oil security tax and carbon tax. For example, a \$5-per-barrel security tax increases the crude-oil price index to 107.5, and the carbon tax adds another \$2.30 per barrel, or 3.5 percent, raising the crude-oil price index to 111.[13] Therefore, the combined effect of the two taxes is to increase the price of crude oil by 11 percent. For purposes of calculating the 2050 prices, it is assumed that the base prices of the three fuels are unchanged in real terms and that the taxes were implemented at their earliest point—2009—and escalate thereafter. Whereas the security tax is held constant in 2007 dollars at \$5 per barrel, the carbon tax quintuples by 2050 in real terms. In 2050, the combined taxes raise the price of crude oil by 25 percent.

For natural gas and coal, there is no justification for a security tax, only a carbon tax. Natural gas is our cleanest fossil fuel, containing only 117 lbs of $CO_2$ per million Btu, compared with coal's 205 lbs of $CO_2$ per million Btu. A ton of bituminous coal containing 24 million Btu will result in 2.46 tons of $CO_2$ emissions. It is not surprising, therefore, that a \$5-per-ton $CO_2$ tax increases the 2007 price of natural gas by only 4.7 percent and, by 2050, by 23.5 percent. In contrast, a \$5-per-ton carbon tax applied to coal would result in a tax of

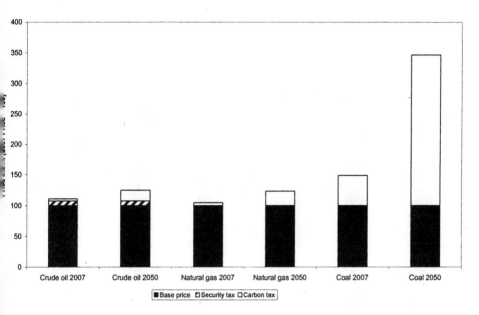

igure 6.1
mpact of a carbon tax and a security tax on fossil fuel prices
ased on author calculations using data from DOE (2008a).

$12.40 per ton, raising the price of coal from $25.16 per ton to $37.56 per ton—
a 49 percent increase. By 2050, coal prices would increase by 256 percent. Future price changes of this magnitude would greatly affect fuel choices for new
power plants or encourage carbon-sequestration projects.

Although the effects of the carbon and security taxes are particularly relevant
to the major industrial users who must choose among these fuels and alternatives, we should also consider the impact of these taxes on consumer prices for
gasoline, heating oil, natural gas, and electricity (generated from coal). These
measures give us a sense not only of the macroeconomic implications of the
taxes but also of their ability to encourage conservation by residential consumers. As shown in figure 6.2, the combined effects on gasoline prices are only
7 percent initially and 17 percent by 2050. For heating oil, the price increases are
6 percent initially and 14 percent by 2050. For residential natural-gas prices, the
effects are very small—2 percent initially and 11 percent by 2050.

The explanation for these comparatively modest price increases for residential consumers is simple. Natural gas is a low-carbon fuel, and the cost of the gas
is only a small part of the overall costs, which include pipeline and local distribution costs. The most significant effect of the taxes would be felt by residential

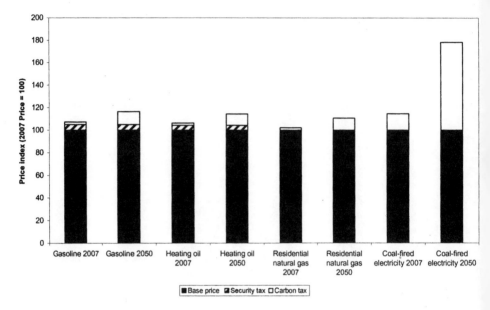

Figure 6.2
Impact of a carbon tax and a security tax on consumer energy prices
Based on author calculations using data from DOE (2008a).

electricity customers served by coal-burning plants. The carbon tax would raise
these prices by 14 percent initially and by 78 percent by 2050. Although no taxes
are welcomed, the proposed magnitude of the initial carbon taxes is by no
means onerous and should not provoke substantial macroeconomic disruptions. Indeed, for these reasons, even China and India might find such increases
palatable.

The really good news is the long-run effects that these taxes would set in mo-
tion. Knowing that the carbon tax will quintuple over the next forty-plus years,
consumers and producers would begin altering their investment decisions today. The decision to buy a more or less fuel-efficient car, air conditioner, refrigerator, or other appliance would surely be affected by the anticipation of the
carbon tax rising by 48 percent (in real dollars) in ten years and 119 percent in
twenty years. Likewise, planners of a new power plant would have to take into
account that the price of coal—which initially will have increased by 49 percent with the imposition of the carbon tax—will more than double in twenty
years. Surely, such expectations would completely change the way future energy investments are considered.

Even though a number of European countries have adopted carbon taxes, these taxes are neither indexed to inflation nor set to increase by a certain percentage each year. Because they do not increase in real terms in the future, they do not have the impact that an escalating tax rate would have on current and future energy investments. An advantage of the carbon tax proposed here is that its immediate effect on fuel prices *would not be that onerous,* yet the fact that the tax escalates significantly overtime at a known rate should trigger an immediate impact on current investment decisions regarding coal-burning power plants and other alternative fuels.

It is often argued that the United States should adopt, as an alternative to a carbon tax and an oil security tax, a hefty gasoline tax of, say, $1 per gallon. Indeed, one of the policy prescriptions proposed by a blue-ribbon panel sponsored by the Council on Foreign Relations was a $1-per-gallon gasoline tax.[14] Although using taxes to modify economic behavior is generally a good idea, if we are to balance the trade-offs between cheap, clean, and secure energy correctly, it is important that the magnitude of the tax reflect the externality it is designed to correct. Since there are 42 gallons in a barrel and roughly half of each barrel of oil is converted into gasoline, a $1-per-gallon gasoline tax translates into about a $21-per-barrel tax on oil, which is far higher than the estimated security and carbon externalities, which together would total about $7.30 per barrel. In effect, we would sacrifice a lot of cheapness to attain only incremental improvements in security and carbon abatement.[15] For example, a gasoline tax is not suitable for correcting the security externality associated with oil because the tax should encourage conservation of *all* petroleum products, not just gasoline, which accounts for less than half of petroleum consumption. Likewise, a gasoline tax, which does nothing to reduce coal or natural-gas consumption, is not a suitable weapon for attacking global warming.

**The Revenue Potential of the Proposed Taxes**

A $5-per-ton $CO_2$ tax and a $5-per-barrel oil security tax would generate significant federal tax revenues. By contrast, tradable emissions permits that are simply given to existing polluting firms would not result in any federal revenue and would not insulate consumers from higher fuel costs. Estimating the revenue implications of these taxes goes well beyond the scope of this analysis, but one simple calculation will provide policymakers with an idea of their potential.

For simplicity, assume that despite a growing economy, future fossil-fuel consumption remains constant at 2007 levels and the taxes were implemented in 2009.[16] Under this assumption, estimated tax revenues would be $37 billion from the carbon tax and $36 billion from the oil security tax, for a total of $73 billion. Over time, this figure is likely to rise substantially, if only because the carbon tax is to be increased annually by the rate of inflation, plus 4 percent. For example, the carbon tax quintuples (in real terms) by 2050. At current emissions rates, carbon-tax revenues could rise to $185 billion (in 2007 dollars). Assuming an inflation rate of 3 percent per year, carbon-tax revenues would be $590 billion in 2050 dollars. The oil security tax would add another $120 billion in 2050 dollars. Clearly, these taxes could be a huge generator of future tax revenue at the same time that they steer the economy toward lower emissions and less dependence on oil. Not only would such tax revenue be a boon for the U.S. Treasury, but revenue-starved developing countries adopting security and carbon taxes would clearly find them attractive revenue generators as well. Perhaps even India and China would find such revenue sources superior to its other methods of generating revenues.

### Overcoming Objections to Taxes

Despite the clear merits of the proposed energy taxes, many Americans are likely to oppose them on philosophical as well as macroeconomic grounds. To many, the word "tax" is a four-letter word. Indeed, we could soften some of the more visceral objections by labeling it an "environmental and security fee" instead of a "tax." Nevertheless, people like my good friend Wayne Findley will see it for what it is—a tax. Wayne's point is that increased tax revenues will only be an invitation for increased federal spending and waste. Additionally, the Wayne Findleys of our electorate will point out that until recently energy prices have risen sharply, making it even more difficult for people to make ends meet.[17] How can such objections be overcome?

MAKE ENERGY TAXES REVENUE NEUTRAL

As part of any energy-tax legislation, the tax revenues should be earmarked for offsetting reductions in income and payroll taxes and for increases in the earned income tax credit. The impact of the new taxes on consumers' pocketbooks would thus be offset by reductions in other taxes. Revenue-neutral energy taxes have an important advantage over cap-and-trade proposals. A cap-and-trade system would leave consumers with higher energy prices, but there would be no offsetting tax reductions. Under cap-and-trade systems in which the biggest carbon emitters receive emissions permits for free, the windfall profits from owning these permits accrue to the large carbon emitters, not to consumers. Indeed, it is paradoxical that many policymakers endorse a cap-and-trade system but are reluctant to endorse carbon and security taxes for fear of public opposition. A revenue-neutral system of energy taxes would have much greater benefits to the public at the expense of the large carbon-emitting industries.

MACROECONOMIC IMPACTS ARE MINIMIZED

The macroeconomic effects of revenue-neutral energy taxes would likely be minimal for two reasons. First, although consumers as a group would pay more for energy, the offsetting tax reductions would neutralize the effects of the energy taxes. Second, because of the relatively small magnitude of the initial carbon and oil security taxes, they would be unlikely to cause any major short- or long-run macroeconomic disruptions. As shown in figure 6.2, the percentage price increases for petroleum products and natural gas would be well within the range of existing fluctuations. Coal prices would be significantly affected, but the relevant issue is their impact on the residential prices of electricity generated by coal. Even then, the initial effect would be about a 14 percent increase. Furthermore, because the carbon-tax rate would be increased over time, its effects would occur gradually.

Opponents of a carbon tax who argue that emissions-allowance trading (with prices of $30 or more per ton of $CO_2$) is preferable to a carbon tax (of $5 per ton) fail to consider two realities. Because of the extreme inflexibility of the energy system in the short run, very high carbon prices are not likely to reduce emissions appreciably more than a $5-per-ton tax with built-in escalators would. Yet the effect of such high carbon prices on electricity and petroleum prices could be six times that of the carbon tax. In the long run, both may have fairly similar impacts because the gradually rising carbon-tax rate would induce investments today in anticipation of those higher future prices. Allowance prices of $30 per ton, coupled with wildly gyrating prices as in the European Union, would have serious macroeconomic repercussions. The carbon tax has far superior macroeconomic consequences because it starts at a much lower level and provides an orderly transition to a low-carbon world. Consequently, India and China in particular should view a carbon tax as far more palatable than a cap-and-trade system.

### Administering the New Taxes

Now let's consider how a carbon tax and an oil security tax would work in practice. The simpler of the two would be the oil security tax, which would be assessed on a per-barrel basis. It would be collected from each refinery in the United States for the barrels of crude oil delivered to it each month. Likewise, importers of refined petroleum products would be required to pay an equivalent tax per barrel at the port of entry into the United States. The same tax per barrel would be owed on crude oils of differing quality because from a security perspective there is no distinction in value. And since, as noted earlier, the fungibility of crude oil makes it impossible to separate secure from insecure oil, all crude oil would also be subject to the same tax regardless of whether it originated in a secure or insecure region.

A carbon tax would work similarly to a security tax, but with some important differences. The basic notion behind a carbon tax is that it would be assessed on the basis of the tons of $CO_2$ produced by the use of a fuel.[18] Different types of coal and crude oils have different Btu and $CO_2$ contents that are masked in power plants and refineries, so the carbon tax on a fossil fuel must be assessed at the point of its first purchase or consumption, whichever is first. For example, a carbon tax would be collected at the point of sale from the coal mine to the first purchaser (the power plant). For petroleum products, the tax would be assessed at the refinery gate or at the port of entry. For natural gas, the tax would be assessed at the point of first sale following its production at the wellhead or, for imports, upon entry into the United States. It is also important to note that fuel imports would be subject to the same tax, whereas fuel exports would not.[19]

Finally, power plants investing in carbon-sequestration technologies would be allowed to claim tax credits for $CO_2$ abatement based on the percentage of $CO_2$ they can demonstrate they have sequestered. Otherwise, there would be no special tax credits such as the clean development mechanism (whereby domestic emitters of $CO_2$ claim tax credits for reduced emissions abroad) or domestic tax credits (whereby domestic farmers receive subsidies for growing carbon-absorbing plants).

### A Brief Recapitulation

Taxes are a superior method for solving the problem of balancing the competing goals of cheap, clean, and secure energy. An oil security tax coupled with a carbon tax would

- provide a more level playing field for new technologies to compete against the incumbent fossil fuels;
- take much of the decision making away from politicians and interest groups and let the market decide which technologies are best;
- encourage conservation of energy by raising energy prices;

- eliminate the uncertainty of wildly fluctuating emissions-permit prices, providing instead a more predictable environment for business to make long-lived capital investments;
- minimize macroeconomic disruptions, because of the phased increases in taxes over time; and
- be revenue neutral because of offsetting reductions in income taxes.

## A PRICE-BASED ENERGY POLICY

As we have discussed at length, global warming and oil security are worldwide problems that are optimally dealt with through international cooperation. As emphasized in chapter 5, achieving *universal* cooperation, however, seems unlikely. If the United States were a small country, the choice would be easy—do nothing, be a free rider, and hope for the best. But that is obviously not the case. Under the club approach—involving an organization of the world's large carbon emitters—prospects for cooperation appear reasonably good, particularly if the United States plays a significant leadership role. The United States provides leadership in many ways, and abdicating it in the areas of global warming and oil security is unacceptable on geopolitical, ethical, and pragmatic grounds.

The smart energy policy advocated here can be summarized as follows:

- Embrace the goals of cheap, clean, and secure energy.
- Reject the petro-nationalist mindset (and its corollary, oil independence), and accept the reality of a global oil market.
- Trust markets to provide cheap energy.
- Recognize that, because of externalities, market prices will not by themselves fully reward clean and secure energy.
- Focus energy policy on "getting the prices right," which means imposing a carbon tax on fossil fuels and an oil security tax to reflect the true cost of these fuels.
- Set the $CO_2$ tax at $5 per ton, *rising at 4 percent per year in inflation-adjusted dollars* for the foreseeable future—a rate based on the best available studies.
- Set the oil security tax at $5 per barrel, to be adjusted annually for inflation.
- Continue to fund and expand federal R&D, with an emphasis on basic research, taking advantage of the level playing field provided by the new taxes. R&D project selection should be made by the U.S. Department of Energy on the basis of technical and economic promise, with minimal intervention by Congress.

Even though these policy prescriptions are both simple and reasonable, they may not be readily adopted. Despite the abundance of evidence that the existing policy mishmash isn't working, Congress is not likely to recognize the error of its ways and reform itself. The existing system provides great powers to enrich various interest groups, so without strong external pressures, changes of the type envisioned here will not happen. Broad segments of the scientific, media, and professional communities must push for the adoption of these ideas. Finally, in order to gain traction with the general electorate, congressional leaders must be able to explain in simple terms why getting the prices right is both a simple and a smart energy policy.

With these policies in place, the United States can regain world leadership in the field of energy and environmental policy and use its influence to seek cooperative action. We will not be alone, because world leaders are increasingly coming to the realization that these problems are real. Once these policies have been adopted, policymakers must then be patient, resisting the temptation to react to each new hurricane or upheaval in the Middle East. They must recognize that markets have been phenomenal providers of new energy technologies and will, given time and the right prices, obtain the desired balance between cheap, clean, and secure energy.

# Notes

**INTRODUCTION**

1. For details, see figure 1.2.
2. Volumetrically, ethanol contributed 4.7 percent of 2007 gasoline supplies, but it takes 1.5 gallons of ethanol to achieve the same effective consumption of regular gasoline.
3. Author's calculations drawn from USDA (2008), McElroy (2006), and DOE (2008c).
4. It should be recognized that a cap-and-trade system accomplishes the objective of raising the cost of fossil fuels and relies on the price system. Indeed, cap-and-trade systems can be designed to function similarly to a carbon tax, but they are more susceptible to political manipulation.
5. See Goulder (2003) and Goodstein (2004).
6. Since the effect of the carbon tax is likely to fall more on lower-income workers, adjustments to the earned income tax credit could be part of an overall reduction in income-tax rates.
7. Parry (2007).
8. Here we define petro-nationalism as the use of the coercive powers of the state to override the market as a means of providing petroleum and thereby gain some strategic advantage vis-à-vis other nations.

**CHAPTER 1. THE THREE CONFLICTING GOALS OF ENERGY POLICY**

1. See figure 1.2 later in the text.
2. Gow (2006).
3. See *Washington Post* (2005); Shadid (2007); *Philadelphia Inquirer* (2005); and Global Energy Decisions (2005).
4. See *Biofuels Security Act of 2007*, S 23, 110th Cong., 1st sess. (January 4, 2007).
5. McElroy (2006).
6. Fox and Shwedel (2007).
7. For a calculation, see McElroy (2006).
8. See Searchinger et al. (2008) and Fargione et al. (2008).
9. Relatively little attention has been directed toward making major technological breakthroughs in *truly new* technologies like cellulosic ethanol, which would use grain sorghum stalks or switchgrass. Compared with corn-based ethanol, cellulosic ethanol has the potential to double the yield per acre. Fortunately, U.S. energy policy is supporting an $80 million demonstration project on this intriguing but unperfected technology. See *Biofuels News* (2000).
10. Cars that run on electricity, which may be generated by a variety of emissions-producing sources, are still considered zero-emissions vehicles.
11. U.S. Department of Labor.
12. In economists' jargon, "elasticity" means the responsiveness of demand to a price increase or decrease. Formally, elasticity, as it relates to energy consumption, measures in absolute terms the percentage change in energy consumption in response to a given percentage change in the price of energy. Inelasticity refers to a response less than unity—that is, the percentage reduction in consumption is smaller than the percentage price increase.
13. U.S. Department of Labor.
14. In the range of 0.05 to 0.1. For example, with a price elasticity of demand of 0.1, a 10 percent price increase reduces consumption by only 1 percent. For evidence, see H. Huntington (1993).
15. Data is from the National Bureau of Statistics of China.
16. *Economist* (2007c, 90).
17. Intergovernmental Panel on Climate Change (2007).
18. BP (2008).
19. Adler (2003).
20. See Cohen (2007).
21. BP (2008).
22. It is important to note that oil reserves are *known* deposits that can be recovered at *current* prices with *existing* technology. Reserves do not include undiscovered deposits or oil in existing fields that will become recoverable in the future if technology improves or prices increase. Oil reserves, therefore, clearly do not constitute the ultimate resource base. If they did, the world would have run out of oil long ago. For example, world oil reserves were estimated at 611 billion barrels in 1970. In the thirty-five years that followed, the world consumed 853 billion barrels. Even more astounding, in 2005 there were 1,278

billion barrels of reserves left! Current oil reserves are analogous to the food in a grocery store. When these current reserves are taken off the shelf, new supplies, potentially costing more, will be found through exploration and further development of existing oil fields. The world will not run out of oil any time soon—but what will it cost to replenish our reserves in the future, and where will they come from?

23. Griffin and Steele (1986).
24. S. Huntington (2003).
25. Power Partners Resource Guide (2007).
26. DOE (2007c, table 2).
27. Socolow and Pacala (2006).
28. Implicitly, these calculations must be based on ethanol from sugar cane, not corn-based ethanol; furthermore, these calculations do not account for $CO_2$ emissions associated with changes in land use.

## CHAPTER 2. THE END OF CHEAP OIL?

1. See Mouawad (2008).
2. The OECD countries are basically the developed nations in Europe, North America, and Asia (Japan).
3. See IEA (2007, 16).
4. Data is from the National Bureau of Statistics of China.
5. See Herberg (2008).
6. See Zellner (2004).
7. For yield and crude-oil characteristics, see Energy Intelligence Group (2006).
8. See Nightingale (2008).
9. IEA (2007, 54).
10. See Nightingale (2008).
11. Verleger (2008).
12. Energy Intelligence Group (2006)
13. See OPEC (2008, 3).
14. See Brown, Virmani, and Alm (2008).
15. Brown, Virmani, and Alm (2008, 6).
16. Jacobe (2008).
17. See IEA (2006).
18. See Griffin and Steele (1986, 293–297).
19. Basically, an oil futures contract is the obligation to take delivery of 1,000 barrels of West Texas Intermediate crude oil at Cushing, Oklahoma, at some future date. At the time of delivery, the barrels can be sold on the spot market. The owner of the futures contract profits to the extent that the spot price at delivery exceeds the contract purchase price.
20. Heston and Rouwenhorst (1994).
21. OPEC (2008).
22. De Long et al. (1990).
23. See Goldman (2008).
24. See Campbell (2005) and Tverberg (2008).

25. Hubbert (1956).
26. See Campbell and Laherrere (1998) and Campbell (2005).
27. See Lynch (2002).
28. Simmons (2005).
29. See *Economist* (2007b).
30. Blas (2008).
31. The change attributable to non-OPEC production includes natural-gas liquids and inventory changes because it is calculated as demand growth less the change in OPEC crude-oil production.
32. Petroleum Industry Research Foundation (1977).
33. Adelman (1972).
34. Petroleum Industry Research Foundation (1977).
35. Spot prices refer to one-time sales of a tanker load of crude oil as distinguished from the official prices for long-term contract sales.
36. Griffin and Steele (1986).
37. See the discussion in chapter 1 under the heading "Cheap Energy: The Lifeblood of a Growing Economy."
38. This expectation assumes that oil in particular and energy in general are indispensable inputs—that is, to produce a dollar's worth of GDP, a fixed amount of oil and energy are necessary.
39. For an economic analysis of this program, see Griffin and Steele (1986).
40. Suslow (2005).
41. See Griffin and Xiong (1997).
42. See Griffin and Xiong (1997).
43. For GDP growth rates, see CIA (2008).
44. CIA (2008). The growth rate is based on the period 2000 to 2007.
45. Simmons (2005).
46. DOE (a).
47. Fox and Wilpert (2006).
48. Reservoir engineering constraints limit the rate of current production relative to the remaining reserves because faster production can severely reduce ultimately recoverable reserves. As an approximate guide, petroleum engineers often use a reserves-to-production ratio of 10 or less.
49. See DOE (2006).
50. Baker Institute Energy Forum (2007).
51. Baker Institute Energy Forum (2007).
52. Baker Institute Energy Forum (2007).
53. Romero and Krauss (2007).
54. Baker Institute (2007).
55. Teece (1982).
56. This was a U.N. program that allowed Iraq to increase production to generate revenue to buy food.
57. See Kramer (2008).

58. Using a sophisticated model of the world oil market that incorporates cartel incentives, I have reached similar conclusions. See Griffin and Xiong (1997).

59. Griffin and Schulman (2005).

60. See Griffin and Schulman (2005).

61. See Workshop on Alternative Energy Strategies (1977, 140).

62. The Canadian oil sands are oil-bearing sands that are usually surface-mined like strip-mined coal. The bitumen is then separated from the sand by hot water and centrifuges. After the removal of sulfur and coke, the remaining product is a type of high-quality crude oil.

63. National Energy Board (2006).

64. Stranded gas supplies are located in areas sufficiently far from major consuming areas that they cannot be transported by pipeline. Consequently, their value is quite low. In the past, natural gas was burned off (or "flared") as an unwanted by-product of oil production in many remote areas.

65. Lyne (2004).

66. See Bryant (forthcoming).

67. See Griffin and Steele (1986, ch. 8).

## CHAPTER 3. OIL SECURITY IN AN INCREASINGLY INSECURE WORLD

1. BP (2008).

2. Shadid (2007).

3. Vietor and Evans (2004).

4. See Barnes and Jaffee (2006).

5. Doran (2004).

6. Clawson and Henderson (2005, ix).

7. For survey results, see Vietor and Evans (2004).

8. Barnes and Jaffe (2006).

9. Griffin and Steele (1986, 123–124).

10. Leiby et al. (1997).

11. Brown and Yucel (2002, 204.

12. Parry and Darmstadter (2003).

13. Friedman (2006).

14. Here we define petro-nationalism as the use of the coercive powers of the state to override the market as a means of providing petroleum and thereby gain some strategic advantage vis-à-vis other nations.

15. Adelman (1990).

16. Yergin (1993, 303–368).

17. Gholz and Press (2004).

18. Yergin (2006, 77).

19. See Adelman (1984).

20. Gulen (1999, 125–139); Bachmeier and Griffin (2006, 55–71).

21. See the discussion of explanations 2 and 4 for oil price increases since 2004, in chapter 2.

22. DOE (2008c). Transportation costs are estimated by subtracting the average freight-on-board cost from the average landed cost. Recently, transportation costs have soared because of capacity constraints.

23. West Texas Intermediate crude has a gravity of 40.8 degrees and a sulfur content of less than 0.5 percent. Alaska North Slope crude has a gravity of 27.5 degrees and a sulfur content of 1.1 percent. Saudi Light crude has a gravity of 33.5 degrees and a sulfur content of 1.77 percent. Malaysian Tapis Blend crude has a gravity of 44 degrees and a sulfur content of only 0.03 percent.

24. Bachmeier and Griffin (2006).

25. DOE (2007a).

26. Adelman (1990).

27. DOE (2007a).

28. Refineries are assumed to be located in the consuming countries with capacity sufficient to process local consumption.

29. The price elasticity of demand measures the responsiveness of the quantity consumed to a price increase. Formally, it is measured as the percentage change in quantity consumed divided by the percentage change in price.

30. Oil-producing countries are assumed to consume no oil domestically.

31. In reality, rather than there being a single world oil price, prices of various crude oils tend to exhibit stable, long-term price differentials, reflecting differences in quality and transportation costs. Depending on the capacity utilization of tankers and complex refineries, these differentials will vary over time; nevertheless, as shown in figure 3.3, all four crude-oil prices move together.

32. Assuming a short-run price elasticity of demand of 0.1 implies that a 10 percent price increase is necessary to produce a 1 percent reduction in consumption. Likewise, to achieve a 10 percent reduction in consumption, a 100 percent price increase is necessary.

33. Assuming a short-run price elasticity of demand of 0.1, a 100 percent price increase is necessary to reduce consumption by 10 percent. Likewise, to induce a 50 percent reduction in consumption, a 500 percent price increase would be required.

34. The term "effective" price would allow for command-and-control policies that restrict use but leave the nominal price unchanged.

35. Over time, as demand for oil from Countries 1 and 2 falls with Country B's transition to oil independence, it is reasonable to assume that both Countries 1 and 2 will invest in only enough capacity to meet Country A's demand for oil.

36. To see the math, assume Country A's predisruption world price was $100 per barrel and Country B's price with the $100 tariff was $200 per barrel. To reduce world (outside of Country B) demand from 50 to 25 barrels, the world price must rise to $520 per barrel. For Country A, a price of $520 per barrel implies a 420 percent price spike, forcing it to reduce its consumption by 21 barrels per day. In Country B, given a short-run demand elasticity of 0.1, an increase in its domestic price from $200 to $520 per barrel (a 160 percent increase) would cause B's consumers to reduce consumption by 4 barrels (16 percent), freeing up exports to A of 4 barrels. This example assumes no short-run ability of B to increase production beyond 25 barrels.

37. Bielecki (2002) makes the same point.

38. One exception is the Arab oil embargo of 1973–1974, in which the Arab oil producers instituted an embargo against the United States and the Netherlands for their support of Israel. Because the embargo did not include other major consuming nations, non-Arab oil supplies destined for other consuming countries were simply diverted to the United States and the Netherlands. Since then, disruptions have involved at most two producers.

39. The probability that any one country will experience a supply disruption in a given period (i.e., that there will be a disruption affecting 20 percent of the world's oil supply) is given by the following formula:

$$\Pr(X = 1) = \binom{5}{1} \times (0.05)^1 \times (1 - 0.05)^{(5-1)} = 5 \times (0.05) \times (0.95)^4 = 0.204$$

40. $\Pr(X = 2) = \binom{10}{2} \times (0.05)^2 \times (1 - 0.05)^{(10-2)} = 45 \times (0.05)^2 \times (0.95)^8 = 0.075$

41. $\Pr(X = 4) = \binom{20}{4} \times (0.05)^4 \times (1 - 0.05)^{(20-4)} = 4,845 \times (0.05)^4 \times (0.95)^{16} = 0.013$

42. Bohi and Toman (1996); Gholz and Press (2004).

43. Bohi and Quandt (1984, 14–17).

44. Verleger (1993).

45. DOE (2008c).

46. Since the price data are reported for weekday trading days, I have reported average gasoline production on a weekly basis, understanding that this includes Saturdays and Sundays. All data are drawn from DOE (2008c).

47. Boutique gasoline blends were devised by the EPA to allow individual air-quality regions to reach their mandated air qualities. Conventional gasoline imports generally will not meet the specific blending characteristics of the boutique blends.

48. Griffin and Steele (1986).

49. Leiby et al. (1997,66).

50. Parry and Darmstadter (2003). Additional support for a $5 tax was provided by the National Research Council (2002).

51. In any event, even if a $5-per-barrel tax in 2002 would have represented, say, a 20 percent tax, there is no justification for a $26-per-barrel tax when the price of oil is $130 per barrel. A percentage tax would be justified only if the intent of the tax was to capture economic rents that OPEC would otherwise attempt to collect. That, however, is not the intent of this security tax.

52. Yergin (2006, 77).

### CHAPTER 4. CLIMATE CHANGE AND THE SEARCH FOR CLEAN ENERGY

1. Intergovernmental Panel on Climate Change (2007).

2. Intergovernmental Panel on Climate Change (2007).

3. Griffin (2003a).

4. Loosely speaking, radiative forcing is the change in the difference between the incoming

radiation energy and the outgoing radiation energy in a given climate system. Radiative forcing is measured in watts per square meter.

5. Wigley (1999).
6. Intergovernmental Panel on Climate Change (2001).
7. Intergovernmental Panel on Climate Change (2001, 2007).
8. For a discussion of the carbon cycle, see Schlesinger (2003).
9. Intergovernmental Panel on Climate Change (2007, 2).
10. Intergovernmental Panel on Climate Change (2001).
11. Other greenhouse gases are also projected to increase, but generally at much slower rates than $CO_2$, making $CO_2$ the primary contributor to radiative forcing. See Intergovernmental Panel on Climate Change (2001, appendix 2).
12. Socolow (2005).
13. Intergovernmental Panel on Climate Change (2001).
14. Intergovernmental Panel on Climate Change (2007, 9; 2001, 25).
15. North (2003, 64).
16. DOE (2001).
17. Basically, carbon sequestration involves capturing the $CO_2$ and injecting it in back into a geologic formation or into deep ocean depths where it becomes a liquid.
18. Goulder (2003).
19. The social discount rate, $r$, is measured in real terms after excluding inflation.
20. Manne (2003).
21. Stern (2007).
22. Nordhaus (2006).
23. Schelling (1995).
24. Nordhaus (1991); Cline (1992); Fankhauser (1995); and Tol (1995). Midpoint estimates of $CO_2$ concentrations and temperature increase were computed by International Panel on Climate Change (2001).
25. Mendelsohn and Neumann (1999).
26. Mendelsohn (2003).
27. Mendelsohn (2003).
28. Since plants feed off of $CO_2$, increased concentrations act as a fertilizer for plants.
29. Smith, Lazo, and Hurd (2003) and Mendelsohn (2003).
30. Nordhaus and Boyer (2000).
31. Tol (1998).
32. Nordhaus and Boyer (2000).
33. This claim is usually predicated on the assumption that fossil fuels were not used in the production or transportation of these biofuels or in the cultivation of the corn or grains used to produce the biofuels.
34. Edmonds and Sands (2003).
35. Electric Power Research Institute (2006).
36. In the IGCC process, coal is first transformed into a gas, which is then used to power a combined-cycle power plant such as a plant now fueled by natural gas.
37. Energy Modeling Forum (1995).

38. Manne (2003); Nordhaus (2008).

39. Nordhaus (2008).

40. Tol (2005).

## CHAPTER 5. CLIMATE CHANGE AND THE DIFFICULT SEARCH FOR INSTITUTIONS AND POLICIES

1. Victor (2006).

2. Stavins (2003).

3. Stack gas scrubbers have been installed in the emissions stacks of power plants to eliminate sulfur oxides because coal tends to be a high-sulfur fuel.

4. Nordhaus (2006).

5. So called because of the "caps" in the form of total emissions permits and the "trade" in permits being bought and sold.

6. Kruger, Oates, and Pizer (2007).

7. Victor (2006).

8. Victor (2006).

9. Manne (2003); Nordhaus (2008).

10. See Ellerman, Buchner, and Carraro (2007, 360–361) for a discussion of how allowances were allocated.

11. Wara (2007).

12. Victor (2006).

13. OECD (2006).

14. Indeed, David Gow (2006) predicts that in 2010, European emissions will be about 1 percent below 1990 levels. Although Kyoto's targets may not be reached, it seems clear that in the absence of the Kyoto targets, the emissions of these economies would have grown substantially with economic activity.

15. OECD (2006).

16. Data calculated from CIA (2008).

17. See Houser et al. (2008).

18. See Victor (2006).

19. Coal has a higher $CO_2$ content than natural gas. Furthermore, the thermal conversion efficiency of a coal-fired plant is about 34 percent as opposed to 62 percent for a natural-gas-fired combined-cycle plant.

20. Victor (2006).

21. Lane (2006).

22. Lane (2006, 70–73).

23. National Commission on Energy Policy (2007).

24. Edmonds and Stokes (2003).

25. Production for 2007 is from *BioFuels Journal* (2008).

26. See discussion in chapter 1 and McElroy (2006).

27. Kruger, Oates, and Pizer (2007).

28. See Paltsev et al. (2007).

29. See *Climate Stewardship and Innovation Act of 2007*, S 280, 110th Cong., 1st sess. (January

12, 2007); *Global Warming Reduction Act of 2007,* S 485, 110th Cong., 1st sess. (February 1, 2007); *Low Carbon Economy Act of 2007,* S 1766, 110th Cong., 1st sess. (July 11, 2007); and *Safe Climate Act of 2006,* HR 5642, 109th Cong., 2d sess. (June 20, 2006).

30. See *Low Carbon Economy Act of 2007,* S 1766, 110th Cong., 1st sess. (July 11, 2007) and *Keep America Competitive Global Warming Policy Act of 2006,* HR 5049, 109th Cong., 2d sess. (March 29, 2006).

31. Paltsev et al. (2007, 53).

32. This assumes that the base prices of these fuels were unaffected by the price of the allowances.

33. Manne (2003) and Nordhaus (2008).

34. See Goulder (2003) and Goodstein (2004).

35. Since the effect of the carbon tax is likely to fall more on lower-income workers, adjustments to the earned income tax credit could be part of an overall reduction in income-tax rates.

36. Parry (2007).


### CHAPTER 6. A SMART ENERGY POLICY

1. DOE (2006).

2. Chemlink Consultants.

3. *Economist* (2007a, 79).

4. DOE (2007c, table 2).

5. DOE (b).

6. Electric Power Research Institute (2006).

7. Vaitheeswaran (2005).

8. Lovins et al. (2004).

9. See Goulder (2003) and Goodstein (2004).

10. Since the effect of the carbon tax would likely fall more on lower-income workers, adjustments to the earned income tax credit could be part of an overall reduction in income-tax rates.

11. Parry (2007).

12. Nordhaus (2008) adopts a lower rate of escalation than does Manne (2003).

13. The 2007 average price of crude oil was $66.30, so a tax of $5 per barrel would raise its price by 7.5 percent. Thus, the price index would rise to 107.5.

14. Council on Foreign Relations (2006).

15. To justify substantially higher gasoline taxes than those implied in figure 6.2, we must be able to identify other externalities, such as traffic congestion in certain large cities. In Europe, high gasoline taxes are popular in large part because they reduce traffic congestion. Likewise, in highly congested areas of the United States, special local taxes may be warranted. See Parry, Walls, and Harrington (2007). As a device aimed primarily at enhancing security and reducing carbon emissions, however, such high tax rates do not seem justifiable.

16. Obviously, a comprehensive study of future revenues should factor in both short- and

long-run price responses to the demand for these fuels, as well as the effects of increasing economic activity.

17. I owe this consideration to my hunting buddy Wayne Findley, who, during a hunting trip to West Texas, argued for a hundred miles (or six gallons of gasoline) that he would accept such a tax only if Congress was prevented from spending the money.

18. The tax per barrel would vary depending on the petroleum product because the $CO_2$ content per barrel will vary. For example, a barrel of gasoline produces 0.41 tons of $CO_2$, which implies a tax of $2.05 per barrel assuming a $5-per-ton carbon tax.

19. The United States is a significant exporter of coal. Imposing the tax on coal exports would simply hurt U.S. coal companies and would not reduce coal consumption outside the United States; foreign coal producers would simply provide the coal in place of the U.S. companies.

# References

Adelman, Morris A. 1972. *The World Petroleum Market.* Baltimore: Johns Hopkins University Press.

———. 1984. "International Oil Agreements." *Energy Journal* 5 (3): 1–5.

———. 1990. "Mineral Depletion, with Special Reference to Petroleum." *Review of Economics and Statistics* 72 (1): 1–10.

Adler, Jerry. 2003. "The Day the Lights Went Out: From Scarce Water and Gasoline to the Warmth of Neighbors and the Kindness of Strangers, a Portrait of Life in the Darkness." *Newsweek,* August 25, 44–51.

Bachmeier, Lance J., and James M. Griffin. 2006. "Testing for Market Integration: Crude Oil, Coal, and Natural Gas." *Energy Journal* 27 (2): 55–71.

Baker Institute Energy Forum. 2007. *The Changing Role of National Oil Companies in International Energy Markets.* Baker Institute Policy Report 35. Houston, Tex.: James A. Baker III Institute for Public Policy of Rice University. Also available online at http://www.rice.edu/energy/publications/PolicyReports/BI_Study_35-1.pdf.

Barnes, Joe, and Amy Myers Jaffe. 2006. "The Persian Gulf and the Geopolitics of Oil." *Survival* 48 (1): 143–162.

Bielecki, J. 2002. "Energy Security: Is the Wolf at the Door?" *Quarterly Review of Economics and Finance* 42 (2): 235–250.

*BioFuels Journal.* 2008. "Ethanol Production Caps Year with Continued Growth"

March/April, 60. Also available online at http://www.nxtbook.com/nxtbooks/grain journal/biofuelsjournal_20080304.

*Biofuels News.* 2000. "Colloquies Explore Key Resource for Cellulosic Fuels and Chemicals." Spring/Summer, 1–4.

Blas, Javier. 2008. "Supply-Side Squeeze Explains Oil's Relentless Rise in Record Territory." *Financial Times* (London), April 16.

Bohi, Douglas R., and William B. Quandt. 1984. *Energy Security in the 1980s: Economic and Political Perspectives.* Washington, D.C.: Brookings Institution.

Bohi, Douglas R., and Michael A. Toman. 1996. *The Economics of Energy Security.* Boston: Kluwer Academic Publishers.

BP. 2008. *Statistical Review of World Energy 2008.* http://www.bp.com/statisticalreview.

Brown, Stephen P. A., and Mine K. Yucel. 2002. "Energy Prices and Aggregate Economic Activity: An Interpretive Survey." *Quarterly Review of Economics and Finance* 42 (2): 193–208.

Brown, Stephen P. A., Raghav Virmani, and Richard Alm. 2008. "Crude Awakening: Behind the Surge in Oil Prices." *Federal Reserve Bank of Dallas Economic Letter* 3, no. 5 (May).

Bryant, Henry. Forthcoming. "Effects of a Variable Ethanol Subsidy or Higher Renewable Fuels Standards on U.S. Agriculture." In *Biofuels, Food, and Feed Tradeoffs,* ed. Joe Outlaw, James A. Duffield, and David P. Ernstes. Oakbrook, Ill.: Farm Foundation.

Campbell, Colin J. 2005. *Oil Crisis.* Brentwood, U.K.: Multi-science Publishing.

Campbell, Colin J., and Jean H. Laherrere 1998. "The End of Cheap Oil." *Scientific American,* March, 78–83.

Chemlink Consultants. Gas to Liquids Technology Worldwide. http://www.chemlink.com.au/gtl.htm (accessed July 26, 2007).

CIA. *See* U.S. Central Intelligence Agency.

Clawson, Patrick, and Simon Henderson. 2005. *Reducing Vulnerability to Middle East Energy Shocks: A Key Element in Strengthening U.S. Energy Security.* Policy Focus 49. Washington, D.C.: Washington Institute for Near East Policy.

Cline, William R. 1992. *The Economics of Global Warming.* Washington, D.C.: Institute of International Economics.

Cohen, Ariel. 2007. "Europe's Strategic Dependence on Russian Energy." Heritage Foundation. Backgrounder 2083, Nov. 5. http://www.heritage.org/Research/Europe/bg2083.cfm.

Council on Foreign Relations. 2006. *National Security Consequences of U.S. Oil Dependency.* Independent Task Force Report 58. New York: Council on Foreign Relations.

De Long, J. Bradford, Andrei Shleifer, Lawrence H. Summers, and Robert J. Waldmann. 1990. "Positive-Feedback Investment Strategies and Destabilizing Rational Speculation." *Journal of Finance* 45 (2): 374–397.

DOC. *See* U.S. Department of Commerce.

DOE. *See* U.S. Department of Energy.

Doran, Michael Scott. 2004. "The Saudi Paradox." *Foreign Affairs,* January/February, 35–51.

*Economist.* 2007a. "Bright Idea." December 1, 79.

———. 2007b. "OPEC Is Back in Charge of the Oil Price," July 19, 74.

————. 2007c. "Too Hot to Touch," December 1, 90.

Edmonds, James A., and Ronald D. Sands. 2003. "What Are the Costs of Limiting $CO_2$ Concentrations?" In Griffin 2003a, 140–186.

Edmonds, James A., and Gerald M. Stokes. 2003. "Launching a Technology Revolution." In *Climate Policy for the 21st Century: Meeting the Long-Term Challenge of Global Warming,* ed. David Michel, 153–186. Washington, D.C.: Center for Transatlantic Relations.

Electric Power Research Institute. 2006. "Generation Technologies in a Carbon-Constrained World." Paper presented by Steven R. Specker at the Resources for the Future Policy Leadership Forum, Washington, D.C., March 30.

Ellerman, A. Denny, Barbara K. Buchner, and Carlo Carraro. 2007. "Unifying Themes." In *Allocation in the European Emissions Trading Scheme,* ed. A. Denny Ellerman, Barbara K. Buchner, and Carlo Carraro, 339–369. Cambridge, U.K.: Cambridge University Press.

Energy Intelligence Group. 2006. *International Crude Oil Market Handbook, 2006.* New York: Energy Intelligence Group.

Energy Modeling Forum. 1995. *Integrated Assessment of Climate Change.* EMF 14.Palo Alto, Calif.: Stanford University.

EPA. *See* U.S. Environmental Protection Agency.

Fankhauser, Samuel. 1995. *Valuing Climate Change: The Economics of the Greenhouse.* London: Earthscan.

Fargione, Joseph, Jason Hill, David Tilman, Stephen Polasky, and Peter Hawthorne. 2008. "Land Clearing and the Biofuel Carbon Debt." *Science,* February 29, 1235–1238.

Fox, Glenn, and Kenneth Shwedel. 2007. "North American Ethanol Bioenergy Policies and Their NAFTA Policy Implications." Paper presented at the Fourth Annual North American Agrifood Market Integration Consortium (NAAMIC) Conference, Cancun, Mexico, June 13–15.

Fox, Michael, and Gregory Wilpert. 2006. "International Energy Agency Increases Venezuela's Oil Production Estimates, Maybe." *Venezeualanalysis.com,* May 15. http://www .venezuelanalysis.com/articles.php?artno=1729.

Friedman, Thomas L. 2006. "The Energy Mandate." *New York Times,* October 13.

Gholz, Eugene, and Daryl Press. 2004. "Protecting 'The Prize': Oil and the National Interest." Paper presented at the annual meeting of the International Studies Association, Montreal, Quebec, Canada, March 17.

Global Energy Decisions. 2005. *Energy Policy Act of 2005: Who Is Left Behind?* http:// www.globalenergy.com/BR05/BR05-energy-policy.pdf.

Goldman, David. 2008. "Costly Oil Could Mean Recession—Soros." *CNN Money.com,* June 3. http://money.cnn.com/2008/06/03/news/economy/energy_manipulation_hearing/ index.htm?postversion=2008060314.

Goodstein, Eban. 2004. *Economics and the Environment.* 4th ed. New York: Wiley & Sons.

Goulder, Lawrence H. 2003. "Benefit-Cost Analysis and Climate Change Policy." In Griffin 2003a, 67–91.

Gow, David. 2006. "Figures Reveal Europe Falling Far Short of Climate Targets." *Guardian* (Manchester). October 28.

Griffin, James M., ed. 2003a. *Global Climate Change: The Science, Economics, and Politics.* Northampton, Mass.: Edward Elgar.

————. 2003b. "Introduction: The Many Dimensions of the Climate Change Issue." In Griffin 2003a, 1–24.

Griffin, James M., and Craig T. Schulman. 2005. "Price Asymmetry in Energy Demand Models: A Proxy for Energy-Saving Technical Change?" *Energy Journal* 26 (2): 1–21.

Griffin, James M., and Henry B. Steele. 1986. *Energy Economics and Policy.* 2nd ed. Orlando, Fla.: Academic Press.

Griffin, James M., and Weiwen Xiong. 1997. "The Incentive to Cheat: An Empirical Analysis of OPEC." *Journal of Law and Economics* 40:289–316.

Gulen, S. Gurcan. 1999. "Regionalization in the World Crude Oil Market: Further Evidence." *Energy Journal* 20 (1): 125–139.

Herberberg, Mikkal. 2008. "Supply Side to Blame." *San Francisco Chronicle,* April 29.

Heston, Steven L., and K. Geert Rouwenhorst. 1994. "Does Industrial Structure Explain the Benefits of International Diversification?" *Journal of Financial Economics* 36 (1): 3–27.

Houser, Trevor, Rob Bradley, Britt Childs, Jacob Werksman, and Robert Heilmayr. 2008. *Leveling the Carbon Playing Field: International Competition and U.S. Climate Policy Design.* New York: Peterson Institute for International Studies and World Resources Institute.

Hubbert, M. King. 1956. "Nuclear Energy and the Fossil Fuels." Paper presented at the Southern District Division of Production, American Petroleum Institute, San Antonio, Tex., March 7–9. Reprinted in *Drilling and Production Practice,* 7–25. Also available online at http://www.hubbertpeak.com/hubbert/1956/1956.pdf.

Huntington, Hillard G. 1993. "OECD Oil Demand: Estimated Response Surfaces for Nine World Oil Models." *Energy Economics* 15 (1): 49–56.

Huntington, Samuel P. 2003. *The Clash of Civilizations and the Remaking of World Order.* New York: Simon & Schuster.

IEA. *See* International Energy Agency.

IHS. 2006. Mimeo (on file with author).

Intergovernmental Panel on Climate Change. 2001. *Climate Change, 2001: The Scientific Basis; Contribution of Working Group I to the Third Assessment Report of the Intergovernmental Panel on Climate Change.* Cambridge, U.K.: Cambridge University Press.

————. 2007. "Summary for Policymakers." In *Climate Change, 2007: The Physical Science Basis; Contribution of Working Group I to the Fourth Assessment Report of the Intergovernmental Panel on Climate Change.* Cambridge, U.K.: Cambridge University Press. Also available online at http://www.ipcc.ch/pdf/assessment-report/ar4/wg1/ar4-wg1-spm.pdf.

International Energy Agency (IEA). 2006. *World Energy Outlook, 2006.* Paris: IEA. Also available online at http://www.iea.org/textbase/nppdf/free/2006/weo2006.pdf.

————. 2007. *Medium-Term Oil Market Report.* Paris: IEA. Also available online at http://omrpublic.iea.org/currentissues/mtomr2007.pdf.

————. 2008. *Oil Market Report,* May 13. Available online at http://omrpublic.iea.org/omrarchive/13may08full.pdf.

Jacobe, Dennis. 2008. "Majority of Americans Support Price Controls on Gas." *Gallup.com,* May 28, 2008. http://www.gallup.com/poll/107542/Majority-Americans-Support-Price-Controls-Gas.aspx.

Jones, Donald W., Paul N. Leiby, and Inja K. Paik. 2004. "Oil Price Shocks and the Macroeconomy: What Has Been Learned Since 1996." *Energy Journal* 25 (2): 1–32.

Kramer, Andrew J. 2008. "Deals with Iraq Are Set to Bring Oil Giants Back." *New York Times,* June 19.

Kruger, Joseph, Wallace E. Oates, and William A. Pizer. 2007. "Decentralization in the EU Emissions Trading Scheme and Lessons for Global Policy." Resources for the Future Discussion Paper 07-02. Washington, D.C. Also available online at http://www.rff.org/Documents/RFF-DP-07-02.pdf.

Lane, Lee. 2006. *Strategic Options for Bush Administration Climate Policy.* Washington, D.C.: AEI Press.

Leiby, Paul N., Donald W. Jones, T. Randall Curlee, and Russell Lee. 1997. *Oil Imports: An Assessment of Benefits and Costs.* Prepared for the U.S. Department of Energy. Oak Ridge, Tenn.: Oak Ridge National Laboratory. Also available online at http://pzl1.ed.ornl.gov/ORNL6851.pdf.

Lovins, Amory B., E. Kyle Datta, Odd-Even Bustnes, Jonathan G. Koomey, and Nathan J. Glasgow. 2004. *Winning the Oil Endgame: Innovation for Profits, Jobs, and Security.* Snowmass, Colo.: Rocky Mountain Institute.

Lynch, Michael. 2002. "The New Energy Crisis: Separating Threats from Hysteria." *Energy Policy* 30 (1): 1–2.

Lyne, Jack. 2004. "Shell Signs on to Build $5B Gas-to-Liquid Plant in Qatar." *Site Selection,* February 2. http://www.siteselection.com/ssinsider/snapshot/sf040202.htm.

Manne, Alan S. 2003. "Energy, the Environment, and the Economy: Hedging our Bets." In Griffin 2003a, 187–203.

McElroy, Michael B. 2006. "The Ethanol Illusion: Can We Move Beyond an Energy Policy Running on Hype and Hot Air?" *Harvard Magazine,* November-December, 33–35, 107.

Mendelsohn, Robert. 2003. "Assessing the Market Damages from Climate Change." In Griffin 2003a, 92–113.

Mendelsohn, Robert, and J. Neumann, eds. 1999. *The Economic Impact of Climate Change on the Economy of the United States.* Cambridge, U.K.: Cambridge University Press.

Mouawad, Jad. 2008. "The Big Thirst." *New York Times,* April 20.

National Commission on Energy Policy. 2007. *Energy Policy Recommendations to the President and the 110th Congress.* Washington, D.C.: National Commission on Energy Policy.

National Energy Board (Canada). 2006. *Canada's Oil Sands—Opportunities and Challenges to 2015: An Update.* Calgary: National Energy Board. Also available online at http://www.neb-one.gc.ca/clf-nsi/rnrgynfmtn/nrgyrprt/lsnd/pprtntsndchllngs20152006/pprtntsndchllngs20152006-eng.pdf.

National Research Council. 2002. *Effectiveness and Impact of Corporate Average Fuel Economy (CAFE) Standards.* Washington, D.C.: National Academy Press.

Nightingale, Alaric. 2008. "Iran Doubles Oil Stored in Tankers, Boosting Rates." *Bloomberg.com,* May 2. http://www.bloomberg.com/apps/news?pid=newsarchive&sid=a52hPWks6OO8.

Nordhaus, William D. 1991. "To Slow or Not to Slow: The Economics of the Greenhouse Effect." *Economic Journal* 101 (July): 920–937.

————. 2006. "After Kyoto: Alternative Mechanisms to Control Global Warming." *American Economic Review* 96 (2): 31–34.

————. 2008. *A Question of Balance.* New Haven, Conn.: Yale University Press.

Nordhaus, William D., and Joseph Boyer. 2000. *Warming the World: Economic Models of Global Warming.* Cambridge, Mass.: MIT Press.

North, Gerald R. 2003. "Climate Change over the Next Century." In Griffin 2003a, 45–66.

*Oil and Gas Journal.* 1970. "World Wide Oil at a Glance." December 28, 92–93.

————. 2006. "CGES: Global Crude Supplies Will Continue to Get Heavier." September 25, 60–62.

OECD. *See* Organization for Economic Cooperation and Development.

OPEC. *See* Organization of the Petroleum Exporting Countries.

Organization for Economic Cooperation and Development (OECD). 2006. *Energy Prices & Taxes—Quarterly Statistics,* 3rd Quarter.

Organization of the Petroleum Exporting Countries (OPEC). 2008. *Monthly Oil Market Report,* May.

Paltsev, Sergey, John M. Reilly, Henry D. Jacoby, Angelo C. Gurgel, Gilbert E. Metcalf, Andrei P. Sokolov, and Jennifer F. Holak. 2007. *Assessment of U.S. Cap-and-Trade Proposals.* MIT Joint Program on the Science and Policy of Global Change Report 146. Also available online at http://web.mit.edu/globalchange/www/MITJPSPGC_Rpt146.pdf.

Parry, Ian W. H. 2007. "Should We Abandon Cap-and-Trade in Favor of a $CO_2$ Tax?" Weathervane, March 23. http://www.weathervane.rff.org/policy_design/taxes_and_subsidies/Should_We_Abandon_Cap_and_Trade_for_CO2Tax.cfm.

Parry, Ian W. H., and Joel Darmstadter. 2003. "The Costs of U.S. Oil Dependency." Resources for the Future Discussion Paper 03-59. Washington, D.C. Also available online at http://www.rff.org/Documents/RFF-DP-03-59.pdf.

Parry, Ian W. H., Margaret Walls, and Winston Harrington. 2007. "Automobile Externalities and Policies." *Journal of Economic Literature* 45 (2): 373–399.

Petroleum Industry Research Foundation (PIRF). 1977. *Vertical Divestiture and OPEC.* New York: PIRF.

*Philadelphia Inquirer.* 2005. Editorial. "Energy Bill Far from Visionary." July 28.

Power Partners Resource Guide. http://www.uspowerpartners.org/Topics/SECTION1 Topic-NaturalGas.htm (accessed December 20, 2007).

Romero, Simon, and Clifford Krauss. 2007. "Deadline Nears in Chavez Fight Against Big Oil." *New York Times,* July 10.

Schelling, Thomas C. 1995. "Intergenerational Discounting." *Energy Policy* 23 (4/5): 395–401.

Schlesinger, William H. 2003. "The Carbon Cycle: Human Perturbations and Potential Management Options." In Griffin 2003a, 25–44.

Searchinger, Timothy, Ralph Heimlich, R. A. Houghton, Fengxia Dong, Amani Elobeid, Jacinto Fabiosa, Simla Tokgoz, Dermot Hayes, and Tun-Hsiang Yu. 2008. "Use of U.S. Croplands for Biofuels Increases Greenhouse Gases through Emissions from Land Use Change." *Science,* February 29, 1238–1240.

Shadid, Anthony. 2007. "With Iran Ascendant, U.S. Is Seen at Fault." *Washington Post,* January 30.

Simmons, Matthew R. 2005. *Twilight in the Desert: The Coming Saudi Oil Shock and the World Economy.* Hoboken, N.J.: Wiley & Sons.

Smith, Joel B., Jeffrey K. Lazo, and Brian Hurd. 2003. "The Difficulties of Estimating Global Non-market Damages from Climate Change." In Griffin 2003a, 114–139.

Socolow, Robert H. 2005. "Can We Bury Global Warming?" *Scientific American,* July, 49–55.

Socolow, Robert H., and Stephen W. Pacala. 2006. "A Plan to Keep Carbon in Check." *Scientific American,* September, 50–57.

Stavins, Robert N. 2003. "Experience with Market-Based Environmental Policy Instruments." In *Handbook of Environmental Economics,* vol. 1, ed. Karl Göran Mäler and Jeffrey Vincent, 355–435. Amsterdam: Elsevier Science.

Stern, Nicholas. 2007. *The Economics of Climate Change: The Stern Review.* Cambridge, U.K.: Cambridge University Press.

Suslow, Valerie. 2005. "Cartel Contract Duration: Empirical Evidence from Inter-war International Cartels." *Industrial and Corporate Change* 14 (5): 705–744.

Teece, David J. 1982. "OPEC Behavior: An Alternative View." In *OPEC Behavior and World Oil Prices,* ed. James M. Griffin and David J. Teece, 64–93. London: Allen & Unwin.

Tol, Richard S. J. 1995. "The Damage Costs of Climate Change: Toward More-Comprehensive Calculations." *Environmental and Resource Economics* 5 (4): 353–374.

———. 1998. "New Estimates of the Damage Costs of Climate Change." Working Paper D-98/06. Vrije Universiteit, Amsterdam.

———. 2005. "The Marginal Damage Costs of Carbon Dioxide Emissions: An Assessment of the Uncertainties." *Energy Policy* 33 (16): 2064–2074.

Tverberg, Gail. 2008. Peak Oil Overview—June 2008. http://www.theoildrum.com/files/Peak_Oil_June_08B.pdf.

United Nations. 2008. United Nations Commodity Trade Statistics. http://comtrade.un.org/db/ (accessed June 10, 2008).

U.S. Central Intelligence Agency (CIA). 2008. *The 2008 World Factbook.* Washington, D.C.: CIA https://www.cia.gov/library/publications/the-world-factbook/index.html.

U.S. Department of Agriculture (USDA). 2008. National Agriculture Statistics Service. Corn, Sweet: National Statistics. http://www.nass.usda.gov (follow "Crops and Plants" hyperlink; then select "Vegetables" and "Corn Sweet") (accessed June 15, 2008).

U.S. Department of Commerce (DOC). 2008. Bureau of Economic Analysis. National Income and Product Accounts Table: Table 1.1.5. Gross Domestic Product. http://www.bea.gov/national/nipaweb/TableView.asp?SelectedTable=5&ViewSeries=NO&Java=no&Request3Place=N&3Place=N&FromView=YES&Freq=Year&FirstYear=1970&LastYear=2007&3Place=N&Update=Update&JavaBox=no.

U.S. Department of Energy (DOE). a. Energy Information Administration. Country Analysis Briefs: Saudi Arabia. http://www.eia.doe.gov/emeu/cabs/Saudi_Arabia/Oil.html (accessed June 15, 2008).

———. b. Wind Powering America: Wind Power Economics in New England. http://www.eere.energy.gov/windandhydro/windpoweringamerica/ne_economics.asp (accessed August 15, 2007).

———.2001. Energy Information Administration. *International Energy Annual, 1999.*

DOE/EIA-0219(99). Washington, D.C.: Energy Information Administration. Also available online at http://tonto.eia.doe.gov/ftproot/international/021999.pdf.

———. 2006. "New $CO_2$ Enhanced Recovery Technology Could Greatly Boost U.S. Oil." Press release, March 3. http://www.energy.gov/news/3291.htm.

———. 2007a. Energy Information Administration. *Annual Energy Outlook, 2007, with Projections to 2030.* DOE/EIA-0383(2007). Washington, D.C.: Energy Information Administration. Also available online at http://www.eia.doe.gov/oiaf/archive/aeo07/pdf/0383(2007).pdf.

———. 2007b. Energy Information Administration. *International Energy Annual, 2005.* Washington, D.C.: Energy Information Administration. Also available online at http://www.eia.doe.gov/iea.

———. 2007c. Energy Information Administration. *Renewable Energy Trends in Consumption and Electricity, 2005.* Washington, D.C.: Energy Information Administration. Also available online at http://tonto.eia.doe.gov/ftproot/renewables/062805.pdf.

———. 2008a. Energy Information Administration. *Annual Energy Review, 2007.* Washington, D.C.: Energy Information Administration. Also available online at http://www.eia.doe.gov/emeu/aer/contents.html.

———.2008b. Energy Information Administration. International Petroleum (Oil) Consumption. http://www.eia.doe.gov/emeu/international/oilconsumption.html.

———. 2008c. Energy Information Administration. Petroleum Data, Reports, Analysis, Surveys. http://www.eia.doe.gov/oil_gas/petroleum/info_glance/petroleum.html (accessed June 25, 2008).

U.S. Department of Labor. Bureau of Labor Statistics. 2006 Consumer Expenditure Survey: Quintiles of Income before Taxes. http://www.bls.gov/cex/2006/Standard/quintile.pdf.

U.S. Environmental Protection Agency (EPA). 2008. National Emissions Inventory (NEI) Air Pollutant Emission Trends Data. http://www.epa.gov/ttn/chief/trends (accessed June 10, 2008).

U.S. Geological Survey (USGS). 2000. *World Petroleum Assessment, 2000.* Also available online at http://pubs.usgs.gov/dds/dds-060.

Vaitheeswaran, Vijay V. 2005. *Power to the People: How the Coming Energy Revolution Will Transform an Industry, Change Our Lives, and Maybe Even Save the Planet.* New York: Farrar, Straus, and Giroux.

Verleger, Philip K., Jr. 1993. *Adjusting to Volatile Energy Prices.* Washington, D.C.: Institute for International Economics.

———. 2008. "Facts and Fantasies about Petroleum and Oil Markets: I." *Petroleum Economics Monthly,* April.

Victor, David G. 2003. "International Agreements and the Struggle to Tame Carbon." In Griffin 2003a, 204–229.

———. 2006. "Fragmented Carbon Markets and Reluctant Nations: Implications for the Design of Effective Architectures." In *Architectures for Agreement: Addressing Global Climate Change in the Post-Kyoto World,* ed. Joseph E. Aldy and Robert N. Stavins, 133–160. Cambridge, U.K.: Cambridge University Press.

Vietor, Richard H. K. and Rebecca Evans. 2004. "Saudi Arabia: Getting the House in Order." Harvard Business School Case 9-702-031. Boston: Harvard Business School Publishing.

Wara, Michael. 2007. "Is the Global Carbon Market Working?" *Nature* 445: 595–596.

*Washington Post.* 2005. Editorial. "Energy Deficient." July 28.

Wigley, Tom M. L. 1999. *The Science of Climate Change: Global and U.S. Perspectives.* Washington, D.C.: The Pew Center on Global Climate Change. Also available online at http://www.pewclimate.org/docUploads/env_science.pdf.

Workshop on Alternative Energy Strategies. 1977. *Energy Supply to the Year 2000: Global and National Studies: Second Technical Report of the Workshop on Alternative Energy Strategies.* Cambridge: MIT Press.

World Bank. 2008. *World Development Indicators, 2008.* Washington, D.C.: World Bank. Also available online at http://web.worldbank.org/WBSITE/EXTERNAL/DATASTATISTICS/0,,contentMDK:21725423~pagePK:64133150~piPK:64133175~theSitePK:239419,00.html.

Yergin, Daniel. 1993. *The Prize: The Epic Quest for Oil, Money and Power.* New York: Simon & Schuster.

———. 2006. "Ensuring Energy Security." *Foreign Affairs* 85 (2): 69–82.

Zellner, Wendy. 2004. "Crude Lessons About Oil." *Business Week,* November 15, 2004, 88.

# Index

Page numbers in italics refer to figures and tables.